FLOWER
Garden
PROBLEM
SOLVER

www.jerrybaker.com

FLOWER Garden PROBLEM SOLVER

786 Fast Fixes for Your Favorite Flowers

by Jerry Baker,
America's Master Gardener®

Published by American Master Products, Inc.

Published by American Master Products, Inc. / Jerry Baker

Executive Editor: Kim Adam Gasior
Project Editor: Cheryl Winters Tetreau
Interior Design and Layout: Sandy Freeman
Cover Design: Kitty Pierce Mace
Illustrator: Elayne Sears
Indexer: Nanette Bendyna

Publisher's Cataloging-in-Publication

Baker, Jerry.
    Flower garden problem solver : 786 fast fixes for your favorite flowers / by Jerry Baker.
      p. cm.

    1. Flower gardening.   2. Flowers.   I. Title.

SB405.B24695 2002   635.9
                QBI02-200783

Printed in the United States of America
2 4 6 8 10 9 7 5 3 1 hardcover

Contents

Spittlebugs ❀ Scale ❀ Slugs and Snails ❀ Spider Mites ❀ Thrips ❀ Whiteflies ❀ Deer ❀ Rabbits and Rodents ❀ Bacterial Diseases ❀ Fungal Diseases ❀ Viruses ❀ Cultural Problems

Flower Power Tonics Roundup ... 331

❀ All-Purpose Bug/Thug Spray ❀ All-Purpose Fertilizer ❀ All-Season Clean-Up Tonic ❀ All-Season Green-Up Tonic ❀ Aphid Antidote ❀ Baking Soda Spray ❀ Bed Builder Mix ❀ Beetle Juice Tonic ❀ Bug-Be-Gone Spray ❀ Bulb Bath ❀ Bulb Booster ❀ Bulb Breakfast ❀ Bulb Soak ❀ Caterpillar Killer Tonic ❀ Chamomile Mildew Chaser ❀ Clematis Chow ❀ Compost Booster ❀ Compost Tea ❀ Deer Buster Egg Brew ❀ Disease Defense ❀ Dog-Be-Gone! ❀ Double Punch Garlic Tea ❀ Fabulous Foliar Formula ❀ Flowerbed Bonanza ❀ Flower Defender ❀ Flower Feeder ❀ Flower Flea Fluid ❀ Flower Power Prep Mix ❀ Foundation Food ❀ Fragrant Pest Fighter ❀ Frozen Feed ❀ Fungus Fighter ❀ Garden Cure-All Tonic ❀ Get-Up-and-Grow Iris Tonic ❀ Herb Garden Potpourri ❀ Homegrown Daisy Spray ❀ Hot Bite Spray ❀ Hummingbird Nectar ❀ Magic Mum Booster ❀ Mildew Relief Elixir ❀ Mulch Moisturizer Tonic ❀ Nutrient Boost for Neglected Soil ❀ Perennial Planting Potion ❀ Perfect Potting Mix ❀ Potted Plant Picnic ❀ Powdery Mildew Control ❀ Quassia Slug Spray ❀ Really Rosy Potpourri ❀ Repotting Booster Tonic ❀ Rhubarb Pest Repellent Tonic ❀ Root Revival Tonic ❀ Root Rousing Tonic ❀ Rose Rousin' Elixir ❀ Rosy Clean-Up Elixir ❀ Rosy Feeding Regime ❀ Scat Cat Solution ❀ Seedling Starter Tonic ❀ Seedling Strengthener ❀ Slugweiser ❀ Soil Energizer Elixir ❀ Start-Up Snack ❀ Summer Rejuvenating Tonic ❀ Super Seed-Starting Mix ❀ Super Shrub Elixir ❀ Super Shrub Stimulator ❀ Super Spider Mite Mix ❀ Transplant Tonic ❀ Ultra-Light Potting Soil ❀ Weed Wipeout ❀ Whitefly Wipeout Tonic ❀ Wonderful Weed Killer ❀ Year-Round Refresher ❀ Round Refresher ❀ **Bonus Tonics:** Dead Bug Brew, Hot Bug Brew, Scare-'Em-All Tonic

USDA Plant Hardiness Zone Map ... 356

Index ... 357

Introduction

There's nothing like the pride and joy you feel when looking at your beautiful yard filled with lush leaves and bright blooms. But wait…doesn't that daisy over there look a little droopy? And hey—that rosebush was covered with buds yesterday, but now they're all chewed up. Your border of begonias? It looks like a train wreck! What's going on? You need some serious help—and quick!

Well, never fear, folks: ol' Jer is here! In all my years of growing flowers, first helping in Grandma Putt's garden, and then working in my own, I've come across just about every problem that can rear its ugly little head. And thanks to Grandma's old-time wisdom, plus a little hands-on experimenting, I've figured out how to beat all of 'em. The result? *Jerry Baker's Flower Garden Problem Solver!*

In this how-to helper, you'll discover hundreds of top-notch tips, tricks, and tonics for bringing out the best in your beds and borders, right from the get-go. And if bothersome bugs or funky fungi *do* get a foothold, I've included plenty of hints and super secrets to send those pests packing—*pronto!*

Ready to get growin'? Here's an overview of what you'll find in the following pages, to help you on your way:

❀ **Part 1: "Create a Garden with Flower Power"** is packed with pointers for growing flower gardens with plenty of pizzazz. Never again will you have flowerbeds that look great in spring, but are boring during the dog days. You'll learn how to turn tough sites into fabulous features, and oh, so many ways to create fun and flower-full new gardens. It's all right here!

❀ **Part 2: "A Healthy Garden Is a Happy Garden"** covers all my down-and-dirty tips for building a great garden from the ground up. You'll find all kinds of options for getting a new garden started (nope—digging isn't the *only* way to do it!), plus plenty of tricks for feedin', weedin', and waterin' to get those baby bloomers growin' like gangbusters.

❀ **Part 3: "Favorite Flowers—A to Z"** is the place to turn to when you're at your wit's end, looking for the scoop on specific flowers. From sun scorch on ageratums to mildew on zinnias, I've included a bushelful of problem-solving tips that'll *guarantee* you get the best from each and every flower in your yard.

❀ **Part 4: "Pest and Problem Patrol"** is your quick-and-easy reference for identifying pesky pests and datardly diseases to help you pick just the right control measures. I've also in-cluded a complete summary of all my fantastic Flower Power Tonics, so you'll have 'em right at your finger-tips when you need 'em.

So, if you've got flower garden problems, don't throw in the trowel just yet! You, too, can grow the biggest, brightest, bloomingest beds on the block—*dazzling* daylilies, *breathtaking* begonias, or *ravishing* roses—that'll make your garden the Blue Ribbon winner of the neighborhood!

PART 1

CREATE a GARDEN with FLOWER POWER

Grandma Putt's flower garden was a magical place to me. Flowers bloomed in all colors of the rainbow, and there was something new to see every day. But Grandma didn't rest on her laurels—so to speak; instead, she was always making changes, to build a better garden. And while we planned and plotted, I learned one of the most important lessons Grandma Putt taught me: Making a flower garden isn't a once-and-done affair—and that's a big part of the fun of gardening!

Grandma had loads of tricks that she used to figure out which plants to move around, when to add different colors, and what would make her garden look "just so."

On the pages that follow, you'll find all of Grandma Putt's best tips and techniques on making a beautiful flower garden—plus everything I've learned over the years in my own garden. We'll go over all kinds of designer secrets for perfect garden planning, plus pointers for coping with particularly tricky sites. I've also added an idea gallery chock-full of great tips for planning a garden that's fun as well as flower-full. So try them out, have some fun, and above all, don't be afraid to experiment!

1

Simple Secrets for Fabulous Flower Gardens

✿ When I was just a kid helping my Grandma Putt tend her flowers, I didn't ever wonder *why* her garden looked so pretty—I just knew it did! Turns out, she had all sorts of tricks up her sleeve to make sure her flowerbeds were in just the perfect place, and that the colors always looked beautiful together. Read on to find out how she did it!

Planning Makes Perfect

When the urge to start a new garden strikes, it's tempting to grab your checkbook and head to the local garden center for a shopping spree. But if you spend a bit of time planning before you shop 'til you drop, you'll be glad you did. The best way to start the garden you've always dreamed of—and to make sure it grows like gangbusters—is to look at your yard and decide where you want flowers the most.

Leave Lawn Mowing Behind

Don't waste time trimming grass around trees—plant flowers there instead!

Tired of spending every weekend behind a lawn mower? Replacing some or all of your grass—especially on those hard-to-mow sites—with beds of ground-covers and perennials is the way to go. You'll need to invest some time and energy up front to get the plants off to a good start, but they'll more than repay you with year after year of no-mow beauty!

Spread the Wealth

All too often, flowerbeds get pushed up against the edges of the yard, where they look like chairs lined up against the wall, ready for a dance. You wouldn't arrange furniture that way (unless you were having friends over for a hoedown!), so why do it for flowers?

Instead, look for places in your yard where a touch of color would mean the most. A patch of blooms along the driveway, for instance—or on either side of your front door—is a great way to welcome guests. Or how about a bed of colorful, fragrant flowers to enjoy while sitting on your deck? Flowers that you see up close every day will give you far more pleasure than ones planted out along the back lot line!

Put Your Flowers to Work

Flowers are more than just pretty faces—they can work hard, too! Covering steep slopes, hiding your neighbor's junk cars, adding

PROBLEM SOLVED!

Sick of looking at sparse, weedy grass under your trees? Replace that mess with a bed of bright-leaved hostas and other shade-loving perennials! Add shade-appreciating annuals like impatiens (*Impatiens walleriana*), and you'll have cheerful color to enjoy all summer long.

color to that boring backyard; you name it, and flowers can fix it. Why not take a walk around your yard and see what sorts of jobs flowers can do for you? Jot down ideas in a notebook, and maybe even make some simple sketches of what you'd like to see. When it comes time to plan a new flowerbed, just whip out your notes, and the job's half done!

It's in the Bag

Having trouble picturing what a new flowerbed will look like? Grab some trash bags, sticks, sheets, and boxes, and "build" the garden right on the spot! Bags filled with fall leaves make great stand-ins for bushy or mounding plants. Stakes (draped with sheets for extra bulk) and cardboard boxes are other good plant stand-ins.

Arrange your stand-ins where you'd like flowers to be. Look at your "garden" from all angles, especially if you want the real thing to hide an ugly view or add privacy to a sitting area. Sure, you might get some strange looks from your neighbors—but they'll quickly turn into glances of admiration when your perfectly planned garden's in all its glory!

GRANDMA PUTT'S
Handy Hints

It's easy to see what's on the surface of a site, but how about what's under your feet? Take this tip from my Grandma Putt: Before she decided to plant in a particular area, she'd grab a shovel and dig a test hole about 1 foot deep. In the process, she'd find out if that spot had lots of rocks, if it was hard and compacted, or if it was filled with tree roots—all factors that encouraged her to look elsewhere!

Simple Shapes Save Work

Here's a simple step that can save you hours of aggravation! Before settling on a final shape for your flower garden, think about how you'll mow around it. Flowerbeds with scalloped or zigzag edges may look nice, but they take lots of extra time to trim, since you have to keep backing up the mower and going forward again. Gentle curves, though, are a breeze to mow around—and straight edges are absolutely the easiest option of them all!

Bricks set in a bed of sand make a super edging strip. They look great and make mowing a snap, too!

The Path to Success

When you design your dream garden, don't ignore those well-worn paths your family and visitors use every day. They offer a great way to organize your overall design! It's also darn near impossible to keep your family from using them. So if you can't beat 'em, spruce up those well-worn tracks in the lawn—such as the one out to the driveway or garage—by planning gardens that run along, not across, them. If you want a bed to cross an established path, use stepping stones to direct visitors through it; that'll keep 'em from compacting the soil and trampling your flowers.

It's Okay to Look Down on Your Garden!

Grandma Putt's favorite spot for thinking about garden design was up in her attic, where she would lean as far out of the windows as she could to look down on her yard. She

FLOWER POWER TONICS

Bed Builder Mix

If you have a site that you'd like to fill with flowers someday, it's never too soon to start the soil-building process. Scrape off the weeds and grass with a sharp spade, then add a dose of my super-duper mix.

40 lbs. of bagged topsoil
10 lbs. of compost
5 lbs. of bonemeal
1 lb. of Epsom salts

Mix all of these ingredients in a wheelbarrow or garden cart, spread a 2- to 3-inch layer over the entire site, and then top the bed with mulch. Add the plants whenever you're ready! ❋

swore the bird's-eye view led to some of her best garden ideas ever!

From her window vantage point, Grandma could see just how all of the flowerbeds, shrubbery, and other features fit together. She also could tell where new walkways or other features should go, and whether the colors she liked best were spread evenly through the garden. Then she'd come back down to earth to fine-tune her planting plans.

Mapmaker, Mapmaker...

Planning individual gardens is a good start, but before you start digging, here's a tip: Take things one step further and draw an overall plan for your yard. Like a road map, a landscape plan helps guide you as you plant gardens and plan new ones.

Start by making a simple "base map," then use it to create your overall plan. Your base map doesn't need to be fancy—just grab a piece of graph paper and draw an outline of your yard to scale—¼ inch on paper equals 5 feet in your yard, for example. Draw in the permanent features, like your house, then fill in trees, shrubs, and existing gardens, and voilà—your base map is complete!

Trace Your Way to a Great Garden

To use your base map for designing, place a sheet of tracing paper over the top of it, then draw out your ideas. As one sheet gets scribbled up, just add another on top, transfer the ideas you like best, and start again! Once you're happy with your design, make a clean copy of your overall plan.

Jerry's TIMELY TIPS

"If you take only one piece of advice about your new garden, let it be this one: Keep your first flower garden small. A small plot is easy to plan, plant, and take care of, so you're guaranteed success right from the start. It's a snap to make a small garden bigger—but it's sad to have to make a too-big garden smaller, or give up on it altogether."

Picture-Perfect Planning

Your best garden design tool is as close as your camera bag! And no, you don't need a fancy set-up, either: A state-of-the-art digital camera and an inexpensive point-and-shoot can give equally good results.

Take pictures from your house out toward where you want a flower garden, or from the property line back toward your house. To get a view of your entire yard, take a series of pictures from a single point, and tape them together. Get enlargements of your best shots, then place tracing paper over them. (Photocopies are inexpensive enough to draw on directly.) Sketch in new plants and other features over the pictures, and you'll have a great idea how your finished design will look *before* you turn the first spadeful of soil!

Lay Out the Hoses

Once you've figured out where you want a bed to be, try "drawing" it right on the lawn just like my Grandma Putt did—with garden hoses! Arrange hoses in the shape you're planning, then fine-tune the size and shape until you're happy with the result.

Your base map should show any existing features that might affect your overall yard design. So make sure you mark down these features on your map as you draw:

- ☑ House
- ☑ Garage
- ☑ Driveway
- ☑ Patios, porches, or decks
- ☑ Other buildings (toolsheds, gazebos, etc.)
- ☑ Utilities (air conditioners, meters, septic fields, etc.)
- ☑ Paths and walkways (paved and unpaved)
- ☑ Walls and fences
- ☑ Existing trees and shrubs
- ☑ Existing beds and borders
- ☑ Unattractive views
- ☑ Steep slopes
- ☑ Wind direction
- ☑ Very wet and very dry sites

No Drain, No Gain!

Most flowers hate soggy soil, so it's critical to check your site's drainage before you finalize your choices. Dig a hole about 10 inches deep and 4 to 6 inches wide, fill it with water, and let it drain overnight. The next day, fill the hole with water again, then wait 10 hours and recheck.

If the hole still has water sitting in it, you'll either need to limit yourself to growing flowers that can tolerate "wet feet," or else improve the drainage of the area. The simplest solution is raising the soil level by spreading several inches of topsoil over the site. To keep the soil from washing away, support the sides of the bed with low stone walls, bricks, or landscape timbers.

Terrific Tips for Great Garden Color

Are you a new gardener with no idea of which plants to pick for your first flowerbed? Or a long-timer with a flower garden that just needs a little help? Either way, I've got all the answers you need right here!

Feature Flowers with Foliage

Once you've been smitten by fabulous flowers, it's easy to overlook leaves. But leaves play a key role in keeping your garden picture pretty. Flowers come and go through the season, but the leaves are always there, so of course, you want them to look good!

The greens of leaves highlight the flower colors and set off individual blooms. Ideally, you want perennials with leaves in many shades of green—from grayish through deep blue-green. Look for perennials with leaves in various textures, too, like strappy-leaved yuccas and ferny-textured yarrows (*Achillea*).

Heat 'Em Up, or Keep Your Cool

Nervous about picking colors for a new garden? Take a tip from the pros, and choose colors with a similar "mood." See, garden designers often describe colors as being warm or cool, based on the feeling you get when you look at them. Cool colors—the colors of water—are blue, violet, purple, and green; they make you feel calm and relaxed. Warm colors, on the other hand, are bright yellow, red, and orange—fiery hues that are vibrant and exciting. Choose hues that reflect your personality, and you're sure to enjoy your new "mood garden."

It's Sew Simple

When my Grandma Putt couldn't decide on a color scheme for a new garden, she'd turn to an unexpected place—her sewing basket! She'd take a pretty floral print destined for the quilt she was working on, then pick and plant perennials with flowers in the same colors.

To try this approach yourself, choose a piece of fabric you like— a patch from a quilt, a favorite blouse, or even a piece of upholstery. Plan your flower garden to feature those colors, and it's sure to be sew-perfect!

Get the Blues

How many times have you brought home a flower that's supposed to be blue, only to find out it's really purple or violet when it finally blooms? If you really want a rich sky blue, here are your best bets for perennials: blue flax (*Linum perenne*), delphini-

Great gardeners know that the real secret to a super flower garden isn't the flowers at all—it's the leaves! Sounds crazy, I know, but think about it: What do you look at while you're waiting for your plants to bloom, or after they're finished flowering? The foliage! So when you pick out plants for your garden, look for those that have pretty leaves as well as showy flowers, and you're guaranteed to have the best-looking garden on the block from spring to frost.

"For a garden color scheme that's sure to please, plant flowers in colors that accent or repeat shades you've used to decorate the inside of your home. When you pick out curtains, wallpaper, or upholstery for your living room or bedroom, you stick to colors you like— and it makes sense to use them in your garden, too! As an added bonus, the flowers you pick outdoors will perfectly complement your interior decor."

ums, and plumbago (*Ceratostigma plumbaginoides*). If your soil is on the acid side, you'll also get stunning, true-blue blooms from big-leaved hydrangea (*Hydrangea macrophylla*). Two easy-to-grow annuals come in true blue, too: larkspur (*Consolida ajacis*) and bachelor's buttons (*Centaurea cyanus*).

Cool It!

I love bright flowers, but sometimes they can be...well, a little **too** bright! If you're worried about color clashes in your beds and borders, try this designer trick: Separate them with clumps of plants that have cream-colored flowers or cream-and-green-marked leaves. Drifts of silver-leaved plants like dusty miller (*Senecio cineraria*), lavenders, and wormwood (*Artemisia absinthium*) also make peace between clashing combatants, as do white-striped ornamental grasses, such as variegated Japanese silver grass (*Miscanthus sinensis* 'Variegatus').

Flowers to Count On

Sure, annuals and bulbs are super sources of garden color, but long-blooming perennials are really the backbone of any great color scheme. Here's a list of some free-flowering perennials that are sure to fill your garden with color all summer long—and then some!

Balloon flower (*Platycodon grandiflorus*): Pinch off dead flowers regularly for bloom from summer to fall.

Daylilies (*Hemerocallis*): Plant ever-blooming and reblooming daylilies such as 'Happy Returns', 'Pardon Me', 'Little Grapette', and 'Stella de Oro'.

Hollyhock mallow (*Malva alcea*): Rosy pink blooms appear from early summer to fall.

Pincushion flower (*Scabiosa*): 'Butterfly Blue' and 'Pink Mist' flower from late spring to frost.

Thread-leaved coreopsis (*Coreopsis verticillata*): 'Moonbeam' produces pale yellow flowers from early summer to fall.

Trim Those Bloomers

Ever wish your favorite flowers would last longer? With a little of my garden magic, you can bring tired perennials back to life and enjoy blooms for months longer than everyone else! Simply cut back bushy plants like catmints (*Nepeta*) by a half to two-thirds after their main summer showing of flowers. They'll be back in bloom within a few weeks, and flower their fool heads off for the rest of the growing season. This trick works on yarrows (*Achillea*), too—to encourage repeat bloom, just trim back to a leaf joint where you can see a tiny flower bud emerging.

PROBLEM SOLVED!

Want to make a real splash in your yard—and simplify your planning at the same time? Choose just three or four favorite perennials that have compatible colors and the same soil and sun needs. Arrange them in a series of large drifts, with no fewer than three or five of each plant in each cluster. If you have the room, repeat this simple scheme throughout your yard to create a design that's simple but show-stopping.

Low-growing lady's mantle, flat-topped yarrow, and spiky mulleins add cheerful summer color to any sunny spot.

Garden Design 101

Making a great garden design may seem like a deep, dark mystery, but it's really a snap if you use some of my simple, sure-fire techniques! I've found that messing around with garden shapes and plants is a great way to figure out what works and what doesn't in a garden.

Bed and Border Befuddlement

There are two terms you'll come across again and again as you read about flower gardening—beds and borders. Understanding the difference between them will help you settle on the best shape, style, and location for your own flower garden.

Beds are located on the edge of a lawn, or around a deck or patio. They're seen from several sides and are usually enjoyed from up close, so details matter. Stick to long-blooming plants that have great-looking leaves.

Borders run lengthwise along a fence, lot line, walkway, or building. They're usually seen only from one side, so the tallest plants go toward the back. Borders are longer than they are wide, and they can be rectangular or have curving edges. And since you'll look at them from a distance, masses of color are more important than fine details.

FL❀WER POWER TONICS

Soil Energizer Elixir

Whatever kind of garden you're planning, you'll get great results if you perk up the soil before planting with this energizing elixir!

1 can of beer
1 cup of regular cola (not diet)
1 cup of liquid dish soap
1 cup of antiseptic mouthwash
¼ tsp. of instant tea granules

Mix these ingredients in a bucket or container, and fill a 20 gallon hose-end sprayer. Overspray the soil in your garden to the point of run-off (or just until small puddles start to form), then let it sit at least two weeks. This recipe makes enough to cover 100 square feet of garden area. ❈

Is an Island in Your Future?

To create a garden that's a joy to stroll around, consider an **island bed** set somewhere in your lawn. These free-form plantings really do look like islands of flowers surrounded by a sea of turf grass. Larger is better here—a small island looks like a little postage stamp. Make yours at least twice as wide as the tallest plant in the center.

Do Your Homework

Putting a plant in the wrong place is a sure-fire recipe for a disappointing garden. So before you pick out any flowers for your yard, I want you to take a good, hard look at the site. Watch how much sun or shade it receives, and also note the soil type and any other conditions that will affect the flowers you want to grow there.

Landscape Lingo

Beds and borders can contain just one kind of plant (such as an annual bed, or a perennial border) or a combination of annuals, perennials, and bulbs (commonly just called a flowerbed or flower garden). The term **mixed border** or **mixed planting** refers to a grouping of many different kinds of plants: annuals, perennials, bulbs, herbs, ornamental grasses, shrubs, and even small trees.

Now, it's time to make your plant list. Start with *your* favorites, then page through "Favorite Flowers—A to Z," starting on page 134, where you'll find all of *mine*! As you add each plant to your list, compare its growing requirements to the conditions your site has to offer. (The "Grow It!" part of each entry—which summarizes each plant's growing needs—makes this a snap to do.) If each plant on your final list thrives in the sunlight and soil conditions that your site has to offer, then you're well on your way to success.

Bubble, Bubble—It's No Trouble!

Okay, you've settled on a site and a shape, and you know at least some of the plants you'd like to grow. What's next? I suggest drawing a bubble diagram, which is a simple planting plan for your new garden. To make one, draw an outline of your garden to scale on graph paper. A large scale is best—something like ½ or

1 inch on paper equals 1 or 2 feet in the garden. Use a pencil to start drawing bubble-like shapes that are roughly to scale, to represent individual plants or groups of similar plants.

Draw in the big plants first. Shrubs can easily be 5 or 10 feet wide, so they'll need plenty of space. Add smaller bubbles around them to represent clumps of perennials, which range from 1 to 3 feet across. Write the plant name and the number of plants in each bubble, and presto—you're a whole lot closer to creating your dream garden!

Color Your World

Want an even better idea of how your new garden will look? Grab some colored pencils and start coloring in your bubbles! Fill each one with a color that matches the flowers you've selected. For a season-by-season look at your design, make copies of your diagram for spring, summer, and fall, then color in the bubbles that will be in bloom during each season.

Dynamic Duos

I can sum up the secret pros use to create great plant combinations in one word: contrast. To add interest to any bed or border, pair vase-shaped plants, such as irises or ornamental grasses, with shrubby, broader-leaved ones, like peonies. Mix soft-textured, mounding plants, like hardy geraniums (*Geranium*), with stiff plants like yuccas, or lacy-leaved ferns with large-leaved hostas. The more variety in your garden, the more beautiful it will look!

FLOWER POWER TONICS

Summer Rejuvenating Tonic

Whenever Grandma Putt's carefully planned annual gardens started to look a little tired in late summer, she'd pinch 'em back hard and give 'em a good drink of this potent pick-me-up.

¼ **cup of beer**
1 tbsp. of corn syrup
1 tbsp. of baby shampoo
1 tbsp. of 15-30-15 fertilizer
1 gal. of water

Mix all of these ingredients, then slowly dribble the solution onto the soil around your annuals. Within two weeks, they'll be real comeback kids! ✳

Plants on the Move

Whatever you do, don't get too uptight about getting your garden perfect right from the get-go. If you end up with a planting you don't like, just use the best garden design tool of all—a shovel. It's no big deal to dig up a plant that clashes or just doesn't quite fit in. Move your plants around until you're happy with the arrangement, and in the process, you'll become a better designer and gardener!

Picture This!

To really bring your on-paper plan to life, use magazines and catalogs to reproduce it in full color. Cut out pictures of the flowers you are planning to grow, then arrange the cut-outs in a collage, according to your diagram. While all the cut-out pictures may not be the same size, you can get a pretty good idea of the garden picture you'll be planting.

PENNY WISE

You've created the perfect plan, but when you add up all the plants you need to buy—well, let's just say your bank balance is less than perfect. Now what? Don't start over—revise your plan to use less expensive options. Check your yard for clumps of perennials that you could divide, or ask friends and family members for divisions and cuttings. You might even decide to grow your own flowers from seed—that's a great way to get dozens of new plants for only a few bucks, so give it a try!

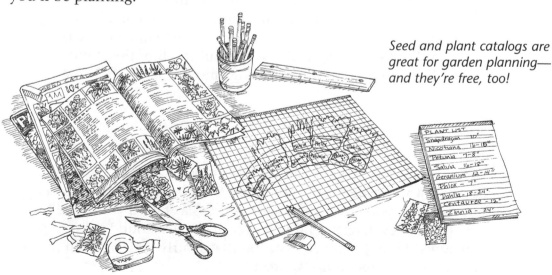

Seed and plant catalogs are great for garden planning— and they're free, too!

Mix It Up!

Hey, folks—if you're going to make a flower garden, you want it to be the best on the block, right? Well, listen up—the key to an out-of-the-ordinary flowerbed is out-of-the-ordinary plants! The prettiest gardens I've ever seen include just about everything but the kitchen sink. They have perennials, for sure, but also annuals, bulbs, flowering shrubs and small trees, ornamental grasses, vines, herbs, and even vegetables. It's easy to mix eye-popping plants to make gardens that are the envy of the neighborhood.

Elbow Out Weeds

Perennials aren't proud, so they don't mind "rubbing elbows" with other kinds of plants. They're just as happy growing alongside annuals or shrubs as they are with other perennials. Besides adding extra height and seasonal interest, these other plants offer another advantage when used to round out a perennial-packed garden: They leave less room for pesky weeds, which will take over if you don't fill the space first! Just remember, all of the plants that you select should thrive in the same amount of sun or shade.

Screening for Solitude

If your backyard is exposed to the whole neighborhood, a mixed planting may be just the ticket. Most perennials aren't tall enough to provide much privacy on their own, but mix in some shrubs, and you can make a garden that's as tall as you'd like it to be! Include evergreens and you even have year-round screening. As an added bonus, a mixed planting that's fairly wide and tall helps muffle sound from a noisy street, too!

Food for Thought

Don't think you have room for both blooms and veggies? Well, think again! Tall, staked tomatoes are actually good-looking plants that can take the place of large perennials in a flower garden. Varieties with tiny, but abundant fruits, like 'Yellow Pear' and 'Sweet 100', are especially attractive. Sweet and hot peppers are super choices, too, for their pretty flowers, nice-looking leaves, and showy fruits. Colorful leaf lettuces, along with curly parsley and spinach, make great edging plants (cover them with a hoop of poultry wire for nearly invisible protection against rabbits). Other eye-catching edibles include kale, leeks, and Swiss chard—especially the red-stemmed 'Rhubarb' or multicolored 'Bright Lights' varieties.

A Bright Idea

To get even more bang for your gardening buck, remember to think about what's below the ground, as well as what's on top! Bulbs are simply perfect for filling the spaces between clumps of perennials. Think spring-bloomers, like crocuses and daffodils, for the early show, as well as later-blooming bulbs, such as lilies (*Lilium*), for super summer color.

Plan Practical Pathways

Since you need to be able to reach in and tend your flowers, 4 feet is generally a good width for most gardens—6 feet if you can reach in from either side. In a mixed planting, though, a single shrub can easily be 4 feet across—so what's a body to do? Make a network of narrow maintenance paths through the bed, so you can

---

GARDEN SMARTS

If you love your garden like I do, you want to enjoy it as long as possible. Well, a typical flowerbed offers little more than mulch to look at through the winter, but a mixed border gives you something to enjoy every single day of the year! Shrubs and small trees featuring colorful bark and twigs, berries, and/or handsome branching habits all add interest through the dreary winter months. And for the rest of the year, color comes easy because you're combining such a wide variety of plants.

---

get to your flowers without squashing the plants or stepping on and packing down the soil. Maintenance paths can be just a foot or two wide, and they can wind around anywhere you want them to, since you're the only one who will use them. To keep them weed-free, cover them with a couple of layers of newspaper topped with mulch.

The Layered Look

To make sure each plant has its chance to shine, pay careful attention to height when you arrange your planting plans. In a border, the tallest plants look

Don't forget to add a bench, so you can rest and enjoy those beautiful blooms!

best toward the back, while in a flowerbed or island planting, they belong in the center. That way, they'll form a backdrop for tiers of smaller plants up front. Use flowering shrubs, ornamental grasses, and even shrub roses for the tallest tiers. Train vines, such as clematis, on pillars or over shrubs for more high-flying color! Smaller perennials, herbs, and annuals are well suited for the lower layers.

Say No to Spreaders

For a successful mixed planting, stay away from fast-spreading groundcovers. They'll just try to take over, and you'll be left with more work than you wanted to keep them in check. Ajuga, yellow archangel (*Lamium galeobdolon*), and plumbago (*Ceratostigma plumbaginoides*) are three to avoid; variegated bishop's weed (*Aegopodium podagraria* 'Variegatum') and ribbon grass (*Phalaris arundinacea* var. *picta*) can be real headaches, too.

Want to make the most out of every inch in your flowerbeds? Fill in the bare spots around your perennials and shrubs with annuals. You can even plant them on top of clumps of spring bulbs that are starting to die back. The annuals will do a bang-up job covering up those yellowing bulb leaves, and they'll fill in perfectly after the bulb foliage completely disappears.

Balance Your Beds

Ever plan a garden that looked...well, sort of lopsided? I did too, until I learned these three simple steps that give gardens a professionally designed look every time!

Step 1: Plant three shrubs for each tree. (Use large shrubs near large trees and smaller shrubs near smaller trees.) Group the shrubs near the base of the tree, but set them a few feet away from the trunk to avoid the tree's roots.

Step 2: Include at least three to five perennials—some larger and some smaller—for each shrub.

Step 3: Finish off around the edges with as many low-growing perennials and annuals as you need to fill the space that's available.

Connect the Dots

The trickiest part of designing a mixed planting? Deciding where it will look the best! If you're stumped, do what I do—plan the bed around trees and shrubs you already have in your yard. Having some already-mature trees and shrubs in your mixed planting will make the whole thing look well-planned, right from the get-go. And at the same time, grouping several trees and shrubs into one bed will cut your mowing and trimming chores, especially if you stick to straight or smooth-curving edges that you can easily mow around.

Terrific Small Trees for Shade

With so many great small trees to choose from, how's a body supposed to know which ones'll look just right in a mixed border? Here are my favorites for somewhat shady spots.

Cornelian cherry (*Cornus mas*): Bright yellow blooms in early spring; red berries later in the season.

Downy serviceberry (*Amelanchier arborea*): White flowers in early spring; edible summer fruit that attracts birds; excellent yellow-to-red fall foliage color.

Eastern redbud (*Cercis canadensis*): Pink flowers in spring; heart-shaped leaves that turn yellow in fall.

Flowering dogwood (*C. florida*): White or pink spring flowers; handsome red berries in summer; purplish red fall leaves.

Hemlocks (*Tsuga*): Evergreen foliage; super year-round screening.

Hollies (*Ilex*): Evergreen hollies offer year-round screening plus winter color; showy berries.

Super Shrubs for Shady Sites

It's easy to find super shrubs for sunny spots, but shady sites can be a bit of a puzzle, right? Not anymore! Here are seven spectacular shrubs that are guaranteed to fill your shaded beds and borders with beautiful flowers—and great-looking leaves, too!

Mountain laurel (*Kalmia latifolia*): Pink, red, or white, spring to early summer flowers; evergreen leaves.

Oakleaf hydrangea (*Hydrangea quercifolia*): White summer flowers; outstanding red fall leaves.

Pagoda dogwood (*Cornus alternifolia*): Yellowish white summer flowers; red-purple fall foliage.

Rhododendrons and azaleas (*Rhododendron*): Pink, white, purple, red, yellow, or orange spring flowers; may be deciduous or evergreen.

Summersweet (*Clethra alnifolia*): Spikes of fragrant white flowers in summer; yellow to golden fall foliage.

Leatherleaf viburnum (*Viburnum rhytidophyllum*): Yellowish-white spring flowers; glossy, evergreen to semi-evergreen leaves.

Witch hazels (*Hamamelis*): Fragrant yellow, red, or orange flowers in late winter; outstanding red or orange fall foliage.

Jerry's TIMELY TIPS

"If you're having trouble picturing what a mixed planting is, think of a woods. There, tall trees shelter smaller understory trees and shrubs, with all manner of perennials covering the ground. Even if your yard currently has only one or two older trees, you can mix-and-match small trees and flowering shrubs around it to create an island bed planting with a woodland feel."

Learn from the Best

Fresh out of ideas for that special spot in your yard? Take my advice—sign up for a garden tour sponsored by a local club or neighborhood association. Jot down notes about problem areas you'd like ideas for, and take them along with a notebook and pencil. As you look at other people's gardens, pay attention to features and plants that would work in your own yard, and be sure to note any plant combinations that catch your eye.

Keep the Color Coming

The next time you're looking for good ideas for your flower garden, put a John Philip Sousa march on your stereo. After all, every gardener wants a plentiful parade of flowers from spring to frost, and what better parade-planning music is there than the good ol' "The Stars and Stripes Forever"? Thinking about your garden as a procession of floats and bands isn't all that crazy, either, because it helps you marshal your flowers into a season-long parade of color!

Plan for Four Seasons

Here's a can't-miss way to plan a garden that's colorful month after month: Just pick a few plants that shine during each season. Keep your choices super-simple by picking spring-, summer-, and fall-bloomers. Or, you can break the seasons down by plants that flower in early, mid-, and late summer. Scatter the flowering plants you've chosen throughout your yard, or arrange them in drifts that bloom together. Then there's something pretty to look at during each season.

Roses in the Snow

Want to have the first blooms on your block each year? Plant hellebores! As their name suggests, Christmas roses (*Helleborus niger*) start blooming in early winter in mild-winter climates. In colder areas, they may not start until late winter, but they're still **much** earlier than most flowers. Lenten roses (*H.* x *hybridus*) pick up where Christmas roses leave off, flowering from late winter to early spring. These dependable perennials are a snap to grow: Just give 'em partial to full shade and average garden soil.

Special Sites for Lovely Flowers—Longer

For the earliest spring blooms—and longer-lasting fall flowers, too—look south, not west, young man (or woman). That's because south-facing sites, especially those against a wall or building, warm up faster in spring. You'll notice they stay warmer much longer in fall, too.

To get the best out of these special sites, tuck in a bunch of hardy bulbs, to start off the show with a bounty of extra-early color. In summer, sunny, south-facing sites tend to get sizzling hot, so fill them with annuals that can take the heat, like narrow-leaved zinnias (*Zinnia haageana*) and ornamental peppers (*Capsicum annuum*). Replace tired summer annuals in fall with a crop of cold-tolerant annuals, like flowering kale (*Brassica oleracea*), and you'll have color well into early winter!

Plan a Spring Fling

Daffodils and tulips are obvious options for early color in beds and borders, but if you want something different, it's time to look beyond bulbs. There's a host of early-blooming perennials that can really get things hoppin', well before the mercury starts risin'!

Low-growing basket-of-gold (*Aurinia saxatilis*), moss phlox (*Phlox subulata*), and rock cress (*Arabis caucasica*) make great groundcovers for early color. Other spring-blooming sun-lovers include bleeding heart (*Dicentra spectabilis*) and columbine (*Aquilegia*).

For cheerful spring color in partial to full shade, consider any or

> ### To the Rescue!
>
> After a long, dreary winter, there's nothing like a burst of color to welcome the return of warmer weather. Plant some of these super-early-blooming bulbs, and you'll have all the bright blooms you could wish for, come spring!
>
> **Common snowdrop** (*Galanthus nivalis*)
> **Glory-of-the-snow** (*Chionodoxa luciliae*)
> **Reticulated iris** (*Iris reticulata*)
> **Snow crocus** (*Crocus chrysanthus*)
> **Winter aconite** (*Eranthis hyemalis*)

all of the following: crested iris (*Iris cristata*), foamflower (*Tiarella cordifolia*), lungworts (*Pulmonaria*), primroses, and violets.

Spring Shrub Spectacular

Masses of yellow forsythia and multicolored azaleas are a sure sign of spring, but if you want something a little more unique for your garden, there are super shrubs for you, too! These seven early-birds flaunt their flowers from late winter to early spring, well before their leaves appear.

Chinese redbud (*Cercis chinensis*): Rosy purple flowers.

Flowering quince (*Chaenomeles speciosa*): Pink, red, red-orange, or white blooms.

Fragrant winter hazel (*Corylopsis glabrescens*): Fragrant, pale yellow blossoms.

Star magnolia (*Magnolia stellata*): Shrub or small tree with fragrant white flowers.

Thunberg spirea (*Spiraea thunbergii*): White flowers.

White forsythia (*Abeliophyllum distichum*): White to palest pink flowers.

Witch hazel (*Hamamelis* x *intermedia*): Yellow or red to red-orange blooms; many selections are fragrant.

Pansies Do Double Duty

Pansies (*Viola* x *wittrockiana*) are perfect for adding patches of early color to spring gardens, as are their close relatives, Johnny-jump-ups (*V. tricolor*). Both are cold-tolerant, and they can flower for months, especially if you snip off the spent blooms before they set seed. But, did you know that these cuties are super for fall color, as well? In mild areas, they'll flower all winter; in cooler climates, they'll bloom until freezing weather, and they'll often live over to bloom again in earliest spring. How's that for getting your money's worth?

Bulbs: A Bright Idea for Early Summer

Plant pansies and violets in fall, and they'll bloom even better in spring!

Bulbs aren't just for spring anymore! These super space-savers keep the color coming well into summer, and it's a snap to tuck them in anywhere your flower garden could use some extra oomph. My all-time favorites for this time of year are the ornamental onions (*Allium*). Hybrids 'Gladiator' and 'Globemaster' both bear round, softball-size, purple blooms, while star of Persia (*A. cristophii*) bears huge, silvery purple clusters up to a foot across! Other hardy bulbs for late spring to early summer bloom include camassias, dogtooth violets (*Erythronium*), Madonna lily (*Lilium candidum*), snowflakes (*Leucojum*), star-of-Bethlehems (*Ornithogalum*), and summer hyacinths (*Galtonia candicans*).

Water Wisely for More Flowers

The dog days of summer can be a tough time to keep flowers looking fresh. What's the problem? Well, if your summer-blooming annuals or perennials tend to develop droopy-looking leaves and stop flowering as the mercury rises, bone-dry soil is often the culprit. Fortunately, regular watering can perk up plants in

Jerry's TIMELY TIPS

"If gaps show up in your flower parade, it's time to go visiting—local gardens, that is. Any time there isn't much blooming in your backyard, walk around your neighborhood and see what's going on in other folks' gardens. You can also visit displays at botanical gardens and garden centers to get more great ideas about what to plant."

Bulb blooms can get lost in the garden if you plant just one bulb here and one bulb there. For a spectacular show, pull out all the stops, and plant them in big bunches! Group little bulbs, like crocuses and grape hyacinths (*Muscari*), in masses of 20 or 30 bulbs. Larger bulbs, like daffodils, look best when planted in drifts of at least 5 to 10 bulbs.

a jiffy, so be prepared to drench those spots once a week during dry weather, and you'll keep the color coming even through those scorching summer spells.

Exposure Exposé

Scorching summer heat doesn't just wilt gardeners; it's also tough on shade-loving plants. To keep shady spots colorful all summer long, it helps to remember that shady spots aren't all the same. A garden that receives morning sun and afternoon shade usually is cooler than one that's shaded in the morning, then baked by the sun all afternoon. Shade-loving plants that can stand a bit of sun—like hostas and astilbes—usually grow best in areas that receive morning sun and afternoon shade, or dappled, all-day shade. Keep the beds with afternoon sun for the sun-lovers that can stand a bit of shade—like coreopsis, for example.

Sunny-Side Up

No matter how carefully you plan and plant your garden, there's one thing you won't have much control over: which way your flowers will face. Flowers like to look toward the sun, so they generally turn to the south and west. This is most noticeable with flowers that have distinct faces, like sunflowers

Looking for months of easy-care color? Daisies just can't be beat!

(*Helianthus annuus*) and daffodils. If you plant a row of sunflowers along the south side of your yard, for instance, they'll have their backs to you all summer.

With plants that feature spiky blooms, like delphiniums—or mounding habits, like thread-leaved coreopsis (*Coreopsis verticillata*)—the flower direction doesn't matter nearly as much. So, if you're planting a bed on the south side of your house, be sure to include plenty of these "faceless" beauties. That way, both you and your neighbors can have plenty of pretty flowers to look at!

A Fall Flower Fling

If your flower garden tends to fizzle out by fall, take a drive down a country road to get some inspiration. Wildflowers that adorn the roadsides in autumn are a super source of ideas for your fall flower garden. Asters top the list for autumn color, but boltonia (*Boltonia asteroides*) also bears clouds of daisy-like fall flowers in white or pink. Include some goldenrods (*Solidago*), too—'Fireworks' has golden blooms that literally explode into flower in fall, just as its name suggests.

Landscape Lingo

If you read the fine print on plant labels and in catalogs, you'll sometimes see terms like **early, midseason,** and **late** used to describe some perennials. These terms apply to each particular plant's bloom time—not to the actual seasons of spring, summer, and fall. Daylilies (*Hemerocallis*) are a good example: All bloom in summer, but those described as "early" flower in late spring to very early summer, while "late" daylilies can flower into fall. Once you know the lingo, you can use these clues to help you pick plants for the longest possible parade of flowers in your yard!

Make Your Own Winter Wonderland

Tired of looking at a boring, brown (or white) backyard all winter? Needle-leaved evergreen trees like pines (*Pinus*) and spruces (*Picea*) are classics for winter color, but they aren't your only options. You can also spice up your mixed borders with more compact, broad-leaved evergreens, such as hollies (*Ilex*), rhododendrons, and leatherleaf viburnum (*Viburnum rhytidophyllum*). For even more excitement, toss in trees and shrubs with colorful bark, like red-twig dogwood (*Cornus alba* 'Sibirica') and paperbark maple (*Acer griseum*).

Let's Keep It Growing

One of the things my Grandma Putt taught me to love about having a garden is that it's always changing. Oftentimes, the change is for the good, as the plants fill in and get bigger and showier. Sometimes, though, there's room for improvement—a plant gets too big, colors clash, or you discover a thug that's crowding out all your other plant buddies. Tinkering with problems—my Grandma called them challenges—makes you a better gardener. It's also half the fun!

Jeepers, Creepers!

Is your garden plagued with empty patches where bare soil shows through? It's time to call in some fast-growing perennials for quick cover. For shade, clumps of vigorous hostas are a great choice—'Francee' and 'Golden Tiara' are two extravigorous, eye-catching selections. Ferns are good choices, too; consider lady fern (*Athyrium filix-femina*) or New York fern (*Thelypteris noveboracensis*). Lily-of-the-valley (*Convallaria majalis*) and spotted deadnettle (*Lamium maculatum*) are also great spreaders for shade. For sun, bee balms (*Monarda*), catmints (*Nepeta*), coneflowers

GRANDMA PUTT'S
Handy Hints

It's fun to fine-tune established beds and borders with new additions, but it can get pretty pricey to keep on buying extra plants. My Grandma Putt was always finding room for new flowers to add to her garden, but she rarely spent a penny on them. Instead, she'd root slips of her favorites, or start new ones from seeds. Besides getting plenty more of her favorites—all for free!—she'd trade her extra plants with gardening friends and neighbors for new treasures.

(*Echinacea* and *Rudbeckia*), daylilies (*Hemerocallis*), snow-in-summer (*Cerastium tomentosum*), thymes (*Thymus*), and yarrow (*Achillea*) are all fast fillers.

Start with the Soil

A bare patch of ground in a garden bed might mean that something's wrong down under. So before you plant more flowers to fill that patch, loosen the soil with a garden fork and work in several shovels full of compost to improve the earth.

Hostas and ferns are a natural choice for fillin' up shady spots quick!

Start with the Big Stuff

If shrubs play a part in your plans, but you can't plant the whole garden right now, it's just plain smart to give them a head start. Figure out where the shrubs are going to go, then remove the lawn in those areas and plant your shrubs. You'll have to trim the grass around them for a season or two, but they'll get some size on them in the meantime.

When you're ready to plant the rest of the bed—or a small section of it—you have two options. Either remove the sod, dig, and plant, or smother the remaining grass with newspapers topped with several inches of topsoil and then mulch. (If you take the latter

PENNY WISE

Big garden, but a small budget? Get serious about growing plants from cuttings, divisions, and seeds. That way, you can buy a single plant and make all the copies you want without spending another dime!

To make caring for lots of baby plants a snap, dig a small garden in a protected area near your house. (Make sure it's handy to the hose, too, so you won't forget to water the little guys often.) Then grow all your treasures in rows until they're big enough to go out into the yard.

approach, smother the grass one season and plant the next. Dig holes for your annuals, perennials, and bulbs right down through the mulch and paper.)

Choose Your Chores

L et's face it, not all gardening chores are created equal. It's a fact of life that you'll enjoy some garden tasks and dislike others. Weeding and edging flowerbeds, for instance, top many people's "could do without" lists. Watering, mowing, and feeding the lawn aren't all that much fun, either. To cut back on these chores, replace your lawn with beds of low-maintenance groundcovers. Plan on eliminating a little lawn each year, so you can easily keep weeds under control until the groundcovers fill in.

What if staking flowers isn't your favorite activity? Replace tall perennials with shorter selections that can stand up without any assistance. Or just let tall plants sprawl onto their neighbors—the effect of flowers mingling together has a nice cottage-garden feel to it.

Jerry's TIMELY TIPS

"Mapping and planning are valuable tools whether you're renovating an old, overgrown garden, or creating a new one. Record the locations of plants and flowers you want to save on your base map, then use sheets of tracing paper over it to experiment with ideas. Deciding just where you want your flowers before you dig will save you a lot of time and effort in the long run!"

Living on the Edge

G iven half the chance, lawn grass will quickly creep into the rich soil in your flowerbeds. So instead of fighting to keep it out, take time to install edging strips whenever you put in a new bed or border. Take it from me—you'll save yourself hours of aggravation later on!

You can buy commercial plastic or rubber edging strips, or make your own from landscape timbers, stones, or bricks. Install edging strips so that the top edge is just slightly above the soil surface. That way, you can mow around the beds with the wheels on one side riding along the strip, trimming as you go! You can also use edging strips to keep vigorous groundcovers from invading their neighbors.

Don't Dig In Just Yet

Moving to a new home may mean an exciting new garden, but it can also mean you've inherited someone else's mistakes. The best first step is to just wait and watch your yard for a full year. Figure out which trees and shrubs you have, and see what perennials and bulbs show up. After that, you can make informed choices about what stays and what goes.

If your new yard is really overgrown, you may need to take action immediately: Pull weeds and cut back rampant spreaders. Once you can see what's what, decide if you want to restore the basic design or undertake a major overhaul. As you work, keep in mind that if a plant is weedy or just plain ugly, it's perfectly okay to dig it up and throw it away. You don't have to save each and every plant that's there, and anyway, you're making room for something new!

Soaker hoses snaked through your beds don't simply make watering a snap—they also keep your water bill in bounds! That's because they deliver water directly to the roots and minimize evaporation. Cover them with mulch and leave them in place year-round, and your watering woes will be a thing of the past.

Use What You've Got

If you're lucky enough to have inherited mature clumps of perennials, dig up overgrown specimens and divide them into smaller pieces. (For more details on dividing your perennials, see "Divide to Multiply!" on page 127.) Plant pieces of the best ones in several spots to add color throughout your yard, and you'll have a professional-looking landscape without spending an extra dime on any of it!

Site-Savvy Solutions

✿ Guess what, folks? I've *never* met anyone whose yard started off with the rich and moist, but loose and well-drained soil the books always say is a must for a great garden! Don't get me wrong—good soil sure is the key to success, but that doesn't mean you can't garden without it; you just need to know the secrets for whipping less-than-perfect soil into shape. In this chapter, you'll find my best tricks for coping with tough soil challenges, as well as other problem sites like shade and high-traffic areas.

Dealing with Dry Soil

Parched perennials and arid annuals are never a happy sight. They'll have droopy, undersized leaves, few flowers, and stunted growth. Sounds pretty gruesome, doesn't it? Fortunately, it's easy to change even the driest site from barren to beautiful—it just takes a little know-how!

Mulch Magic

Where dry soil is a common problem, the absolute best thing you can do is water thoroughly, then add mulch—lots of it! A layer of shredded bark, chopped leaves, or other mulch works wonders to keep the soil moist and cool for great root growth. It keeps the soil from forming a water-repelling crust, and it adds organic matter, too, which helps your soil hold even more moisture for those thirsty roots.

Personal Plant Waterers

Want to give a plant its own personal water supply? Here's how: Make a pinhole in the bottom of a 1-liter soda bottle, then sink the base of the bottle slightly into the soil next to the plant. Keep the bottle filled, and it'll leak a slow, but steady, supply of water—just what newly planted flowers need to get growing!

Baby Those Babies!

Even the most drought-tolerant flowers need "regular" watering until they have a chance to get their roots settled in—so how often is that, and for how long? For annual transplants, that translates into watering once every five to seven days for the first month. Water newly planted perennials once a week for their first growing season in your garden; after that, they should do fine on their own. For even better results, dig deeply before planting—that'll make it easy for new roots to spread—and add a 2- to 3-inch layer of organic mulch (like chopped leaves) after planting, to help keep the soil moist and cool.

PENNY WISE

Rain barrels may be an old-fashioned idea, but their time has come again, if you want to collect free water for your too-dry garden. Modern-day models come with attachments that fit gutter downspouts, plus spigots ready-made for attaching a hose, or for filling watering cans. How handy can you get?

Raised Bed Reversal

You've probably heard about gardening in raised beds—but what about sunken beds? Sounds crazy, maybe, but they're a

Sometimes, you can tell which plants are likely to laugh at dry soil just by looking at them. Here are clues to the traits that make some flowers more drought-tolerant than others:

- ✔ Deep roots that resent being transplant-ed—think of peonies, for instance.

- ✔ Fleshy, thickened roots that hold mois-ture—like daylilies (*Hemerocallis*).

- ✔ Silver or gray leaves with waxy or hairy coverings—such as lavenders and dusty miller (*Senecio cineraria*).

- ✔ Thin, or narrow, leaves—yuccas and many ornamental grasses are good examples.

- ✔ Fleshy leaves and stems—such as sedums and hardy cacti (*Opuntia*).

smart solution where water is scarce.

For best results, start in a low-lying area of your yard, then loosen the soil with a rotary tiller or turn it over by hand. Dig in plenty of compost or peat moss as you go—it helps hold more moisture in the soil. Use some of the loosened soil to build up a low berm around the edge, so the surface of the bed is an inch or so below the surrounding soil level. Voilà—you've got your-self a sunken bed that'll catch and keep plenty of rainwater for happier and healthier flowers.

Soggy Soil Solutions

Squishy spots, where water puddles after a rain, can be a real hassle. They're a pain to mow, and many flowers would rather curl up their roots and die, than soak their feet in standing water. But don't despair—before you send your garden dreams out to sea, try these super tricks for parting the waters.

Well, Well—What a Great Idea!

To deal with excess water that flows from gutters or through drainpipes before it gets to your garden, consider installing a dry well. Dig a hole large enough to hold a 55-gallon barrel. Cut both ends off the barrel, fit it into the hole, and backfill around it. Fill up the barrel with large rocks or coarse gravel, then cover the top with a layer of soil. Use downspout extensions or pipes to direct water to the well, where it'll soak gradually into the soil below.

Drain Your Worries Away

Flexible, perforated plastic pipes are perfect for drying out wet sites. To install them, dig a ditch that gradually slopes away from the area you want to drain and toward where you want to catch the water—a ditch, a nearby pond, or a dry well. (A slope of 3 to 6 inches per 100 feet is fine.) Line the bottom of the trench with coarse gravel, lay the pipe, then add more gravel, and top it with topsoil. Presto—no more soggy spots!

Raising the Roots

Too wet to dig down? Then it's time to grow up—with raised beds, that is! To try this approach, mix 1 part coarse builder's sand with 3 parts compost, rotted sawdust, and/or rotted manure. Dig it deeply into the soil, rake it smooth, and let the site settle for three or four weeks. Then smooth out and round off the site with bagged topsoil before planting. A different option is to build a low frame around the area with rocks or lumber, then fill it with a mix of topsoil and compost. With either method, you'll end up with a well-drained bed above a reservoir of damp soil—ideal for keeping deep-rooted perennials happy during the dry, dog days of summer.

GRANDMA PUTT'S
Handy Hints

When my Grandma Putt had lemons, she made lemonade; when she had a wet area, she made a water garden. She'd fill the area with her favorite moisture-loving flowers, including astilbes, cardinal flower (*Lobelia cardinalis*), hostas, and Siberian iris (*Iris sibirica*). What a great way to get the most flower power for the least amount of effort!

Raised beds are a super solution for soggy sites!

Wet 'n' Wild Flowers

Y ou know, some folks are *happy* to have wet soil, because it lets 'em grow some of the showiest perennials and bulbs you can imagine! Here are eight great, no-fuss flowers that'll thank you every day for giving them the evenly moist soil they adore.

Camassias (*Camassia*)

Great blue lobelia
(*Lobelia siphilitica*)

Ironweeds (*Vernonia*)

Joe Pye weeds
(*Eupatorium*)

Queen-of-the-prairie (*Filipendula rubra*)

Scarlet rose mallow (*Hibiscus coccineus*)

Swamp milkweed
(*Asclepias incarnata*)

Swamp sunflower
(*Helianthus angustifolius*)

PROBLEM
SOLVED!

You can fill soggy sites with great-looking shrubs, as well! Swamp azalea (*Rhododendron viscosum*) bears fragrant pink flowers in late June or July. There are dogwoods that love wet feet, too. Try red-twig dogwood (*Cornus stolonifera*), with dark red stems that are especially showy in winter, plus clusters of white blooms in early summer. Combine it with its cheerful cousin, yellow-twig dogwood (*C. stolonifera* 'Flaviramea'), for a dramatic winter display of color.

Coping with Clay

If you're stuck with heavy clay soil, you may be tempted to give up on your garden and take up pottery as a hobby. I don't blame you, because clay can be one of the toughest gardening challenges of all. It's super-sticky when wet, and rock-hard when dry. But don't despair; read on for some great ideas to help you cope with that cloying clay!

And, the Good News Is...

Clay soil is far from *all* bad. Those tiny particles hold lots of nutrients, making clay soils rich and fertile. They are also the last kind of soil to dry out during a drought.

The secret to growing a great garden on clay is adding plenty of organic matter—not just once, but over and over again. Spread a 2- to 4-inch layer of organic matter over the soil each year—a mix of compost and chopped leaves is fine—and dig it into the soil, if you can; otherwise, leave it on top as mulch.

Slippery When Wet

If you have clay soil, I can't give you better advice than this: Don't even *think* about digging or tilling when the ground is wet! Besides making your job 10 times harder, working soggy clay soil will leave you with a compacted mess—definitely not good conditions for flowers to grow in. So before you dig in, pick up a handful of soil and squeeze it. It should be moist enough to stick together when you open your hand, but dry enough to break apart when you tap the clump lightly with your finger. If it sticks to your hand instead, wait a few days, and test again before digging.

How Dry I Am

Clay soil holds on to water for a long time, but once it dries out, it's *really* dry! The surface cracks, and the soil breaks into cement-like chunks that just shed water. The best solution is to never let clay dry out completely. Before it becomes dust-dry, water it slowly and deeply—soaker hoses are perfect for this—and keep it topped with a layer of mulch, such as shredded bark.

Landscape Lingo

You'll often hear gardeners describe clay as **heavy** soil—and no wonder! The densely packed clay particles hold tight to any water that comes by, making the soil hard to dig and definitely heavy to lift.

Pile It On

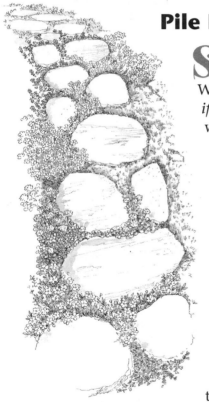

Stepping stones make it easy to reach your plants without squashing the soil.

Some people swear sand's great for loosening up clay, while others insist the opposite's true. Who's right? Here's the real scoop: Sand *can* help, *if* you add enough! Just like organic matter, sand works best when you really pile it on. Spread at least 3 inches of sand over the area, and work it into the top 6 inches of soil. Adding less than that *won't* turn your soil into cement—that's an old wives' tale—but it also won't make a difference in helping loosen up tough clay.

Flower Power Soil Builders

If you're not in a hurry for your new flower garden, try this trick: Prepare the soil as best you can, then sow seeds of some cover crop, like clover or soybeans, in spring or early summer. Mow the tops down in late summer, then till the remains into the soil. Repeat for a second season, if your soil still needs some work. Eventually, you'll have loose, rich, fluffy soil that's a downright joy to dig and plant in.

Salvaging Sandy Soil

If you have sandy soil, you know it. It feels gritty when you rub it between your hands, and you're constantly hauling water to plants that still turn yellow and grow poorly. The secret to successful, sandy-soil gardening is simple: Bulk up your soil to help it hold more moisture and nutrients!

Feel the Burn!

When you exercise, you burn off fat and calories; when sandy soil gets warmed up, it burns up organic stuff! Well, it's not actually the soil that does the burning; it's the tiny critters that live there, breaking down organic matter and making the nutrients available to your plants. Those little, organic critters work overtime in the oxygen-rich conditions of sandy soil, so the nutrients are re-leased faster than your plants can absorb them. Then all that good stuff gets washed down past the roots the next time it rains. To keep this from happening, remember this pair of handy pointers.

❀ Avoid tilling or turning over sandy soil as much as you can. Tilling adds even more air, so the organic matter will disappear even faster.

❀ When you do till or dig, first spread 2 to 4 inches of compost, then work it in as you go. That will give the microbes something to feed on, so they won't deplete what's already in your soil.

To the Rescue!

"All natural" cat box filler—Litter Green® is one brand—is a jim-dandy addition to bulk up sandy soil. It's almost pure alfalfa, so it adds both organic matter and nutrients to your soil.

Undercover Operation

To give sandy soil a never-ending supply of fresh organic matter, always keep it covered with mulch—compost topped with shredded leaves or bark mulch is ideal. Earthworms and other soil organisms will carry the nutrients down to the root zone where they're needed.

Hedge Your Bets

In a seaside garden, salt and wind can be as much of a challenge as the sand is. To cut down on wind-borne salt and create a sheltered haven for your flowers at the same time, surround your garden with hedges of salt-tolerant shrubs. Try some of the following, all of which grow well in sandy soil: American holly (*Ilex opaca*), big-leaved hydrangea (*Hydrangea macrophylla*), forsythias, inkberry (*I. glabra*), junipers, northern bayberry (*Myrica pensylvanica*), and rugosa roses (*Rosa rugosa*).

What's in a Name?

Both common and botanical names offer a super-simple way to find flowers that are suited for sandy soil. Common names that refer to the sea often are applied to plants that thrive there, and thus grow in sandy soil. Sea lavenders (*Limonium*) and sea hollies (*Eryngium*) are two good examples.

In botanical names, look for variations on the word *maritimus*, which means "growing by the sea." Examples here include sea pinks (*Armeria maritima*), sweet alyssum (*Lobularia maritima*), sea kale (*Crambe maritima*), and beach plum (*Prunus maritima*). Of course, many other flowers also thrive in sandy soil, including butterfly weed (*Asclepias tuberosa*), daylilies (*Hemerocallis*), goldenrods (*Solidago*), hostas, peonies, sedums, and yarrows (*Achillea*).

Made for the Shade

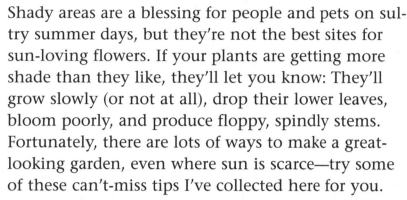

Shady areas are a blessing for people and pets on sultry summer days, but they're not the best sites for sun-loving flowers. If your plants are getting more shade than they like, they'll let you know: They'll grow slowly (or not at all), drop their lower leaves, bloom poorly, and produce floppy, spindly stems. Fortunately, there are lots of ways to make a great-looking garden, even where sun is scarce—try some of these can't-miss tips I've collected here for you.

Spots Make a Splash

Lots of spring-flowering plants thrive in the shade, but come summer, your best bet for color is foliage. Perennials with silver-marked leaves, such as lungworts (*Pulmonaria*) and spotted deadnettle (*Lamium maculatum*) positively glitter in the shade, while 'Burgundy Glow' ajuga contributes multicolored foliage marked with maroon, pink, white, and green. Hostas with green or blue-green leaves that are marked with white and/or yellow are also super choices for adding all-summer color. For brilliant mounds of color, also include some hostas with all-yellow leaves. 'Piedmont Gold' and 'Sum and Substance' are two especially good choices for bringing a touch of sunshine to the shade.

Root Roulette

Besides casting lots of shade, tall trees add another challenge: dense root systems that can suck the water and nutrients right out of

Jerry's TIMELY TIPS

"Sometimes removing a tree limb or two is enough to brighten up a too-shady site. For a day or two, keep a close eye on the site you want to brighten; after that, you should be able to tell if the branch you plan to remove will really let the sun shine in."

My Grandma Putt rarely took a break from her work, but when she did, I knew I'd find her in her shade garden, perched on a bench Grandpa made for her from old barn beams. She always said there was nothing as refreshing as sitting for a spell in the shade among her favorite flowers. So take a tip from Grandma, and make sure you leave space for a bench or chair in one of your shady spots—you'll be glad you did!

any garden you plant directly underneath 'em. If your trees have deep roots, like oaks (*Quercus*) do, you're in luck; shallow-rooted trees, though—like maples (*Acer*)—are a real pain to plant under.

To figure out what's underfoot, use a small spade to gently dig around the trees in your yard. If a solid mass of roots makes digging a bone-jarring job, your best option is to mulch under the tree, and keep flower gardens farther out—beyond where the branch tips end. Believe you me, digging will be a whole lot easier out there!

With their colorful leaves and pretty flowers, hostas are tailor-made for brightening up shady spots.

Get Potted!

Are tree roots making digging too daunting? Potted plants are a perfect way to bring color to those tough sites in the shade. Choose long-blooming annuals like wax begonias (*Begonia semperflorens*) and impatiens (*Impatiens walleriana*) for loads of showy flowers, or coleus for a spectacular show of brightly colored leaves. The larger the container, the better—half-whiskey barrels with holes drilled in the bottom are ideal—because big planters need watering way less often than small pots do.

Solutions for Slopes

Let's face it—gardening on a steep slope can be a nightmare. Soil washes downhill during heavy rains, so it's a hassle to get even the hardiest groundcovers started, let alone pretty perennials and annuals. But don't just give up and ignore that eyesore—good ol' Jerry's here to help you carve great-looking gardens out of even the steepest site!

Quick and Easy Cover-Up

Rushing rainwater carries away soil, and the longer and steeper the slope, the bigger the problem. The secret to saving precious soil is slowing down the water, so it has time to soak in. For a super-simple solution, spread large pieces of burlap over your slope, and fasten it down with wooden pegs. Cut holes in the burlap, and plant right through it. By the time the burlap rots away, your groundcovers will be well established and provide good protection against erosion.

Soaker Hoses Make the Grade

Even drought-tolerant groundcovers need a drink now and then, especially when they're just getting started. If you use a conventional sprinkler, though, the water'll just run off, leaving soil that's dry as a bone. End your watering worries by snaking soaker hoses across that slope, so they run near each plant. Top them with a layer of mulch to cover them up and help the soil hold moisture at the same time. Because these hoses drip so slowly, the water has plenty of time to soak down to the roots.

PROBLEM SOLVED!

To carve out level gardening spaces on a sloping site, build low walls across the slope using stone or landscape timbers. Fill in behind the walls with topsoil, piling it 4 to 6 inches higher than the top of each wall to allow for settling.

Terrific Warped-Wood Terraces

To shore up a slope without spending a lot of time or money, start with lengths of warped, discounted boards—pine four-by-eights are ideal. Start installing your walls at the top of the slope. Either run long boards all the way across a slope, or erect short pieces where each plant will go. (Use them singly or stack them on top of each other to make taller walls.) Drive wooden pegs into the ground to hold the boards in place. Make sure the boards fit firmly against the soil surface, then fill in behind them with soil to make a level planting area. The boards will rot away after a few seasons, but by that time, your slope garden will be well established—*guaranteed!*

Compost on the Move

Try this compost-as-you-go trick to transform a barren slope into a bountiful flower garden. In spring, mark off a strip across a slope that's about 3 feet wide by 4 or 5 feet long. Lightly loosen the soil, then spread leaves, bits of last season's flowers, grass clippings, manure, and some topsoil, too. Add your kitchen scraps and garden trimmings all summer long, and dig 'em in. The following spring, plant flowers or groundcovers in the strip of compost, then start a new strip above or below it. In just a few seasons, you can transform an entire slope, a strip at a time!

Low stone walls are great for terracing slopes, and they make perfect planting sites for rock-garden flowers, too!

Crowd Control

Whether you've got kids running through the yard or a dog that insists on taking a detour through the daisies, people and pet feet can do a real number on your flowerbeds. Either way, you've got smashed plants, compacted soil, and lots of frustration. What's the solution? Redirect that traffic to protect your posies—and save your sanity!

Hedge Your Bets

If your lawn routinely doubles as a soccer or football field, your flowers inevitably suffer. To protect them from trampling feet, falling bodies, and wayward soccer balls, consider surrounding your flower garden with a sturdy hedge. If you don't have room for large shrubs like forsythia, which can withstand the force of a flying football player, consider a row of large ornamental grasses, like miscanthus (*Miscanthus sinensis*)—'Gracillimus' and 'Morning Light' are two handsome selections that form dense clumps reaching 5 to 6 feet tall and wide.

End Mulch Migrations

Bark mulches might all seem the same at first glance, but if you're using them to cover a path, it pays to be picky. I strongly suggest sticking with *shredded* bark, because the pieces tend to knit together. That

---

FL✿WER POWER TONICS

Dog-Be-Gone!

Man's best friend can be your worst traffic nightmare. To keep dogs away from their favorite digging spots, liberally apply this mix to the soil.

2 cloves of garlic
2 small onions
1 jalapeño pepper
1 tbsp. of cayenne pepper
1 tbsp. of Tabasco® sauce
1 tbsp. of chili powder
1 qt. of warm water

Chop the garlic, onions, and jalapeño pepper finely, then combine with all of the remaining ingredients. Let the mix sit for 24 hours, then sprinkle it on any areas where dogs are a problem. ✾

---

makes for a much firmer path than bark *chips*, which tend to slide around underfoot and get pushed off the pathway.

Sounds Like a Super Idea!

There's nothing like sitting a spell in your beautiful flower gardens, but noisy neighbors or nearby traffic can really ruin that quiet time, lickety-split! Thick hedges help muffle sounds, but if you need even more insulation, consider installing outdoor speakers. They're surprisingly easy to install, and you can quickly hook them up to your indoor stereo system.

Now, I'm not suggesting you blast the neighborhood with loud rock and roll. Instead, use your speakers to play "environmental sounds" CDs, like waves crashing on the beach, wind rustling in the trees, or nighttime noises. They will act as "white noise," and help muffle the more unpleasant sounds.

Jerry's TIMELY TIPS

"To enjoy your garden at nighttime without falling into your flowerbeds, consider installing lights along the pathways. Low-voltage lights are a snap to install and safe, even around wet soil. You can buy inexpensive, do-it-yourself kits at garden centers and building supply stores."

The Path to Success

Do family and friends routinely trample your flowers as they cut through gardens, hedges, or what-have-you? It's time to take action! Existing paths are nearly impossible to change, so go with the flow and work them into your garden plan. Here's how:

Step 1: First, dig out (and transplant elsewhere) any flowers that are directly in the path; then widen the path and level it out.

Step 2: Cover it with a material that's different from what you use on your flowerbeds—cement pavers or coarse bark mulch are both top-notch options. Just make sure there's a contrast between the path and your garden, to help remind visitors where to walk.

Step 3: To enforce the new cut-through, line the path with stakes and strings. A row of low-growing perennials or small shrubs on each side of the path is a good added reminder.

Fix-Ups for Faded Foundations

I've seen some really sad foundation plantings in my day—and I'll bet you have, too! Those cute little evergreens look harmless enough when they're new, but then watch out. Without 40 whacks from the clippers every season, they shoot up like skyrockets, and soon, it's "Honey, where's the house?" If this sounds like your yard, never fear—Jerry's here, with a mix of old-time wisdom and newfangled design ideas!

The Foundation of a Great Garden

My Grandma Putt loved tending her gardens, but she didn't love wasting time caring for plants that didn't pull their weight in the bloom department. One big bugbear for her was the boring evergreen shrubs around the foundation of her house. They needed frequent trimming to keep them from blocking her windows, and they didn't produce any pretty flowers to make the work worthwhile.

So one summer, Grandma and I dug out all those losers and replaced them with a mixture of flowering shrubs, like butterfly bush (*Buddleia davidii*) and glossy abelia (*Abelia* x *grandiflora*). These beauties were just the ticket! They made a great back-

PROBLEM SOLVED!

Even plain-green foundation shrubs can "bloom" in summer, if you try my sure-fire secret: Plant annual vines around them! With a little help from you, the climbing stems will wind their way up through the shrub stems—no trellis needed. Morning glories (*Ipomoea*), hyacinth beans (*Lablab purpureus*), and scarlet runner beans (*Phaseolus coccineus*) are all top-notch choices; they offer months of colorful flowers, and they're a cinch to start from seed, too! Or, if you prefer perennial color, consider clematis.

drop for lower-growing perennial and annual flowers, and we could enjoy the blooms from inside, too.

Foil Foundation Weeds

Bored with battling the weeds that always seem to spring up around your foundation shrubs? Here's a handy hint: Fill in the gaps with low-growing groundcovers, like periwinkle (*Vinca minor*), or with vigorous perennials. Plant hardy, spring-blooming bulbs like daffodils and crocuses to come up right through the groundcover, and you'll get twice the beauty from the same amount of space.

Testing, Testing...

Even if you've never bothered testing the soil's pH in the rest of your garden, I strongly suggest you do it for your foundation plantings. (Remember back to chemistry class? pH is a measure of how acidic or alkaline something is, and it ranges from 1.0—very acid—to 14.0—very alkaline.) Most plants grow well when the soil's somewhere between 6.5 and 7.0. Foundation soil tends to be higher than that, though, due to the lime that leaches out of the foundation walls.

Elemental sulfur is super for lowering soil pH, but how much you'll add depends on how alkaline your soil is. A simple pH test takes just a few minutes—you can find inexpensive test kits at your local garden center—and most come with guidelines to help you make any needed adjustments to your soil.

FLOWER POWER TONICS

Foundation Food

Soil along a foundation is often downright awful, at least as far as your plants are concerned. Use the following tonic to build it up and make your plants happy—with a minimum amount of work!

10 parts compost
3 parts bonemeal
2 parts bloodmeal
1 part kelp meal

Mix the ingredients in a garden cart or wheelbarrow. Spread a thin layer (about a half-inch or so) over the entire planting, and lightly scratch it into the soil around shrubs. Add a new layer each year. Top it with shredded bark or other mulch. ❀

Jerry's Garden Idea Gallery

🌸 With so many flowers to choose from, how does anyone decide just what to grow? Well, when you're planning a party, a theme helps you pull all the details together—decorations, what to serve, you name it—and that's true for a garden, too. So if you're fresh out of ideas for your new garden, take a stroll through my idea gallery to get those creative juices flowing again!

Roses and Company

Roses sure look lonely planted alone in a bed, all by themselves, but there's no law that says they have to be that way. My Grandma Putt always mixed her favorites in with other flowers to make gardens that were chock-full of blooms all summer long. Besides looking great, the roses she paired with other plants always seemed twice as healthy as those stuck off by themselves. Try growing roses this way once yourself, and you'll discover the secret to rose-growing success!

For Cryin' Out Loud!

Roses have a reputation for being pest- and disease-prone, but with a little know-how, it's perfectly possible to have problem-free roses—without spraying. And, here's one of my best tips to start you off: Try planting onions under your roses! Companion planting experts swear that onions and their relatives protect roses from blackspot and mildew (two pesky fungal diseases), as well as aphids.

Ordinary onions aren't pretty enough to add to flowerbeds, but many of their relatives are real eye-catchers. Chives, for instance, make a handsome edging for beds containing roses. Other low-growing, ornamental onions that make rousing rose companions include yellow-flowered lily leek (*Allium moly*), rose-purple to pink-flowered nodding onion (*A. cernuum*), and mauve-pink (*A. senescens*).

FLOWER POWER TONICS

Really Rosy Potpourri

Don't let fall call an end to your rosy pleasures—mix dried pink, red, and white petals together to make this pretty pot-pourri you can enjoy all winter long. For extra color, add 1 cup of dried flowers from delphiniums, bee balms (*Monarda*), or bachelor's buttons (*Centaurea cyanus*).

¼ cup of orrisroot nuggets
2½ tsp. of rose essential oil
3 cups of dried rose petals
1 cup of dried rosebuds
1 cup of dried rose geranium leaves
    and flowers
1 cup of dried lavender flowers
¼ cup of dried, crushed lemon peel

Combine the orrisroot nuggets and the essential oil (both available at craft stores) in a small, airtight glass jar for two days. Mix the remaining ingredients together, add the orrisroot/oil mix, and store in a large, airtight jar for two weeks. Shake the mix daily to blend the scents, then display as desired. ✽

A Flower Shop in Your Backyard

Stumped about what to plant with your roses? Think about the flowers you like to combine for indoor arrangements, then plant them together out in your garden. Some spectacular annual companions for roses—both in and out of the vase—include cosmos (*Cosmos bipinnatus*), dahlias, larkspur (*Consolida ajacis*), mealycup sage (*Salvia farinacea*), statices (*Limonium* and *Psylliostachys*), and zinnias.

Perennials pair well with roses, too. Think of including summer-blooming phlox (*Phlox carolina*, *P. maculata*, and *P. paniculata*), pincushion flower (*Scabiosa columbaria*), and Shasta daisies (*Leucan-*

themum x *superbum*). And don't forget summer bulbs: Gladiolus and lilies (*Lilium*) are absolutely elegant with roses.

Best Bets
for the Big Chill

If you live in the North, where frigid winters freeze most roses to the quick, don't despair! Canadian rose breeders have developed beautiful, super-hardy roses that are also disease-resistant. Look for Prairie Series roses, produced in Manitoba—'Prairie Dawn' is one. Other super-tough roses include 'Champlain', 'Cuthbert Grant', 'Henry Hudson', 'John Cabot', 'Morden Fireglow', and 'William Baffin'.

To the Rescue!

Rose blooms may be the queens of the flower garden, but the plants themselves aren't all that much to look at. Hybrid Teas, Floribundas, and Grandifloras—three of the most commonly grown kinds of roses—are particularly prone to losing their lower leaves. So what's the answer? Cover up those bare ankles with lower-growing flowers! Aromatic-leaved herbs, such as catmints (*Nepeta*) and lavenders, are especially nice; they add beautiful, purple-blue flowers that look great with all colors of roses, and their aromatic leaves may also help send pests packing.

A low hedge of lavender is a top-notch option for edging rose beds.

An Herb-and-Flower Garden

Sure, it's great to have a garden that *looks* pretty—but how about one that *tastes* good, too? Sound impossible? Not when you add blooming herbs and edible flowers to your beds and borders! To make your herb-and-flower supply super-handy, keep the patch as close to your kitchen door as possible. That way, you can pop out whenever the mood strikes you and gather what you need in a jiffy!

Jerry's TIMELY TIPS

"There are two essential rules to remember when using edible flowers. First—not all flowers are edible, so before you use a flower in your kitchen, always be absolutely, 100 percent sure you've identified it correctly, and that it is edible. And second—only use flowers that haven't been sprayed with any kind of garden chemicals."

Pretty Tasty

Edible flowers are far from rare or exotic; in fact, some are actually quite common. Think of broccoli, for example: We usually eat the clustered flower buds, but if they burst into bloom before harvest, you can still enjoy the bright yellow flowers in salads and stir-fries. Squash, pumpkins, and zucchini are also excellent choices, producing huge, golden yellow, edible blossoms that rival any traditional garden flower for good looks. Unless you have room to spare in your flowerbed, though, choose dwarf or bush-type plants; vining types'll spread too far and wide.

Handle with Care

You don't need any special tools to harvest herbs and edible flowers—just a pair of sharp scissors for snipping. You see, yanking on stems or pulling off flowers damages the plants—especially the roots—slowing down growth and reducing your harvest. But with one clean cut, you'll get damage-free leaves and flowers for your kitchen, and the plants that are left can keep producing more for you to pick later!

Please Eat the Perennials!

Take a look around your garden, and be prepared for a surprise: I'll bet you're already growing some edible flowers! Here's a Baker's half-dozen of terrific-looking *and* tasty perennials.

Bee balms (*Monarda*)

Daylilies (*Hemerocallis*, buds or flowers)

Lavenders (*Lavandula*)

Pinks (*Dianthus*)

Violets (*Viola*)

Yuccas (*Yucca*)

Keep mints and other spreaders under control by planting them in a sunken pot.

Make Mints Stay Put

Mints look good, smell great, and taste even better! Give them half a chance, though, and they'll overrun your garden with lightning speed. To make mints behave themselves, plant them in large containers sunk into the soil, so that the rim extends about an inch above the soil surface. (The jumbo pots used to grow trees and shrubs are ideal.) Check on them periodically to make sure that the meandering mint roots don't jump the rim and wander where they're not wanted.

Annual Edibles

Never experimented with edible flowers? Then easy-to-grow annuals are just the ticket for getting started. Begin your herb-and-flower patch with several different basils. Both their leaves and flowers are edible, and they come in the pungent, conventional flavor, as well as lemon, cinnamon, anise, and spicy Thai tastes. Other edible annuals include bachelor's buttons (*Centaurea cyanus*), borage (*Borago officinalis*), nasturtium (*Tropaeolum majus*), pansies and Johnny-jump-ups (*Viola tricolor*), pot marigold (*Calendula officinalis*), and snapdragon (*Antirrhinum majus*).

Don't You Dare Eat These!

While the following flowers are pretty in the garden—and beautiful in bouquets—none are *ever* safe for serving as food:

Bleeding hearts (*Dicentra*)

Buttercups (*Ranunculus*)

Clematis (*Clematis*)

Daffodils (*Narcissus*)

Delphiniums (*Delphinium*)

Foxgloves (*Digitalis*)

Hydrangeas (*Hydrangea*)

Larkspurs (*Consolida*)

Monkshoods (*Aconitum*)

Rhododendrons and azaleas (*Rhododendron*)

Rose periwinkle (*Catharanthus*)

The best time to gather edible flowers? Just before their petals begin to unfold, or just as they've opened all the way. Washing flowers is likely to damage them, so it's smart to keep them from getting dirty in the first place; simply keep the soil around them covered with mulch. Harvest only the blooms that are clean and well above the ground. If you still need to clean them up, rinse them lightly with a gentle spray of water.

A Better Butterfly Garden

Ever since I helped Grandma Putt in her garden as a little boy, I've loved butterflies. They seem like floating flowers themselves as they flit from bloom to bloom, sipping nectar. In Grandma Putt's garden, marigolds and zinnias were especially popular butterfly stops. To make a garden where butterflies feel right at home, you'll also want to grow plants that feed caterpillars (baby butterflies), as well as take steps to protect the pupae (the stage where caterpillars transform into adults). For more tips on making your yard a haven for these winged wonders, read on!

Bright-Eyed and Butterflied

If you grow only one butterfly-attracting flower, make it a butterfly bush (*Buddleia davidii*). Also called summer lilac, it produces lilac-like clusters of tiny, orange-eyed blooms that are literally covered with butterflies from midsummer to fall. The flowers are fragrant, too! What more could you ask for?

Crazy for Daisies

Plant a parade of daisies in your garden, and you're sure to see a bounty of butterflies all summer long. All of

GRANDMA PUTT'S Handy Hints

Grandma Putt always planted an extra patch of parsley 'specially for the caterpillars, or larvae, of swallowtail butterflies. Showy swallowtails are worth the extra trouble; they're big, black-and-yellow butterflies that can be more than 3 inches long. When Grandma Putt found the plump, stripy green caterpillars feasting on her kitchen supply of parsley, she'd gently move them over to "their" patch.

these easy-to-grow perennials like full sun and bear cheerful daisies guaranteed to keep butterflies happy: asters, blanket flowers (*Gaillardia*), coneflowers (*Echinacea* and *Rudbeckia*), coreopsis, oxeye (*Heliopsis helianthoides*), Shasta daisies (*Leucanthemum* x *superbum*), and sneezeweed (*Helenium autumnale*).

Weeds That Feed

Looking for an excuse to put off clearing that weed patch in the backyard? Well, consider this: Weedy spots here and there in your yard actually *increase* the number of butterflies you'll see! That's because many caterpillars depend on weeds for food. Burdock (*Arctium lappa*), docks (*Rumex*), milkweeds (*Asclepias*), plantains (*Plantago*), Queen Anne's lace (*Daucus carota*), and thistles (*Cirsium*), as well as many grasses, are all top-notch caterpillar plants.

To keep these butterfly banquets from being unsightly, locate them in an out-of-the-way spot away from the neighbors, and cut off all the flowers *before* they go to seed and spread everywhere.

Make a Mud Puddle...

Ever seen butterflies sitting on a muddy spot along a stream or pond? They're actually probing the mud for water, salt, and other nutrients. To make a similar spot in your own yard, remove weeds from a low spot and water it regularly. If you don't have a natural low spot, dig out a shallow bowl of soil, line it with a square of plastic (the kind used to line water gardens is perfect), refill with soil, and then keep it wet.

To the Rescue!

Annuals are your best bet if you want a butterfly garden in a hurry. Plant a small bed with clumps of the following annuals, then stand back, and watch the show!

Ageratum (*Ageratum houstonianum*)

Bloodflower (*Asclepias curassavica*)

Cosmos (*Cosmos*)

Lupines (*Lupinus*)

Marigolds (*Tagetes*)

Mexican sunflowers (*Tithonia rotundifolia*)

Pot marigolds (*Calendula officinalis*)

Sages or salvias (*Salvia*)

Sunflowers (*Helianthus annuus*)

Sweet alyssum (*Lobularia maritima*)

Sweet peas (*Lathyrus*)

Zinnias (*Zinnia*)

...Or Build a Butterfly Bath

Hey—butterflies get thirsty, too, so why should birds have all the fun? To make your birdbath do double duty, fill it with rounded stones that stick out from the water surface. Then the butterflies can rest on the stones, and get a drink without getting their feet wet.

A Garden That Makes Scents

When I'm searching for blooms that smell good, I don't have much patience for newfangled flowers. Old-fashioned ones—the kind my Grandma Putt grew—are the best bet for filling any garden with fragrance. Here's a bouquet of additional tricks to help you grow the best-smellin' yard on the block!

Choose Just a Few

It's easy to get caught up like a kid in a candy shop when you're choosing fragrant flowers. Try to control yourself at least a little bit, though: Planting too many perfumed blooms in one area will just give you a hodgepodge of mixed-up aromas. Instead, aim for large clumps of a few fragrant flowers that'll fill the air with their signature scents. Clumps of spicy-scented lemon lilies (*Hemerocallis lilioasphodelus*),

GARDEN SMARTS

Wind can be the downfall of a fragrance garden, because it blows away the scents you want to enjoy. So for best results, pick a spot protected from breezes—ideally near a window or outdoor sitting area. Hedges and shrub borders also help cut down on wind, and keep fragrances lingering in the air. Trellises covered with vines are another good option for wind protection.

"The secret to preserving fragrant plants for crafts, like potpourri? Getting them dry lickety-split, before mold and mildew can spoil the scents and colors. Start with a warm, well-ventilated place, like an attic. Darkness is best, but not absolutely essential. Bundle the stems with rubber bands, then hang them from the rafters, a ladder, or a rack suspended from the ceiling. Small bundles dry quickest, so stick to a few stems each. To dry rose petals and small flowers, spread them out in a single layer on old window screens."

sweet August lilies (*Hosta plantaginea*), or richly perfumed Oriental hybrid lilies (*Lilium*) are all unforgettable.

Bundle Up

Want to enjoy flowery fragrances from your garden even in wintertime? Save the dried stalks of fragrant herbs and other scented plants from your garden. Tie up 8- or 10-inch-long bundles of stems with cotton string. Toss a bundle or two into your fireplace, or even on your outdoor grill, for a heavenly reminder of summer. Perfect plants to bundle and burn include basils, bee balms (*Monarda*), lavenders, lemon verbena (*Aloysia triphylla*), mint, rosemary, and thyme.

Bulbs on the Move

Powerfully perfumed bulbs like hyacinths and tuberoses (*Polianthes tuberosa*) can be a bit overwhelming if you plant too many in one place. Instead, grow them in several smaller pots with a few bulbs in each. Keeping them all in one place makes them easier to care for while they're growing, but once their flowers show a touch of color, scatter the pots around on your porch, deck, or patio—and enjoy!

Perfumed Pathways

To sample the fragrance of scented foliage plants, you need to rub or crush the leaves. That makes them a perfect choice for planting along paths, where legs will brush by them, and feet will step on them.

❀ Some of my all-time favorites for perfumed paths include catmints (*Nepeta*), lavenders, lemon balm (*Melissa officinalis*), lemon thyme (*Thymus* x *citriodorus*), and southernwood (*Artemisia abrotanum*).

Thymes and other low-growing herbs are perfect for planting between stepping stones.

❀ Scented geraniums (*Pelargonium*) are also great for edging a walkway. They come in dozens of fabulous fragrances, from apple, lemon, and rose to mint, nutmeg, and coconut.

❀ Between stepping stones, plant mat-forming wild thyme (*Thymus serpyllum*) and Roman chamomile (*Chamaemelum nobile*), which release their spicy or sweet scent as you step on them.

A Humdinger of a Hummingbird Garden

Wanna really bring your garden to life? These aerial daredevils are nothing short of magic in the garden! Hummingbirds can dart from flower to flower with more control than a fighter pilot, hover in mid-air, actually back up in mid-flight, and then zoom away at speeds of 50 to 60 miles per hour.

Reel 'Em in with Red

Patches of scarlet or orange flowers are guaranteed to roll out the red carpet for hummingbirds. But, what if those colors don't really turn *you* on? Don't despair: Flower shape is just as—or even more—important than color. Hummers will visit blooms of many

colors, including pink, white, lavender, and purple. What they *really* like is just about any bloom with a tubular or trumpet shape. Once they discover a particular patch offers nectar—whatever the flower color—they'll visit it again and again.

Shade and Spiders

Why this odd combo? Hummingbirds need both a shady spot and nearby spiderwebs to build a nest and raise a family. They build their tiny nests in shady spots, using milkweed and thistledown surrounded by bits of leaves, lichen, and bark, all stuck together with silk from spiderwebs. While there's not much you can do to attract spiders, it's smart to leave any webs you do find, to keep your hummers happy.

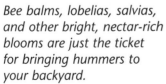

Bee balms, lobelias, salvias, and other bright, nectar-rich blooms are just the ticket for bringing hummers to your backyard.

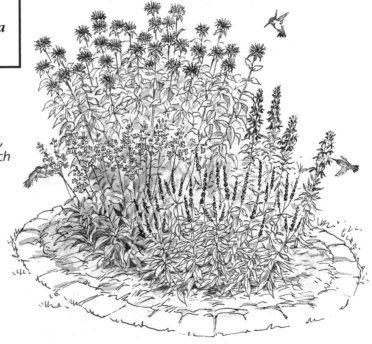

Best Bets for Hummers

Hummingbirds like lots of different flowers, but like people, they have some special favorites. So fill your yard with these nectar-rich blooms, then stand back to enjoy the summertime show!

Annuals: Flowering tobaccos (*Nicotiana*), petunias, salvias, snapdragon (*Antirrhinum majus*), verbenas, and zonal geraniums (*Pelargonium*).

Bulbs: Crocosmias, gladiolus, lilies (*Lilium*), and magic lilies (*Lycoris*).

Perennials and biennials: Beardtongues (*Penstemon*), bee balm (*Monarda didyma*), cardinal flower (*Lobelia cardinalis*), daylilies (*Hemerocallis*), foxgloves (*Digitalis*), hostas, phlox, red-hot poker (*Kniphofia*), and yuccas.

Vines: Honeysuckles (*Lonicera*), morning glories (*Ipomoea*), and trumpet vine (*Campsis radicans*).

Bath Time!

Hummingbirds visit conventional birdbaths, but to really make them happy, install a fountain that sends up a fine mist. You can find these at places that specialize in supplies for feeding wild birds. All kinds of birds are attracted to water, but hummingbirds find these mist fountains especially enticing. They'll actually fly right through the mist to bathe in midair.

FL✳WER POWER TONICS

Hummingbird Nectar

Hummers will visit a feeder all summer long, once they get the idea it's filled with nectar. You can buy packets of nectar mix, but making your own is easy and inexpensive.

1 part white sugar (not honey, which hosts bacteria harmful to hummers)
4 parts water
A few drops of red food coloring (optional)

Boil the mix and let it cool before filling the feeder. Once hummers start coming, decrease the solution to about 1 part sugar and 8 parts water. No, this isn't the old bait-and-switch tactic—there's a good reason for diluting the solution. Hummingbirds can sometimes suffer a fatal liver disorder if they get too much sugar.

Replace the nectar every three days or so—every other day, if temperatures are above 60°F. Wash the feeder with soap and scalding water. Rinse thoroughly. Otherwise, the nectar and/or feeder can host hummingbird-harming bacteria. ✳

Go Wild with Wildflowers

Still searching for the perfect garden theme? Well, then, how about an all-American garden? No, I don't mean red, white, and blue flowers—I mean plants that are native to the good ol' US of A! To make your wildflower garden a sure-fire success, stick to plants that grow naturally in your area. They're most likely to thrive in the soil and with the amount of rainfall that occur in your climate—all with a minimum of effort from you!

Let the Sun Shine In

If you go about it the right way, getting a wildflower patch going is just as easy as any other garden. The first step is to kill weeds and grass, but don't sweat it—let the sun do the work for you!

PENNY WISE

Sure, seeds are cheap; but, if you want fast results from a new meadow garden, plants are *definitely* the way to go! You don't need to buy big plants, though; look for small starts, called plugs, available from wildflower specialists. For an even cheaper alternative, grow your own plugs from seeds.

Step 1: In early summer, dig up the turf with a sharp spade, and lightly till the soil.

Step 2: Dig a shallow trench around the plot, then water the whole area until the ground is sopping wet.

Step 3: Cover the site with a sheet of clear plastic, and bury the edges in the trench. The sun will heat up the ground and cook any weed seeds and grass roots.

Step 4: In late summer, simply take off the plastic, rough up the soil *slightly*, and away you go!

Be a Smart Shopper

If you decide to buy plants to start your wildflower garden—instead of growing them yourself from seed—avoid buying plants that were dug from the wild. People who collect wildflowers destroy our country's precious natural areas, and buying the plants they sell just encourages more collecting. Good garden centers sell nursery-propagated plants, and are proud of that fact. Here's how to tell if plants have been grown in a nursery or collected from the wild:

Nursery-propagated plants. These look healthy, and uniform, with plants centered in pots that are filled with uniform soil mix.

Wild-collected plants. These often look like they were just potted up, with plants sitting off-center in the pots. They often seem large for the pots they are in, but they have few roots, and their leaves and stems are often broken. Two other clues: weeds in the pots, and very cheap prices.

To the Rescue!

Even if you have a shady yard, you can still have an all-American wildflower garden. Here are eight great native shade perennials to consider:

Crested iris (*Iris cristata*)

Foamflowers (*Tiarella*)

Heucheras (*Heuchera*)

Snakeroots (*Cimicifuga*)

Spiderworts (*Tradescantia*)

Wild bleeding heart (*Dicentra eximia*)

Wild blue phlox (*Phlox divaricata*)

Wild cranesbill (*Geranium maculatum*)

Drifting Away

For a knock-your-socks-off wildflower garden, try this trick: Instead of mixing dozens of different plants, choose only two or three kinds, then set them out in drifts. Stumped by what to plant? Look at local roadsides and meadow areas, and identify the showiest flowers you see. Search them out in seed catalogs, or look for their cultivated relatives at your local garden center.

A Formal Affair

If you like to keep your yard in apple-pie order, a formal flower garden might be just the thing for you. That doesn't mean you have to sacrifice beauty for elegance, though—you can have both! My Grandma Putt's whole yard brimmed with flowers, for instance; it's just that some parts were fancier than others. Her most formal garden had four square beds edged with lavender and divided by two brick paths, with a birdbath in the center. If that sounds like something you'd enjoy in your own yard, here's how to do it!

FLOWER POWER TONICS

Wonderful Weed Killer

Nothing spoils the look of a formal garden quicker than weed-filled paths. Use this tonic to kill weeds in gravel walks, or in cracks between bricks or stones in walkways.

1 gal. of white vinegar
1 cup of table salt
1 tbsp. of liquid dish soap

Mix all of the ingredients together until the salt has dissolved. Spray the solution on weeds, or pour it along cracks to kill weeds. Don't spray it on plants that you want to keep, and don't pour it on soil that you plan to garden in someday! ✿

Pointers for "Proper" Garden Plots

Not sure just what makes a *formal* garden? Well, here are some clues:

✿ The beds are in a geometric shape: square, rectangular, triangular, oval, or circular.

✿ The beds are often arranged in pairs to create a sense of order and balance.

✿ Walkways are usually straight and always feature crisp edges; they're typically made from brick, stone, or gravel.

✿ Formal gardens also may feature brick or stone walls, or fences with a simple, elegant design.

Hedges for Edges

This gem of a garden has all the trademarks of a formal planting: symmetrical beds, straight paths, and even a sundial in the center!

While classic formal gardens are often outlined by miles of close-clipped mini-hedges, you can have a formal design without facing those maintenance monsters. First, choose dwarf shrubs for your evergreen hedges; they'll need only a light trim here and there. Also, don't shear your evergreens into rectangles and globes. (Once you start, you'll have to keep trimming them several times a summer to keep them looking neat.) Instead, opt for rounded, more natural-looking shapes that mirror a plant's natural growth habit. Want even less work? Hedges of low-growing perennials, such as lilyturfs (*Liriope muscari*), need little or no pruning.

Pick Pairs to Please

That "everything in its place" look of a formal garden is due to a balanced design. A tree or shrub on one side of the garden, for instance, is paired with a matching plant on the other side. You can plant everything in pairs, or pick just a few main features to repeat—like a particular perennial, or some special pots—and mix up the rest.

If you have two existing beds filled with different flowers, you can still give them a pleasing, formal touch; simply plant the same small tree in the center of each bed. Dwarf shrubs marking each corner, or a low hedge as an edging, will also do the trick.

To the Rescue!

If you want a fancy, low edging hedge that doesn't require a lifetime commitment, then annuals are the answer! Joseph's coat (*Alternanthera ficoidea*) and blood leaf (*Iresine*) both have downright dazzling foliage, and they're a snap to shear into a low hedge that'll last all summer. To create the appearance of a hedge quickly, space the plants close together, then pinch them often to encourage branching.

Get Potted!

Want to decorate your porch or patio with something that's a little different than those good ol' red geraniums? Pots overflowing with an abundance of annuals are always eye-catching, so don't be afraid to experiment! After all, if a combo doesn't work out, you can mambo those plants out to the garden, or simply try again next season.

Container Considerations

Here's the secret to show-stopping container gardens that are a snap to care for: Start with the biggest pots you can manage. Large containers hold more soil, so they need to be watered less often—and that translates into less work for you!

Pea-Nutty Pots

A word to the wise—big planters weigh a ton, even before they're filled with soil. To lighten the load, fill the bottom third of each pot with Styrofoam "peanuts," then fill the rest of the container with potting mix. Water thoroughly, and add more mix so it comes to within an inch or two of the rim. Gently firm it down, then you're all set to plant.

Flash Floods

A sprinkle here and a splash there don't do anything for thirsty flowers—especially when they're growing in containers. When you water, flood the soil surface, let the water soak in, and flood it again. Keep it up until water comes out of the hole in the bottom of the pot.

A Shady Idea

Believe you me—scorching summer sun can dry out even well-watered pots in a New York minute! If you aren't home during the day, give pots a spot where they'll be shaded during the afternoon hours. That way, if they do dry out, the plants won't shrivel before you have a chance to water in the early evening.

Best Bets for Containers

The trick to creating professional-looking container combinations is to include good-looking foliage

A collection of potted plants lets you have lots of color, even where there's no space for a garden!

along with beautiful blooms. Here are some of my favorite container choices to get you going:

ANNUALS FOR FOLIAGE

Blood leaf (*Iresine*)

Coleus (*Solenostemon*)

Dusty miller (*Senecio cineraria*)

Licorice plant (*Helichrysum petiolare*)

Ornamental sweet potato (*Ipomoea batatas*)

Persian shield (*Strobilanthes dyerianus*)

Polka-dot plant (*Hypoestes phyllostachya*)

Purple fountain grass (*Pennisetum setaceum* 'Rubrum')

Scented geraniums (*Pelargonium*)

FLOWER POWER TONICS

Potted Plant Picnic

Container plants need lots of energy to stay chock-full of flowers, so whatever you do, don't skimp on the fertilizer! Here's a meal your potted plants are sure to appreciate.

2 tbsp. of brewed black coffee
2 tbsp. of whiskey
1 tsp. of fish emulsion
½ tsp. of unflavored gelatin
½ tsp. of baby shampoo
½ tsp. of ammonia
1 gal. of water

Mix all of the ingredients together and feed to each of your potted perennials and bulbs once a week. ❀

LONG-BLOOMING ANNUALS

Bacopas (*Bacopa*)

Begonias (*Begonia*)

Dwarf cannas (*Canna*)

Heliotrope
(*Heliotropium arborescens*)

Marigolds (*Tagetes*)

Ornamental peppers
(*Capsicum annuum*)

Petunias (*Petunia*)

Salvias (*Salvia*)

Verbenas (*Verbena*)

Zonal geraniums
(*Pelargonium*)

A Free-for-All Cottage Garden

Cottage gardens are perfect for anyone who simply can't resist any pretty plants they see. These gardens feature every kind of flower, along with vines, shrubs, herbs, and edibles, all mixed up in whatever arrangement looks good to the gardener. The beds can be square, oval, or free-form, while garden ornaments range from rustic to whimsical. Since there are no real rules, cottage gardens are as individual as the people who plant them!

Sow Where They'll Grow

To create that cottage-y look right from the start, scatter the seed of your favorite flowers in patches all through your garden. To ensure big, healthy bloomers, loosen the soil in each spot first, work in a handful of compost, and then sow. Gently firm each area to make sure the seeds and soil are touching. If you don't get rain, water the patches daily until seedlings appear.

Once your garden-sown seedlings have two or three sets of leaves, thin some of them out, to give the remaining plants enough elbow room. Cut off the smallest plants with scissors, or use a small trowel to dig up extras and move them to a new spot.

The More, the Merrier!

There's always room for just one more plant in a cottage garden! Empty spaces between perennials, for instance, make great spots for homeless annuals. In summer, once garden centers start their end-of-season sales, pick up some extra plants, cheap. For best results, pinch back the top growth, and loosen overcrowded roots

with a knife or the tip of a pencil before planting. This harsh treatment encourages a growth spurt, so these transplants will need to be well watered for a few weeks. Most annuals you treat this way will respond with gusto, and bloom right up to frost.

Cheerful Color Combos

A cottage garden is the perfect place to put *every* flower you love, regardless of whether the colors are compatible. Shocking combos—hot pink rose campion (*Lychnis coronaria*) next to gold-and-maroon gloriosa daisies (*Rudbeckia hirta*), for instance—are all part of a cottage garden's charm.

Pop-Up Flowers

Self-sowing annuals and biennials are the backbone of any cottage garden. They'll pop up dependably in different spots from year to year, so you never know quite what to expect—but you know it'll look great!

ANNUALS

Bachelor's buttons (*Centaurea cyanus*)

Cosmos (*Cosmos bipinnatus*)

Larkspur (*Consolida ajacis*)

Love-in-a-mist (*Nigella damascena*)

Nasturtium (*Tropaeolum majus*)

Poppies (*Papaver*)

Pot marigold (*Calendula officinalis*)

Spider flower (*Cleome hasslerana*)

BIENNIALS

Dame's rocket
(*Hesperis matronalis*)

Foxglove
(*Digitalis purpurea*)

Hollyhock
(*Alcea rosea*)

Mulleins (*Verbascum*)

Rose campion
(*Lychnis coronaria*)

Plant 'Em, Pot 'n' All!

Many self-sowing annuals just curl up their roots and die at the thought of transplanting. That makes it pretty tough to get them going, if you don't want to sow their seeds directly into the garden. To make transplanting them as low-stress as possible, try this trick: Sow the seeds in individual peat pots to minimize root disturbance at transplanting time.

When setting out the seedlings, be sure to tear off the top rim of the peat pot, so that it doesn't extend above the soil surface. Otherwise, the pot will dry out, and the roots won't be able to push through it to the soil beyond. After that first year, self-sowers will take care of the seed-starting process themselves!

Color Combos to Go

Planting a garden in your favorite colors is a sure way to put a smile on your face. Choose a single color, such as an all white or all blue-and-purple planting, or try a special combination, like blue-and-yellow or red-and-white, as your theme. Either way, picking plants by color is a super trick for simplifying your garden planning!

Celebrate Your Colors

For a riotous color-theme garden that's a celebration of school spirit, plant a bed in your school colors—red and gold, purple and orange, gold and black. While flowers will provide most of the color, don't overlook foliage, either— especially if colors like maroon or black are part of the picture. Cannas with maroon leaves are a good choice for dark foliage; ornamental peppers (*Capsicum annuum*) with purple or nearly black leaves are available, too!

Keep Your Cool

If you have a tiny yard, consider a cool-color theme garden. Cool colors—blue, violet, purple, and green—make things look farther away than warm colors—yellow, red, and orange—do. They'll make your small yard look a bit bigger, and hey, every little bit helps!

Look Beyond Blooms

Flowers are the most obvious element in a color-theme garden, but they aren't your only option; other features can help carry out the idea, too! Plants with variegated leaves are great as part of a white or yellow theme, for example. And even subtler features, like colorful stems or berries, can help carry the idea throughout the garden. Don't forget accessories, either, such as a painted picket fence behind an all white garden, or a robin's-egg blue pot in a pastel-theme planting.

A special plant in your yard can be all the inspiration you need to pick a color theme. A pink-flowered crabapple (*Malus*), for instance, looks super surrounded with beds of pink annuals and perennials. And a maroon-leaved Japanese maple (*Acer palmatum*) can be the centerpiece of a garden filled with plants that echo its rich color in flowers and foliage.

Plan a Party Garden

Still stumped for ideas? Let your social calendar help you pick a color theme! If you host an annual picnic on the Fourth of July, for instance, a red-white-and-blue garden is a must. Or, if you're planning a garden wedding or formal summer party, start the season off right by planting flowers in an all-white theme.

Plant a Pattern

Whether you want a flowerbed that's shaped like a rainbow, a butterfly, or the Stars and Stripes, start by preparing the soil and raking it smooth. Use a long stick to "draw" the pattern you want in the soil. "Erase" it with a rake and redraw it until you're satisfied, then set out bedding plants or sow seeds in the pattern's spaces. Fill in around the main shape with a plain green or silver-leaved annual to create a neutral background that'll help the pattern stand out. For best effect, choose plants that all mature at about the same height.

Light Up the Night

Time to get the kids to school. Time to leave for work. Time to make dinner. But no time to enjoy the garden? Sure there is! The trick is to plan a garden that looks great when you have time to enjoy it—in the evening.

Light-colored flowers seem to glow long after dusk—and even all night long, when the moon is up. As an added bonus, many evening-opening flowers release rich scents in the still night air.

A Bright Idea

When planning a garden for evening strolling, be sure all the paths are level and easy to negotiate, especially after dark. Cement stepping stones are easy to see after dark, making them a better choice than dark pavers or mulch. You might also consider adding a low-voltage lighting system; it's easy to install and relatively inexpensive. Use these lights to illuminate tricky spots, such as steps, where visitors could stumble. Catalogs and well-stocked garden centers now offer solar-powered lights, as well.

White Shines at Night

For a garden that's easy to see in the evening, choose plants with white or very pale yellow blooms. Flowers with large petals, such as lilies (*Lilium*), show up best, but masses of small blossoms, like white-flowered impatiens or pinks (*Dianthus*), are also effective. Leaves marked with white shine after sunset, too. Try 'Francee', 'Patriot', 'So Sweet', and 'Wide Brim' hostas, as well as spotted deadnettle (*Lamium maculatum*).

Jerry's TIMELY TIPS

"If you usually get home from work after dark, be sure to plant a patch of fragrant, night-flowering annuals such as four-o'clocks (Mirabilis jalapa) *and flowering tobacco* (Nicotiana sylvestris) *right next to your garage. They'll welcome you home every evening, all season long."*

Silver Shines after Sunset

Plants with woolly white or silver leaves sure do show up beautifully in the evening—especially when there's a full moon. My all-time favorite silvery annual is dusty miller (*Senecio cineraria*); it's practically indestructible! If you're in the market for a perennial instead, try English lavender (*Lavandula angustifolia*), lamb's ears (*Stachys byzantina*), rose campion (*Lychnis coronaria*), and Russian sage (*Perovskia atriplicifolia*), or any of the silvery wormwoods (*Artemisia*).

Dusky Delights

Flowers that scent the air after sunset add a touch of magic to any evening garden. Here are my top-five favorite fragrant flowers for nighttime:

Dame's rocket (*Hesperis matronalis*)

Flowering tobacco (*Nicotiana alata* Nicki Series, *N. x sanderae* 'Fragrant Cloud', and *N. sylvestris*)

Heliotrope (*Heliotropium arborescens*)

Moonflower (*Ipomoea alba*)

Night-scented stock (*Matthiola longipetala*)

Make garden paths easier to see at night by lining them with silver-leaved plants, such as lavender.

They Just Make Scents

If you're searching for a great container plant for your patio or deck, look no further than angel's trumpets (*Brugmansia*). These shrubby plants produce pendant, 10-inch-long trumpet-shaped blooms that are intensely scented at night. (Unless you live in a frost-free climate, bring

GARDEN SMARTS

Flowers with evening fragrance are most noticeable just after sunset, when the air is still and humid and the temperature begins to cool down. To get the most pleasure out of your perfumed plants, select a sheltered spot for your night garden, so the scents won't blow away. Or plant fragrant flowers all around the edge of an outdoor sitting area, so you can enjoy them no matter which direction the breeze is coming from.

these beauties into a 45°F room for the winter.) A similar annual plant, *Datura metel,* is commonly called moonflower. It bears fragrant, upward-facing trumpets. Note: All parts of both plants are poisonous if they're ingested.

PART 2

A Healthy Garden
Is a
Happy Garden

My Grandma Putt was downright fussy about her flowers—at least when it came to getting them in the ground. They had to be in just the right spot, and she never planted one without a splash of one of her tonics, plus a shovelful of compost to keep the roots happy. Sure enough, that little bit of TLC always got her flower garden up and growing like gangbusters!

Over the years, I've relied on Grandma's gardening secrets to keep my flowerbeds in top shape—and I've learned lots of new tricks along the way. I'll talk about the down-and-dirty details of getting your soil in top shape, how to buy the best plants for the least dough, and how to get 'em in the ground. And if pests or diseases are foolish enough to rear their ugly heads among your flowers—well, let's just say we have a few surprises in store for *them!* I'm also dying to tell you about my tried-and-true techniques for multiplying your favorite flowers by seeds, cuttings, and divisions. With these tricks up your sleeve, you'll have lots of plants to swap with your gardening friends and neighbors, too. So what are we waiting for?

Give Your Plants a Happy Home

❀ You've got the perfect plan for your new flower garden, and you're ready to turn that dream into reality. Well, then—say it with me—*let's get growing!* In this chapter, you'll find all the down-and-dirty details on bed building, smart shopping, trouble-free transplanting, and lots more. So read on, friends, and get ready for your best flower garden ever!

Making Your Bed (Flowerbed, That Is!)

Sure, getting a new spot ready for growing flowers takes some work. But when you do it correctly, right off the bat, your flowers will repay you with year after year of the healthiest plants and best darn blooms you've ever seen!

Fun in the Sun

Simply guessing how much light a site gets just isn't good enough if you want the best flowers on the block. To pick the perfect plants for any area, watch it for a full sunny day to see just how much sun or shade it gets. Sun-lovers, like roses and peonies, need a spot with *at least* eight hours of direct sun daily. Plants that grow in partial sun need about four hours of direct sun, while those that grow in partial shade need either a few hours of direct sun, or a site with bright, but tree-filtered, day-long shade. Shade plants don't demand any direct sun, but they do need good, bright light all day.

Test the Waters

If your soil has any drainage problems, the time to find out is *before* you plant! It's easy to do: First, water the area very thoroughly—really drench it. Then wait two days, dig a 6-inch-deep hole, and feel the soil at the bottom. If it's dry, your soil doesn't hold enough water to keep flowers happy. On the other hand, if it's still sopping wet, poor drainage is a problem. The solution for both sites is the same: Dig lots of organic matter, like chopped leaves, into the soil.

Don't Be a Pain in the Grass

If you're like most folks, weeds and grass stand between you and the flower garden of your dreams. To get your flowers flourishing quickly, try one of these three tricks:

1. Scalp weeds and grass by cutting them down, as close to the soil surface as possible. Cover the site with a thick layer of newspaper (8 to 10 sheets). Spread several inches of bagged topsoil over the paper, top with an inch of mulch, and plant.

To the Rescue!

Soil in your new garden area not as fluffy and fertile as you'd hoped it would be? The cure for what ails it is simple: Compost—and *lots* of it! Build a pile right on the site, and you'll have a steady supply just where you'll need it most.

2. Use a sharp spade to slice off lawn grass about an inch below the surface, then loosen the soil, and dig a 1- to 2-inch layer of compost into the top 8 inches of soil with a garden fork. It's hard work, but I guarantee you'll have a great garden in no time!

3. Till the site, grass and all. Wait two weeks, then till under the new crop of weeds that have sprouted. Repeat until the weeds are discouraged, then till one more time to work a 1- to 2-inch layer of compost into the soil. Now you're ready to plant!

Green Grass Is Gold...

Gold for your compost pile, that is. If you're removing grass from a new garden site, pile it upside down (roots up) on your compost pile. Once it dies and rots, it yields gardener's gold—nutrient-rich compost. One warning, though: Watch pieces of sod treated this way to make sure they don't sprout roots into your compost pile and start growing. You may have to turn them over once or twice before they give up the ghost.

Stumped?

If there's a tree stump stuck right where you want your garden, don't give up; just try these tips:

❀ Set a birdbath or large container on top of it.

Ready to get that garden started? Use a sharp spade to cut around the edge of the new bed, then slip the blade under the turf and roll it up in strips for easy removal.

What's the easiest way to pick plants for a new garden? Let your site do it for you! Figure out what the area has to offer—what kind of soil, how much sun and shade, and so on—then choose plants that will thrive there, just as it is. They'll naturally be strong and healthy, and you won't have to fuss around trying to fix the soil or cut down trees to get more light!

❀ Bury it with soil and plant shallow-rooted annuals on top.

❀ Drill holes in the stump to speed the rotting process.

❀ Mound soil around it and plant vines, like pumpkins or gourds, to cover it up.

Living on the Edge

Once you've put some sweat equity into getting the grass off your new garden area, you don't want it creeping in again when you turn your back—that's for darn sure! To stop grass in its tracks, install edging strips—right from the get-go!

Most garden centers sell a selection of edging materials, from inexpensive plastic strips to sturdy, long-lasting aluminum ones. Either way, set them so the top of the strip is just above the soil surface. That way, you can mow right along the edge of the lawn, with one wheel of the lawn mower just inside the strip, neatly trimming as you go.

PROBLEM SOLVED!

Woody-stemmed weeds like poison ivy are a major problem anywhere they crop up. You can kill them with heavy-duty herbicides, but if you'd rather not spray, try smothering them using these three easy steps:

Step 1: Cut plants to the ground, then cover the site with large pieces of corrugated cardboard.

Step 2: Top the cardboard with a thick layer of mulch (about 6 inches, or more, if you have it).

Step 3: After a year has gone by, use a sharp spade to dig down through the mulch and cardboard, to plant.

Grow Up!

If your yard lacks privacy, soil berms—raised mounds of soil spruced up with flowers and shrubs—may be just what you need. To build a berm, outline the shape you'd like with a dusting of lime or flour. Spread a base of several inches of gravel within the outline, topped by 1 to 2 feet of heavy clay soil. Then spread another foot of good topsoil, mixed with compost, and set out your chosen plants. Mulch the berm to help hold the soil in place and to keep the weeds down.

Economical Organics

No matter what kind of soil you have, digging in lots of organic matter is the best way to make it even better. These free (or almost free) soil amendments are super sources of organic matter.

Chopped leaves. Pick 'em up off the lawn with a bagging lawn mower, then use as mulch, or work 'em into the soil.

Compost. Homemade is cheapest, but bagged is inexpensive, too.

Grass clippings. Free and readily available.

Hay, sawdust, or straw. Mix with bloodmeal as you work it into the soil, to speed decomposition.

Manure (from cows, horses, poultry, or rabbits). Spread only well-rotted manure in the garden; let fresh manure dry before working it into the soil. And for health reasons, don't use droppings from cats or dogs in your garden.

Super Soil-Prep Pointers

There's just no getting around it: Great soil is the key to a great garden. Fortunately, you don't have to dig for hours and hours—or throw your back out of whack—to build the best soil on your block.

No-Dig Build-a-Bed

Too tired—or too busy—to even *think* about digging a new bed? Well, my friends, give those digging tools away! You'll never use 'em again, once you try this super bed-building method.

Step 1: Cover the grass on your site with several layers of newspaper. (Dunking them in a bucket of water first will help keep them from blowing away after you spread them out.)

Step 2: Top the newspaper with a couple inches of compost.

Step 3: Add more layers on top of the compost: chopped up plants or leaves, straw, hay, fresh grass clippings, bagged topsoil, or soil moved from elsewhere in your yard.

Step 4: Continue adding layers until the pile covering your new bed is anywhere from 10 inches to 2 feet tall, then top with more compost.

Step 5: Plant the following spring, once the pile has settled and the materials have made a rich compost.

To give your plants an extra-deep root run in a layered bed, first till the site, weeds and all. Then cover the site with a thick mat of newspapers (10 sheets or so), and layer away.

Take Your Time

When you're getting a new flower garden going, there's no rule that says you have to do all of the work in a single after-

Jerry's TIMELY TIPS

"In rocky soil, digging with a spade or a garden fork is a sure way to try your patience! Instead, invest in a mattock. This pickax-like tool has a flat blade on one end and an ax-like one on the other. In any soil, it's terrific for chopping trenches to install edging strips, whacking weed roots, or loosening heavy soil. If rocky soil's your problem, jam the flat blade under the rock, and pry it out with ease. Mattocks come in several sizes, so pick up one that feels best to you."

Don't feel like digging? Then build your garden from the ground up! Simply cover the grass with newspapers, then add layers of soil, compost, leaves, and other organic materials.

noon—or even a single season. Tackle the chore in chunks at your own pace—a bit this season, more the next. Plant the newly completed sections as you go, so you can enjoy the fruits of your labor, before you start the next section.

pH Matters

Whatever way you choose to start your garden, I want you to do one more thing: Get a soil test kit from your local Cooperative Extension Service office (look under "Government Services" in your phone book to find it), and have your soil tested. Or, at the very least, get a pH test kit from your local garden center.

You see, the pH of your soil affects how available nutrients will be to the roots of your plants. For example, your soil may have plenty of potassium, but if the pH is too acidic, that nutrient is tied up with other elements in the soil, and not available to your plants. A simple soil test will tell you what the pH is, and how to make any needed adjustments for the flowers you want to grow.

Shop Smart, the Baker Way

When spring fever strikes, it's tempting to head to the garden center and snatch up every plant you see. But, if you try some of my tips each time you shop, I *guarantee* you'll get more bang for your gardening buck!

Inspect the Troops

Before laying down your hard-earned dough, be sure to give every plant you want to buy a good once-over. (If you need glasses to read, wear them to inspect your plants, too!)

❀ Take a close look at the flowers, stems, and leaves—both the tops and bottoms—for signs of pests, like aphids and whiteflies.

❀ Check for brown, black, gray, or white spots on stems or leaves, because these can be signs of disease.

❀ Look at the overall plant to see if it has yellow leaves, or spindly stems with few leaves.

❀ Carefully tip the plant out of its pot. Healthy roots are usually white, yellow, or a bright shade of brown—not black or rotted, or wound around each other.

If you spot any or all of these problems, put that pot back on the shelf. Believe you me, a sick plant is no bargain at any price!

Forget Flowers— For a While

Sure, pots of annuals and perennials smothered in blooms are a pretty sight, but they're not necessarily the best buy. It takes a lot of energy to make all of those flowers, so blooming plants have less to spare for making the new roots they need to adapt to life in your garden. Please take my word for it: You'll get much better results in the long run if you buy

Pot-bound perennials—those that have outgrown their nursery containers—*can* be a bargain, if you're willing to do a bit of extra homework, that is. At end-of-the-season sales, snatch up over-crowded pots of hostas, daylilies (*Hemerocallis*), and any other perennials that are easy to divide. When you get home, dump them out of their pots and tease apart the clumps with your fingers, or use a sharp knife to divide them.

If you end up with very small divisions, you may want to pot them up and grow them in a protected spot until they have healthy roots. Otherwise, plant them out in your garden right away—just make sure you water them regularly until they've settled in.

You can buy good transplants for a great price at grocery and discount stores—*if* you shop smart. Most discounters buy their stock from good wholesale growers, but the plants start to suffer when they've been sitting on the sidewalk, frying in the sun. So, ask a manager when their next plant delivery is scheduled, then show up to shop shortly thereafter. You should be able to find plenty of plants that are still happy and healthy.

Buy compact, bushy transplants—not tall, spindly seedlings that are past their prime!

ones that have healthy stems and leaves, but few or no flowers.

Seeds or Plants?

The answer basically boils down to time or money. Purchased plants are more expensive than starting from seeds, but—in the case of perennials, at least—they'll bloom more quickly. They're also the way to go if you want to get a new garden started in a hurry. Seeds, on the other hand, are far cheaper than purchased plants—you can grow dozens of annuals or perennials for the price of a single packet of seeds!

YES!   **NO THANKS**

Successful Sowing Secrets

If you're one of those folks who thinks seed-starting takes too much time and trouble, then you've never tried it the Baker way. Read on for my best-ever seed-sowing tips, and you'll have your new flower garden up and growing before you know it!

It's as Easy as One-Two-Three!

Come spring, there's always lots to do and never enough time, so it's easy to forget seed-sowing time. Here's help for getting your annual flowers up and growing with a minimum of fuss.

Step 1: In late winter, sort your seed packets into two piles—those you'll sow directly in the garden, and those you'll need to start indoors. (Read the packets to see which belongs where.)

Step 2: Separate the "outdoor" packets into cool-weather annuals, which get sown before the last frost date, and warm-weather annuals, to be sown after that date. (Don't know the last frost date for your area? Ask at a local garden center, or contact your county's Cooperative Extension Service office.)

To get a head start on spring chores, prepare your seedbeds in late summer or fall. Then come spring, they'll be ready to sow whenever you are! Whether you're making a big bed or a small one, spread an inch or two of compost over the area, then dig or till it into the top 6 to 8 inches of soil. Then rake the bed smooth, removing any rocks, breaking up dirt clods, and disposing of the weeds.

Step 3: Put each pile into an envelope and label it. Then pick sowing dates and mark them on your calendar, listing which annuals get sown when. When it comes time to sow, you'll be all ready to go!

When in Doubt, Wait!

After a long winter, it's tempting to get out in the garden on the first nice day, to get your seeds sown. That's fine for cold-tolerant annuals, but it just doesn't work for warmth-loving ones, like marigolds and morning glories (*Ipomoea*). In chilly soil, these seeds are far more likely to rot than sprout. So in cold, wet years when spring seems forever in coming, don't sow warm-season seeds by the last frost date; wait until the soil has warmed up to at least 50°F. Don't worry that your flowers'll be late; they'll spring up quickly and catch up to the others by midsummer.

Divide and Conquer

No doubt about it: Flowers look simply fabulous planted in large patches. But if you're like me, you run out of seeds well before you've filled the space you'd hoped to. Well, here's a sure-fire solution: Count up the number of patches you'd like to have, and divide the seeds in the packet into that many piles on pieces of scrap paper. Fold up each piece of paper to make a little carrying packet, then simply tap the seeds out over each patch. Voilà!

Press for Success!

Seeds have to be in contact with the soil around them, so that they can soak up the moisture they need in order to sprout. To ensure good seed-to-soil contact, gently press down the soil after sowing seeds. Don't worry about hurting the seeds; you're actually doing them a big favor by firming them in!

GRANDMA PUTT'S
Handy Hints

"Don't plant your corn until the oak leaf is as big as a squirrel's ear" was a saying my Grandma Putt used to rely on to help decide when to start her flower garden, as well as her vegetable garden. See, she knew corn was a warm-weather annual. So, once the oak leaves were the right size for planting corn and other warm-weather veggies, she knew it was time to sow the seeds of warm-weather annual flowers, too, like nasturtiums (*Tropaeolum*) and zinnias.

Let There Be Light

Here's another super seed-starting secret: Some seeds—like the ones listed below—need light to germinate, so you definitely *don't* want to cover them with soil after sowing. Just press them lightly into the soil surface, then mist with water often to keep them moist until they sprout.

Beefsteak plant (*Perilla frutescens*)
Farewell-to-spring (*Clarkia amoena*)
Four-o'clocks (*Mirabilis jalapa*)
Gloriosa daisies (*Rudbeckia hirta*)
Mignonette (*Reseda odorata*)
Portulaca (*Portulaca grandiflora*)
Stocks (*Matthiola*)
Sweet alyssum (*Lobularia maritima*)

Keep 'Em in the Dark

For some seeds, darkness is a must for good germination. So when you sow those listed below, make sure you cover them thoroughly with soil; that way, they'll be in good shape for sprouting.

Annual phlox (*Phlox drummondii*)

Bachelor's buttons (*Centaurea cyanus*)

Chinese forget-me-not (*Cynoglossum amabile*)

Evening primrose (*Oenothera biennis*)

Flora's paintbrush (*Emilia coccinea*)

Larkspur (*Consolida ajacis*)

Poppies (*Papaver*)

Pot marigolds (*Calendula officinalis*)

Jerry's TIMELY TIPS

"Regular spring rains usually keep the soil moist for newly sown seeds, but one dry spell can wipe out all your baby plants before they even get started. So check them daily to make sure your seedbeds stay moist, and keep a watering can handy to give them a small shower, if needed."

All Shook Up

Empty herb and spice jars—the ones with those plastic shaker lids that have holes in 'em—are absolutely perfect for sowing seeds. Drop a seed into one of the holes to make sure it'll fit through, then fill, and shake to sow! Mixing some white play sand with the seeds before sowing makes it super-easy to see where you've already sprinkled. After sowing, use a rake or your hands to lightly cover the seeds and gently pat down the soil. And don't forget to add a label, so you'll remember what you sowed where!

A Seedy Cover-Up

Floating row covers—the kind used in vegetable gardens—can be a huge help in the flower garden, too! They protect seedlings from chilly, drying winds, help hold in moisture, and protect the soil surface from pounding raindrops—which can cause a crust to form. They'll also keep hungry birds from gobbling up your flower seeds, and prevent rascally rabbits from snacking on your seedlings.

Get It on Tape

Pre-spaced seed tapes make planting a snap, but they can cost a pretty penny, too. So, take a winter evening or two, and make your own; they're fun to do!

Step 1: Dissolve 1 tablespoon of cornstarch in 1 cup of water over medium heat. Stir constantly, until the mix boils and turns translucent and gel-like.

Step 2: While it cools, cut several paper towels lengthwise into 1-inch-wide strips. Write the name of the seed you're sowing on each strip with a waterproof pen.

Step 3: Spoon some of the cornstarch mix into a plastic sandwich bag, squeeze it into one corner, and cut a tiny hole in that corner.

Step 4: Squeeze out small cornstarch dots along each paper-towel strip, spacing the dots as far apart as the seeds should go. Place a seed on each dot.

Step 5: Once the strips are dry, roll 'em up and store 'em in a plastic bag until planting time.

Picture-Perfect Planting

The day your indoor-grown seedlings go out into the garden, they'll face all sorts of stresses they haven't known before—strong sun, drying winds, and critters galore. Here are some of my best tips to help your future flowers over these hurdles, and get 'em growing in a jiffy.

Boot Camp for Baby Plants

Seedlings that have been coddled in your home or in a greenhouse need toughening up before they're ready for the garden. To get them ready for transplanting, give them a good drink, then set them outside in a shady, protected spot, such as under shrubs or along the north side of your house. Leave them outdoors for an hour or so the first day, then bring them back in. Gradually increase the amount of sun they receive, and the number of hours they're outdoors, over the course of a week. Transplant 'em when they can stay outdoors all day without drooping. Check daily to see if they need watering—small pots sure dry out fast in the wind and sun.

Help indoor-grown seedlings get used to the great outdoors by setting them in the shade of a tree or shrub.

Drippy Days Delight Transplants

Cloudy, drizzly weather is perfect for moving seedlings to the garden, so get out your rain gear! Your youngsters will settle in more quickly without being baked by the sun, and you won't have to worry so much about watering when you're done planting.

Tough Love for Transplants

If you tip a young plant out of its pot and see a rootball that's all wrapped up, set those roots on the right road before you plant. Use a knife or screwdriver to make shallow cuts along the sides of the root ball, then plant as usual. This harsh treatment encourages the roots to branch out, so they'll grow out into the soil, and not continue their circling ways.

GRANDMA PUTT'S
Handy Hints

Not home during the daytime to move seedlings in and out? Try Grandma Putt's simple three-step system for hardening-off seedlings in a jiffy:

Step 1: Pick a protected location under a shrub, and water the ground there thoroughly.

Step 2: Water your seedlings too, then set them on the spot. (Make sure they'll be shaded all day.) Spray the shrub foliage above them, as well, until it drips with water. This'll help keep the young plants from drying (and dying) out during the day.

Step 3: Repeat the process over the course of a week, moving the seedlings into more sun each day.

Perennial Planting Potion

To make sure your flowers get growing on the right root, feed them this powerful potion.

½ can of beer
¼ cup of ammonia
2 tbsp. of hydrogen peroxide
1 tbsp. of liquid dish soap
2 gal. of warm water

Mix all of the ingredients together, and soak the soil around each transplant. You can also sprinkle it around your blooming beauties throughout the summer. ✤

Water While You Work

A trowel or shovel isn't the only essential transplanting tool—keep a watering can nearby as well! Moisten the soil in each hole, pop in a transplant, then water it right away. Don't wait to water until you've finished a whole row or bed; by that time, the first plants may have dried out and even started wilting.

Funny Hats for Your Flowers

If you can't transplant on a cloudy day, give your seedlings their own personal sun hats! Gather up bushel baskets and cardboard boxes, and set them over the young ones as you plant. (Poultry wire draped with burlap works well, too.) If you use boxes, prop them up on one side to let some air in. Let your plants keep their caps on for a day or so, then take them off, and let the sun shine in!

A Snip in Time

It may seem cruel, but pinching or snipping off the tops of the stems, and removing any flowers, actually does your transplants a big favor. They'll put more energy into growing new roots, so they'll settle in quicker. Plus, they'll come back a whole lot bushier, with lots more blooms—and that's what flower gardening is all about!

Settle 'Em In

Freshly dug soil is light and fluffy—perfect for plants. It settles back down during the first few weeks, though. So if you're planting immediately after digging, set your transplant slightly higher in the soil than you normally would. Once the soil settles, they'll end up at the same depth as when they were growing in their pots.

Critter Control

You may see a neatly planted flowerbed, but believe you me, rabbits and other pesky critters see an "all-you-can-eat salad bar" sign! Transplants are most at risk from these hungry little fellas during their first week in the garden, so protect them from the get-go by covering them up with small cages made of poultry wire. (Take off the cages once plants start growing, or leave them on and let the stems grow right up through them.) Animal repellents work well at transplant time, too, since they keep critters from developing a taste for your transplants. Apply hot-pepper spray, or sprinkle bloodmeal around transplants as soon as you set them out.

Get Your Fill

Following the spacing advice on plant labels is a smart thing to do. But when you look at your newly planted perennial garden, you may not think so—you'll probably see more soil than plants! Perennials take a year or two to put down good roots before they fill in up top, but in the meantime, those gaps provide a perfect place for weeds to get started. So here are two options for a great-looking and weed-free perennial garden right from the get-go:

❀ Set your young perennials closer together than recommended, then plan to dig 'em up again in a year or two and move 'em to their correct spacings.

❀ Buy trays of inexpensive annuals, like marigolds, petunias, or salvias, and use them to fill the spaces between properly spaced perennials. They'll crowd out any weeds until the perennials get big enough to shade the soil themselves.

FLOWER POWER TONICS

Root Revival Tonic

Use this terrific tonic to give your bare-root perennials and roses some refreshment before they go into the garden.

¼ **cup of brewed tea**
1 tbsp. of liquid dish soap
1 tbsp. of Epsom salts
1 gal. of water

Let the plants sit in this tonic for up to 24 hours. It'll rev up those tired roots and get them ready to grow—*guaranteed!* ❀

Post-Planting Wrap-Up

Got your seeds sown and your transplants planted? Good for you! But don't take a break quite yet; a new flowerbed needs a little extra attention until the plants are settled in and growing like gangbusters. So check your garden each day during the first week after planting, then at least several times a week for the first season. Keeping an eye on things lets you nip problems in the bud—literally!

Jerry's TIMELY TIPS

"All first-year perennials need to put their energy into making new roots, not seeds, so make sure you snip off flowers as soon as they fade. And if the spring-planted perennials you started with were bare-root, I want you to cut off all the flower buds for that year, to direct energy to root growth. I know it's hard, but I promise you'll thank me later, when your perennials repay you with a bounty of blooms in years to come!"

Keep the Water Coming

By far, the most important thing you can do for your new garden is to water regularly. Unless Mother Nature comes through with some April showers, you'll want to water every day or two for the first week, so the soil doesn't dry out. For the rest of that growing season, make sure your new garden gets at least 1 inch of water per week, either from rainfall or by watering. Mulch new beds, too—that'll be a big help to hold moisture in the soil.

Be the Weed Police

As you stroll around your yard, make it a point to pull any weeds as soon as you see 'em—especially in new beds. Keep a few extra annuals or some mulch on hand to fill in the gaps that are left, and you'll stop pesky weed problems right in their tracks.

Invite Your Flowers to Tea

Want to get your bloomers off to a super-fast start? Treat 'em to a dose of homemade compost tea. This solution is a snap to brew and makes a super, all-around pick-me-up. Simply put several shovelsful of compost or manure (I usually use cow, horse, poultry, or rabbit droppings) into a large trash can. Fill the can to the top with water. Allow the mixture to sit for a day or two, stirring it several times each day.

To serve the tea to your plants, dilute it with water until it's light brown. Give each plant about a cup of this tea every two weeks, and your feeding worries will be over!

Don't Lose It—Move It!

Let's face it: Even the best-planned gardens sometimes need a little adjustment once they've been growing for a while. So if you see something that didn't quite turn out as you'd hoped, don't be afraid to tinker with your design. It's best not to move perennials when they're in full bloom, but before or after that is usually fine. Try to keep a good amount of soil with the roots when you dig, and water thoroughly once you've settled the plants in their new homes. If you move plants during the hotter months of summer, give them a bit of shade, and water them daily until they've recovered.

FLOWER POWER TONICS

Root-Rousing Tonic

Want to get your new flowers off to a fabulous start? Well then, you can't do better than giving each one a generous dose of this excellent elixir!

1 can of beer
1 can of regular cola (not diet)
1 cup of liquid dish soap
1 cup of antiseptic mouthwash
1/4 tsp. of instant tea granules

Mix all of the ingredients in a large bucket, then pour into a 20 gallon hose-end sprayer and spray liberally over all of your flowerbeds. ❋

Keep 'Em Happy and Healthy!

✿ The secret to a healthy, beautiful flower garden isn't working *harder*—it's working *smarter!* In this chapter, we'll discuss dozens of ways to keep your plants in their prime, my best tips and tricks for feedin', weedin', and waterin', and a plethora of pointers on outwitting pesky pests and dastardly diseases.

Trimmin' Time

Sometimes it's the little things that make a big difference. Removing spent blooms and cutting back plants when they need it will keep the flowers comin' and your garden looking great— from spring until frost!

The Kindest Cuts

We all know that pinching off spent flowers is a great way to keep annuals, like snapdragons (*Antirrhinum majus*), cosmos, and dahlias, looking super all season long. But did you know that the same pinch can keep many *perennials* in bloom for weeks—or even months—longer than they'd normally be? It's true!

When you're removing spent flowers or cutting back your perennials, look for tiny buds in the leaf axils (where a leaf joins the stem). Cut just above these joints, and you'll have new flowers in a jiffy! All of these perennials form extra flower buds:

Balloon flower
   (*Platycodon grandiflorus*)

Peach-leaved bellflower
   (*Campanula persicifolia*)

Phlox (*Phlox*)

Pincushion flowers (*Scabiosa*)

Shasta daisy
   (*Leucanthemum* x *superbum*)

Speedwells (*Veronica*)

Stoke's aster (*Stokesia laevis*)

Yarrows (*Achillea*)

Shear Beauties

Giving bushy perennials a haircut is a great way to keep 'em lookin' good all summer long—no stakes required! They'll bounce back with handsome, compact mounds of foliage that won't flop over. Many will even send up another round of flowers to boot! After the main flush of flowers has faded, use your pruners or hedge shears to trim the following perennials down to 2 or 3 inches above the ground:

Candytuft (*Iberis sempervirens*)

Catmints (*Nepeta*)

Columbines (*Aquilegia*)

Germander (*Teucrium chamaedrys*)

Hardy geraniums (*Geranium*)

Lady's mantle (*Alchemilla mollis*)

Mountain bluet (*Centaurea montana*)

Pinks (*Dianthus*)

Spiderworts (*Tradescantia*)

Thread-leaved coreopsis
   (*Coreopsis verticillata*)

GRANDMA PUTT'S
Handy Hints

Come fall, Grandma Putt's garden was just filled with chrysanthemums. They all stood up straight and tall, even though she never bothered staking them. Her secret? She'd pinch off the stem tips twice between late spring and early summer. She never pinched them after the Fourth of July, because she knew late-pinched shoots wouldn't have time to make flowers before the cold weather set in.

Hands Off!

Pinching works wonders with many flowers, but before you start trying it on everything in sight, keep this in mind: It only works on multi-stemmed plants. *Don't* try it on perennials or bulbs that have single-stemmed blooms, like daylilies (*Hemerocallis*), hostas, or true lilies (*Lilium*). They won't branch, and you'll be stuck with a bunch of stick figures—all stems and no blooms!

A Lot Off the Top to Stop the Flop

If you dislike staking as much as I do, you're always on the look-out for easier ways to keep your flowers on the straight and nar-row. Well, here you go: Whack 'em back! When they are 12 to 18 inches tall, cut 'em back by about half; for even shorter, bushier plants, repeat the trim about a month later. A mid-summer trim really helps rein in these towering annuals and perennials:

Boltonias (*Boltonia*)

Brazilian vervain (*Verbena bonariensis*)

Cosmos (*Cosmos bipinnatus*)

Ironweeds (*Vernonia*)

Joe Pye weeds (*Eupatorium*)

New England aster (*Aster novae-angliae*)

Perennial sunflowers (*Helianthus*)

Sneezeweeds (*Helenium*)

Landscape Lingo

Pinching got its name because you really are pinching the plant—pressing your thumb and forefinger together to remove stem tips by cutting them off be-tween your fingernails. Don't have long enough nails to give a good pinch? If the growth is brittle enough, simply snap off the stem by pressing the top of the stem to one side. For hard or woody stems that are too tough to remove with your fingers, use garden shears or scissors to snip the tips.

SOS—Save Our Seedheads!

Self-sowing flowers are super time-savers, since you don't need to worry about starting them yourself each year. But when they produce too many seeds, these beauties can get a little out of hand and end up all over your yard. Fortunately, there are two easy ways to have the best of both worlds!

One option is to remove all of their flowers after the first main flush of bloom, then let some of the follow-up flowers set seed. This works great with bushier plants like bachelor's buttons (*Centaurea cyanus*) and cosmos (*Cosmos bipinnatus*). Spiky blooms like larkspur (*Consolida ajacis*) and foxglove (*Digitalis purpurea*) call for a slightly different system—cut their flower spikes back halfway after the flowers fade. That way, some seeds can form, but not *too* many.

PROBLEM SOLVED!

If powdery mildew always makes unsightly white spots on your garden phlox (*Phlox paniculata*) or bee balm (*Monarda didyma*), pruning is a good first line of defense. In spring or early summer, snip off a third to a half of the stems in the clump, right at ground level. This reduces crowding and improves air circulation, so that the funky fungi can't get a grip!

It's for the Birds!

If you're a bird lover like I am, you might want to leave the seedheads on your flowers to provide food for your feathered friends. Perennials with daisy-like blooms are particularly popular, including asters, coreopsis, orange coneflowers (*Rudbeckia*), oxeye (*Heliopsis helianthoides*), perennial sunflowers (*Helianthus*), and purple coneflower (*Echinacea purpurea*). Birds also flock to the seeds of many annuals, including common sunflowers (*Helianthus annuus*), cosmos, love-lies-bleeding (*Amaranthus caudatus*), marigolds, Mexican sunflower (*Tithonia rotundifolia*), and zinnias.

Dis-Buds for You

Would you believe that you can get better blooms by pinching *off* some flower buds? Sounds crazy, I know, but it works—honest! You see, pinching out the smaller side buds from a cluster directs all that stem's energy into the main bud, so you get a bigger bloom. That's how florists get those huge "football" mums, and it

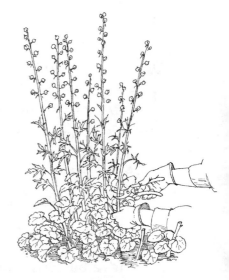

Snip off spent flowering stems just above the leaves to keep plants looking tidy.

works great on dahlias, peonies, and roses, too.

If you'd rather have *more*, but slightly smaller blooms, do just the opposite: Pinch out the main bud on the stem, and let the smaller side buds get all the growing energy.

Prune Away Pests

Psst! Wanna know the absolutely easiest way to get rid of any plant pest *pronto?* Simply pinch or prune off the branches or leaves where they're hanging out! Drop the infested plant parts into a plastic grocery bag, tie it up, and throw it away!

Jerry's TIMELY TIPS

"Pinching off different flower buds on the same plant is a super way to extend its bloom season for several days, or even weeks. On some stems, remove the side buds; on others, remove the main buds. The larger buds will open first, followed by the smaller, side ones."

Hold Their Heads Up

Staking sure isn't my favorite chore, and I'll bet it isn't yours, either! But with some old-fashioned garden smarts, plus a supply of stakes, string, and other basic support materials, you can get those flowers trussed up with a minimum of fuss.

Stake Early, Stake Often

The real secret to successful staking is timing. Waiting until your flowers actually *need* staking is the absolute worst time to do it. It's a big hassle, and the plants'll never look right anyway. Instead, get those stakes in place when the new shoots are only inches out of the ground. It's a breeze to stick in the stakes at this time, and the leafy stems will quickly grow up through to hide the supports.

Let 'Em Lean!

Don't let flopping flowers worry you—at least not all of the time. Sure, flowers with brittle stems, like delphiniums, need staking to keep 'em from breaking off in wind and rain. But in many cases, flowers can look just great when they lean a little on each other! Two of my favorite lean-on-me pairings are peonies spilling into catmints (*Nepeta*), and asters mingling with Russian sage (*Perovskia atriplicifolia*). So before you decide to stake them up, consider letting 'em lean for a season or two to see if you like the more casual look.

An old tomato cage makes a super support for bushy perennials!

Just Say No!

If staking flowers is your least favorite garden job, here's the best advice I can give you: Choose compact cultivars that don't need your support! Unlike their taller parents, these low-growing cultivars stand up straight all on their own.

Ageratum (*Ageratum houstonianum*): 'Blue Danube', 'Blue Horizon'

Balloon flower (*Platycodon grandiflorus*): 'Apoyama', 'Mariesii', 'Sentimental Blue'

Blanket flower (*Gaillardia* x *grandiflora*): 'Baby Cole', 'Dazzler', 'Kobold'

New England aster (*Aster novae-angliae*): 'Purple Dome'

New York aster (*Aster novi-belgii*): 'Niobe', 'Professor Anton Kippenberg'

Shasta daisy (*Leucanthemum* x *superbum*): 'Little Miss Muffet', 'Snow Lady'

Sneezeweed (*Helenium autumnale*): 'Butterpat', 'Crimson Beauty', 'Moerheim Beauty'

To the Rescue!

Stake tips poking up through your flowers can be an accident waiting to happen. You lean over to sniff or pick a bloom, and "Ow!"—you get poked in the arm or eye. There's a simple and safe solution: old tennis or racquet balls. Simply cut a slit or small hole in each ball, and stick it over the top of a stake. If you don't like the color, spray-paint the balls black or dark green before putting them in place.

Believe it or not, old panty hose make perfect plant ties! They're soft and stretchy, so they don't damage plant stems, and a ruined pair or two yield all the ties you'll need for a whole year. Cut across each leg piece to get a bunch of 1- to 2-inch-wide loops. Slide the loops onto one wrist as you head out to the garden, and you've got a supply of perfect plant ties right at hand.

All Tied Up

Figure-eights are aces for fastening plants to stakes or trellises! Attaching stems to stakes this way provides sturdy stem support but with enough "give" for the stem to sway instead of snap off in a gust of wind. Simply wrap a tie—soft twine or yarn is ideal—around the stem, cross the ends between the stem and stake, and then knot the ends together around the stake. Make sure the tie doesn't cut into the stem.

Fix Floppy Flowers—for Free!

Tree and shrub prunings are a super source of free supports for floppy flowers. Simply stick several pruned stems into the ground—cut end down, twiggy end up—around each clump of plants. Snap over the branch tips toward the center of the clump—don't break them off completely—for extra stem support, and get rid of any pointy ends sticking up.

Divide and Conquer

When I was first learning about gardening, I couldn't imagine how digging something up and cutting it to bits could possibly be a good thing. Over the years, I've come to see that some flowers are a little *too* vigorous, and they'll take over the whole back forty if you don't divide 'em. Others grow better after dividing because you get rid of the old, weak growth, which flowers poorly and attracts pests and diseases. Best of all, dividing is a great way to get loads of new flowers for free! So get out there and start chopping up those overgrown clumps—you'll be glad you did!

Do-In Donuts

Clumps of perennials that start looking like donuts are prime candidates for division. The donut syndrome—where a ring of healthy growth surrounds a center where nothing seems to be growing—starts because the center of the clump is filled with old, sickly, or woody growth. Fortunately, there's an easy fix! Simply dig up the entire clump, and toss out any old growth from the center. Cut the healthy growth into chunks, and replant it.

Slice and Dice!

One of my Grandma Putt's favorite tools for dividing clumps of perennials was an old kitchen knife. It had a long, serrated blade that never seemed to get dull. She'd dig up clumps and use it to slice through them like butter.

The Eyes Have It!

Before you chop a clump of perennials into many small pieces, count the "eyes," or buds. Ideally, each new piece should have three to five eyes, along with a good complement of roots, to boot. While divisions that have only a single eye will grow, it's easier to handle slightly larger pieces with more eyes, and they'll fill in far more quickly.

Bulb Basics

After a few years, you'll probably notice that your daffodil, hyacinth,

GRANDMA PUTT'S
Handy Hints

Can't remember what to divide when? I always use Grandma Putt's simple rule of thumb: Divide spring-blooming plants in fall, and fall-blooming plants in spring. She made a few exceptions to this rule, because she knew that Oriental poppies (*Papaver orientale*) and bearded iris (*Iris* Bearded Hybrids) were best off when divided in mid- to late summer.

and tulip blooms just aren't as big and beautiful as they used to be. Chances are, the bulbs are overcrowded and need dividing. Dig 'em up as soon as their leaves have died back after bloom. Break the bulbs apart with your hands (be sure to wear gloves if you're handling hyacinths), then replant the separated bulbs in the garden. It can't get much easier than that!

Leave 'Em Alone

When it comes to division, not all perennials are created equal! Those that grow from thick, carrot-like taproots, as well as those that have extra deep, wide-spreading roots, generally don't tolerate dividing very well. And since they are typically happiest when left undisturbed, there's normally no reason you *have* to divide them. If you do choose to divide the following perennials, be prepared to dig way down to get as many of the roots as you can:

Balloon flower
(*Platycodon grandiflorus*)

Bugbanes (*Cimicifuga*)

Butterfly weed (*Asclepias tuberosa*)

False indigos (*Baptisia*)

Gas plant (*Dictamnus albus*)

Goatsbeards (*Aruncus*)

Lenten roses (*Helleborus*)

Peonies (*Paeonia*)

Consider the Lilies

No garden can have too many lilies, but it can get pretty pricey to buy these beauties. Why bother, when you can grow your own? Most lilies produce small, baby bulbs right above the main bulb, just below the soil surface. Loosen the soil carefully with a hand fork, pick off the babies, and plant them in a nursery bed or a corner of your vegetable garden. After a year or two, move them back to the garden for a great show! Some lilies also form mini-bulbs above ground, right where the leaves join the stems. Pick these off and treat them the same way.

Glad to Know Ya!

Want to grow more of your favorite glads? It's easy to do! When you dig them up in fall for winter storage, break off the withered old corms and discard them; then pick off the cormels that have formed around the new corms. When you replant the following spring, put the fattest corms back in the spotlight, and plant the cormels about an inch deep in a nursery bed or a corner of your vegetable garden. Dig 'em up in fall, then replant the now-larger cormels 2 inches deep the next spring. By the third year, they'll be ready to take center stage!

To make the kindest cuts when dividing perennials, be sure all your tools are clean and sharp. Spades and trowels with sharp blades cut through roots neatly, without ripping or tearing at them. And since clean cuts heal quickly, you'll have fewer problems with rots and other diseases!

Avoid the Ol' Heave-Ho

Late summer and early fall are ideal times to divide your spring-flowering perennials, since they'll have plenty of time to get settled in before their flowering time comes 'round again. The only disadvantage is that these later divisions may *not* have time to grow deep, well-established roots before the cold weather sets in. That means that alternating freezing and thawing can pop them right out of the ground!

To keep your fall divisions in good shape, tuck them into their beds with a thick blanket of loose, lightweight mulch, such as straw or evergreen boughs. And, if you do spot any clumps that have been heaved out of the soil, press them back in when the ground is thawed out during winter warm spells.

Keep These in Check, Please!

Sure, we all like our perennials to be sturdy and strong, but sometimes they can get a little *too* enthusiastic about making themselves at home. Frequent division is the secret to keeping these willing wanderers in their place. Here's a Baker's dozen of perennials that are best divided every two or three years:

Bearded iris (*Iris* Bearded Hybrids)

Bee balm (*Monarda didyma*)

Blanket flower (*Gaillardia* x *grandiflora*)

Chrysanthemums (*Chrysanthemum*)

Coreopsis (*Coreopsis*)

Garden phlox (*Phlox paniculata*)

Mountain bluet (*Centaurea montana*)

Obedient plant (*Physostegia virginiana*)

Shasta daisies (*Leucanthemum* x *superbum*)

Sneezeweed (*Helenium autumnale*)

Speedwells (*Veronica*)

Yarrows (*Achillea*)

GRANDMA PUTT'S Handy Hints

When Grandma Putt wanted to share a special flower with a friend, she didn't bother digging up an entire clump. Instead, she'd use a sharp spade or trowel to cut out a piece—or a few bulbs—from the outside of the clump. She'd wrap the roots in damp newspaper, and send them off to their new home with a smile.

Make sure each new division has some roots and at least one bud or stem.

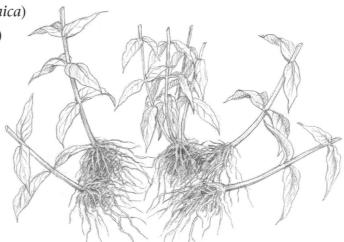

Waterin', Mulchin', and Feedin'

Keeping your plants happy and healthy means more than just taking care of their flowers and foliage—you've got to look down below, too! After all, that's where water, mulch, and fertilizer enter the picture. So let's take a few minutes to talk about some garden smarts in this department, and you'll be all set to keep your flowers in top-notch form, from the tops of their shoots to the tips of their roots!

Water, Water Everywhere

Sprinkling your garden every evening with a hand-held hose may be relaxing for you, but it doesn't do much good for your flowers. The water you supply that way rarely soaks the soil below the top inch, so your plants will form most of their roots close to the surface. This leaves them dependent on a daily water fix, and if you miss a day, they'll wilt at the merest hint of dry weather.

To encourage deep rooting—and cut down on your watering time—the trick is to water thoroughly, then not water again for a week or so. To make sure you've really delivered the goods, stick a finger down into the soil after you think you've watered enough. It should be wet several inches down. If not, continue watering, then check again.

To measure the amount of water an overhead sprinkler delivers, place a few cat food or tuna cans, open end up, on the ground around the flowers you're watering. Run the sprinkler for an hour, then check the depth of the water in the cans. The general rule to remember is that most flowers need 1 inch of water per week during the growing season.

Flower Talk

Not sure when it's the right time to water? Listen to your plants—they'll tell you! Here are some signs to indicate your flowers are thirsty:

❃ Leaves droop slightly during the heat of the day, but recover in the evening once the sun goes down.

❃ Leaves are duller or grayer than normal.

❃ The foliage of fleshy-leaved plants shrivels slightly or feels soft to the touch.

One word of warning: Before you water, always take a look at the soil—pull the mulch aside, if you have to—to make sure the ground isn't actually waterlogged. Plants that have *too much* moisture can show the same symptoms as those that don't have enough.

Say Good-Bye to Watering Woes

If you really want to cut your watering chores to a minimum, make friends with mulch! A 2- to 3-inch-deep layer of this magical material shields the ground from sun and wind, so any water that's already in the soil *stays* there, instead of evaporating away. One tip: If your soil is already dry, water thoroughly *before* you mulch. Otherwise, you'll have to water twice as much, because the mulch will absorb a lot before the moisture makes its way down to the soil below.

FLOWER POWER TONICS

Compost Booster

Whether you use it as a mulch or dig it into the soil to help hold water, you can never have too much compost! To keep your pile cookin', and the compost comin', try the following formula.

1 can of beer
1 can of regular cola (not diet)
1 cup of ammonia
1/2 cup of weak tea water*
2 tbsp. of baby shampoo

Pour this mixture into a 20 gallon hose-end sprayer, and saturate your compost pile every time you add a new, foot-deep layer of ingredients to it.

*Soak a used tea bag and 1 teaspoon of liquid dish soap in a gallon of warm water until the mix is light brown. ❃

Mulch Management 101

There's no doubt that mulch is great for your garden—*if* you apply it properly! What I *don't* want you to do is pile it up around the base of your plants, so it looks like they're rising out of mini mulch mountains. In the same way that mulch holds moisture in the soil, it'll hold moisture against your plants' leaves and stems, and that's an open invitation for fungi, as well as borers, mice, and various other critters. Eliminate these problems by keeping a mulch-free zone that's 2 or 3 inches wide around flower clumps, shrub stems, and tree trunks.

Jerry's Secret All-Purpose Elixir

Here's a super time-saver: an excellent elixir that lets you water and feed your flowers at the same time! To make a bunch of this homemade brew, toss a shovelful of compost into a 5-gallon bucket. Add two heaping handfuls of salt-free alfalfa pellets (available from animal feed stores), then fill the bucket with water. Let the mixture sit for at least two or three days, stirring once or twice a day. Dilute it with water until the tea is light brown before using it to water plants in your garden. Spread the solids from the bottom of the bucket on your flowerbeds for an extra nutrient boost.

Flower-Friendly Feeding

Use these super-simple feeding tips to keep all your flowers happy and healthy:

Annuals. Annuals don't stick around for long, but when they need food, they need it *fast!* Sprinkle a few pinches of dry garden fertilizer (like 5-10-5) around each one at planting time, then fol-

FLOWER POWER TONICS

Nutrient Boost for Neglected Soil

If you have a garden with less-than-great soil, or seem to have lots of yellowed, sick-looking plants, try this sure-fire pick-me-up!

6 parts greensand or wood ashes
3 parts cottonseed meal
3 parts bonemeal

Mix the ingredients together. Add 2 cups of gypsum and 1 cup of limestone per gallon of blend. Apply 5 pounds per 100 square feet a few weeks before planting, or work the mix around established plants. ✳

Flower Feeder

Use this all-purpose food to keep all your flowers flourishing!

1 can of beer
2 tbsp. of fish emulsion
2 tbsp. of liquid dish soap
2 tbsp. of ammonia
2 tbsp. of hydrogen peroxide
2 tbsp. of whiskey
1 tbsp. of clear corn syrup
1 tbsp. of unflavored gelatin
4 tsp. of instant tea granules
2 gal. of warm water

Mix all of the ingredients together. Water all your flowering plants with this mix every two weeks in the morning. ✽

low up with liquid food—like my Flower Feeder tonic—applied every two weeks through the growing season.

Bulbs. Bulbs are around for a long time, so they appreciate a slow but steady supply of food. Mix 2 pounds of bonemeal with 2 pounds of wood ashes and 1 pound of Epsom salts, and sprinkle this mixture on top of flowerbeds where bulbs are growing, just as the shoots emerge from the ground.

Perennials. Like bulbs, perennials enjoy a long-lasting meal. Sprinkle a handful of dry fertilizer (5-10-5 is fine) on the soil around the base of each plant in early spring before you mulch, or pull back the mulch before you feed, then replace it after.

Snack Attack

Are your annuals and perennials lookin' a little frazzled by mid-summer? Foliar feeding—spraying liquid fertilizer or tonic right on their leaves—gives them a snack they can sink their leaves into right away. Simply fill a hose-end sprayer with compost tea or diluted fish emulsion, and spray away!

Weed 'Em and Reap

Nothing can spoil a flower garden quicker than a whole mess of weeds rearin' their ugly little heads. But there's no need to spend all summer battling these bullies—ol' Jer's here to help you fight *smarter*, not harder!

Bubble, Bubble—No Toil, No Trouble!

Weeds between paving stones, in sidewalk cracks, or in gravel paths driving you crazy? Boil up a pot of water, and give 'em a good dousing. One treatment will do in young seedlings, but for older, more stubborn types, pour on the boiling water once a week, until they stop comin' back.

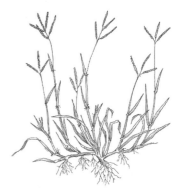

Boiling water is a sure-fire way to get rid of pesky weeds like crabgrass.

Stop These Seedy Characters!

The days may be long, but your gardening time is short—so what's your best weeding strategy? Make a quick sweep through your garden with a bag in one hand and your pruners in the other. Clip off all the weed flowers you see, bag 'em, and toss 'em in the garbage. That way, they won't be making any more seeds for a new weed crop!

Get 'Em Young

No matter what weedy foes you're fighting, baby weeds are always easier to pull than full-grown adults. They also haven't set seeds yet—and as the saying goes, "One year's seeding makes seven years weeding." So make it a habit to always pull weed seedlings as soon as you spot 'em, and you'll save yourself a whole lot of work in the long run!

Know Your Foe

Well, you don't have to know your weeds on a first-name basis, but it sure helps to know something about their habits!

❀ Annual weeds, like chickweed, mallow, and ragweed, are the easiest to wipe out: Pull or dig

Jerry's TIMELY TIPS

"When I see Gene Kelly dancing to 'Singin' in the Rain,' I always think of my Grandma Putt. We always weeded in the rain—well, actually, <u>after</u> a rain. You see, weed roots come up easily when the soil is moist, so after a rain is the best time to attack them. And singin' while you're weedin' makes the work go that much faster!"

them before they flower and set seed, and they won't be back. To say a permanent good-bye, keep after them for a few seasons, to catch any that come up from seeds already in your soil.

❋ Perennials like dandelions, thistles, and ground ivy are tougher. If you leave even a small piece in the ground when you pull them up, you'll have a new weed in its place in a matter of weeks. So dig perennial weeds up, roots and all; zap 'em with my Weed Wipeout tonic; or smother them with 8 to 10 sheets of newspaper topped by mulch.

Flower Fix-Its

My Grandma Putt didn't take any guff from troublemakers that could destroy her precious flowers—and you don't have to, either! The war against pests and diseases starts long before you reach for a sprayer and one of my trusty tonics. If you learn how to be an effective plant inspector, you'll be able to nip most flower problems in the bud (so to speak)!

I Spy

Ready to go on flower patrol? Here's a handy checklist of signs and symptoms to watch for:

☑ Look at the overall health of each plant. Yellowed foliage, wilted leaves or stems, and stunted growth all can signal root or stem pests, as well as diseases.

✔ Brush your hand over each plant, to see if any whiteflies, flea beetles, or leafhoppers jump or fly away.

✔ Look at the leaves. Large, ragged holes usually indicate slugs, beetles, or caterpillars. Turn over a few leaves, too, to check for critters that may be hiding on the undersides.

✔ Inspect the stems and buds carefully, because these are favorite feeding places for pests like aphids and spider mites.

Don't Let Diseases Get Ya Down!

It's easy to stop many diseases in their tracks—*if* you catch them early, and take steps to handle them as soon as you see them.

Spots on leaves. Pick off spotted leaves and toss them in the trash—the sooner, the better!

Mottled green-and-yellow leaves that are crinkled or curled. These are signs that viruses are at work. There's no control, so pull up infected plants and throw them away immediately.

Yellowed leaves, stunted plants, and/or wilting. These symptoms can be due to many possible problems besides diseases, including pests and nutrient deficiencies. To figure out what's bugging your garden plants, turn to Part 4, "Pest and Problem Patrol," on page 308.

Vacuum Your Troubles Away

Your hand-held, rechargeable vacuum cleaner is a perfect pest-control tool in disguise! When you find a bunch of bugs bugging your blooms, run the vacuum lightly over the infested plants. With your other hand, brush the leaves and stems gently to encourage the pests to fly up and be caught in the suction. When you're done, simply dump the pests into a can of soapy water, away from your plants.

Jerry's TIMELY TIPS

"If mice, voles, and other rodents are a problem in your garden, avoid spreading winter mulch. A layer of mulch makes a snug mouse house during the colder months—complete with the crowns and roots of tasty perennials and bulbs for wintertime snacking!"

Garden Cure-All Tonic

At the first sign of insects or disease, mix up a batch of this tonic to set things right.

4 cloves of garlic
1 small onion
1 small jalapeño pepper
Warm water
1 tsp. of Murphy's Oil Soap
1 tsp. of vegetable oil

Pulverize the garlic, onion, and pepper in a blender, and let them steep in a quart of warm water for two hours. Strain the mixture through cheesecloth or panty hose, and dilute the liquid with three parts of warm water. Add the Murphy's Oil Soap and vegetable oil. Mist-spray your flowers with this elixir several times a week. ✽

To Mulch, or Not to Mulch?

In most cases, that's an easy question to answer. Mulch does lots of great things for your garden—it holds in soil moisture, keeps roots cool, and prevents soil from splashing on leaves. On the downside, the cool, damp conditions that are so good for root growth are also perfect for pesky soil-dwelling pests, like slugs, snails, and cutworms. So if you have problems with these creepy crawlies, take all the mulch off for a few weeks, then replace it once you've got the problem well under control.

Crazy Daisy Spray

Who'd have thought that pretty perennials could also pack a punch in the pest-control department? Sun-loving pyrethrum daisies (*Tanacetum cinerariifolium* and *T. coccineum*) are a snap to grow in any sunny spot, and their pink, red, or white daisies contain a potent pest-fighting compound that you can easily extract right at home!

Pick the daisy flowers when they're fully open, and spread them on screens in a warm, dry, dark place. When the flowers are completely crispy, pack them in tightly sealed jars or other containers, and store them in a cool, dark place. To make them into a spray, grind up a few flowers in a mortar and pestle. Mix the dust with a splash of dish soap, dilute it with a cup or two of water, pour the mixture into a hand-held sprayer, and spray wherever pests are a problem. (If the concoction doesn't seem to do in the bugs, use more flowers for the next batch.)

Welcome, Friends!

Of all the insects in your garden, only a few are dastardly plant-attacking pests. Many are beneficial, meaning that they make their buggy livings by attacking and eating the very pests you're fighting! So, instead of trying to wipe 'em all out, learn to recognize these beneficial bugs, and welcome them when they appear.

Lady beetles, or ladybugs, are the best known of these good guys (and gals), but there are many others, too, including:

❀ Assassin bugs

❀ Bigeyed bugs

❀ Centipedes

❀ Lacewings

❀ Praying mantids

❀ Predatory mites

❀ Soldier beetles

❀ Spiders

❀ Wasps and yellow jackets

Pull Up a Stool, Toad!

For a pest-control helper that works cheap, invite a toad to move into your gar-

Don't reach for that pest spray just yet! Beneficial insects may be ready to take care of the bad bugs for you.

FL❀WER POWER TONICS

All-Season Clean-Up Tonic

Apply this tonic in early evening every two weeks during the growing season to keep insects and diseases at bay.

1 cup of liquid dish soap
1 cup of tobacco tea*
1 cup of antiseptic mouthwash
Warm water

Mix the soap, tobacco tea, and mouthwash in a 20 gallon hose-end sprayer, filling the balance of the jar with warm water. Liberally apply this mixture to your beds and borders to discourage insects and prevent disease during the growing season.

*Place three fingers of chewing tobacco in an old nylon stocking and soak it in a gallon of hot water until the mixture is dark brown. ❀

den! To make a place for him to call home, knock a doorway out of the rim of an old clay pot, then nestle it upside down in a shady spot. Then fill a shallow saucer with water to help provide moisture. Why welcome toads? A single one eats between 10,000 and 20,000 insects and other creepy crawlies a year!

Cut Your Losses

Let's face it, folks—sickly flowers that you constantly have to coddle aren't worth the bother. If certain plants in your garden always seem bothered by pests or diseases, just replace 'em! In the long run, it's much less work and worry for you.

If your heart's still set on problem-prone plants, like roses, do some research before you pick replacements, and look for cultivars that have been bred for better pest and disease resistance. There are some great new disease-resistant roses out there—'Knock Out', for instance, is rarely bothered by black spot. If powdery mildew is a menace in your garden, look for mildew-resistant phlox (like 'David') and bee balm (try 'Marshall's Delight' or 'Jacob Kline').

FLOWER POWER TONICS

All-Purpose Bug/Thug Spray

To kill flower garden insects and diseases in one fell swoop, whip up a batch of my all-purpose spray.

3 tbsp. of baking soda
2 tbsp. of Murphy's Oil Soap
2 tbsp. of canola oil
2 tbsp. of vinegar
2 gal. of warm water

Mix all of the ingredients together, and mist-spray your perennials to the point of run-off. Apply in early spring, just as the bugs and thugs are waking up. ✽

FLOWER POWER TONICS

Bug-Be-Gone Spray

Tired of pests having a picnic in your beds and borders? Then use this potent spray to keep bugs at bay.

1 cup of Murphy's Oil Soap
1 cup of antiseptic mouthwash
1 cup of tobacco tea*

Mix all of the ingredients together in a 20 gallon hose-end sprayer, and soak your plants to the point of run-off.

*Place three fingers of chewing tobacco in an old nylon stocking and soak it in a gallon of hot water until the mixture is dark brown. ✽

Putting Your Beds to Bed

Don't think for a minute that the gardening season is over when the first frost nips your flowers! That's a great time to do some garden clean-up, so your flowers will be ready to grow like gangbusters when spring rolls around again.

Trim Time

After frost hits, it's time for a quick bit of clean-up. Pull out dead annuals, and cut back perennials, except for the ones that provide winter interest (like ornamental grasses) or food for birds (like asters). Add the trimmings to your compost pile unless the plant they came from was bothered by pests or diseases; in that case, you're better off throwing it in the trash.

'Sno Joke!

Believe it or not, snow makes great mulch, so pile it on any plants that need a little extra insulation. But don't shovel snow on beds if it's likely to contain deicing salts, because the salt can harm plant roots.

Got Mulch?

If all of your perennials are perfectly hardy in your area, and if they've been in the ground for at least a full growing season, then there's no reason to mulch them every winter. But if you're growing some plants that might not stand the cold, or if you set out new plants in fall, then a cozy winter blan-

FLOWER POWER TONICS

Frozen Feed

To give your perennials a welcome winter snack and a rip-roarin' start in spring, wait until the ground freezes, then apply the following mix.

25 pounds of garden gypsum
10 pounds of garden fertilizer
   (4-2-4 or 5-10-5)
5 pounds of bonemeal

Mix all of the ingredients together, then spread the mixture evenly over your beds and borders. This amount will cover 100 square feet. ❋

ket can make the difference between delightful flowers and dead ones come spring!

Winter Mulch 101

Planning to apply a winter mulch? Wait until the ground has frozen, please, then cover your beds with 6 to 12 inches of a loose, light-weight mulch, like weed-free straw, leaves, or evergreen boughs. (Cut-up Christmas trees make an ideal—and abundant—winter mulch!)

If you use whole leaves, se-lect them carefully. Oak leaves are a good choice, because they're tough and don't tend to mat down over the winter. Thin-ner-textured leaves, like maple leaves, do pack down, and they may smother your plants. Remove winter mulches gradually in spring, once the danger of hard freezes has passed.

Ready for Action!

After a long, tough season of good service, your tools deserve a bit of attention, too. Fall and winter are the perfect times to get your tools back into tip-top shape for spring! Here's what you should do.

❋ Use steel wool or a wire brush to clean any clinging soil off of all tool parts.

❋ Sharpen metal blades, then coat them and other metal parts with light oil to prevent rust. Store them in a dry spot.

❋ Inspect wooden handles. Replace any that are cracked. Sand out chips or scratches, then rub the wood with tung oil before storing.

Fill Your Garden with Flowers— for Free!

If you ask me, making new plants is just like making a little magic! Nothing's better than stickin' an itty bitty seed or cutting into the ground and watchin' it grow into a great big plant. Best of all, it's a whole lot easier than you might think! In this chapter, I've gathered up a bunch of top-secret tips for dividin' and multiplyin' your favorite flowers with no muss and no fuss. They'll be all the healthier for it, and you'll have plenty of plants to fill your yard without going broke in the process!

Seed-Starting Made Simple

Let me tell you, friends—if you want to save a ton of money, do yourself a favor and give indoor seed-starting a try. It isn't rocket science, and it doesn't take a greenhouse or a truckload of fancy-schmancy equipment—just a couple of pots, some seed-starting mix, a few inexpensive lights, and a little time. With 20 bucks or so in supplies, and a little problem-solving know-how, you can grow hundreds of dollars' worth of annual and perennial transplants right in your own home. You can't beat that deal!

Let There Be Light!

Most folks think they're going to grow seedlings on their windowsills, but that's usually not a good idea. Windowsills are narrow, so the pots are likely to fall off, and they're too cool for most seeds to sprout. Plus, few windows get enough light for young plants to really get growing. Instead, I want you to go to your local hardware store or home center and pick up one or two 4-foot shop lights (the kind with two 4-foot fluorescent tubes). Use the chains and S-hooks they come with to hang them over a table or bench. Start with the lights hanging low—no more than 2 inches above the pots. Adjust the hooks as your seedlings grow, so the lights are 4 to 6 inches above their tops.

Yesterday's News = Tomorrow's Blooms

Don't spend a bundle buying plastic pots for seed-starting! With a couple quick twists of the wrist, you can turn old newspapers into super seed-starting pots. You'll need newspaper, scissors, and moistened seed-starting mix, plus a metal or plastic can to use as a form. A 10-ounce soup can works fine for large seeds like zinnias; use 8-ounce or smaller cans to make pots for smaller seeds. Then follow these steps:

Step 1: Cut long strips across an opened-out section of newspaper, making them as tall as the can you're using.

Step 2: Wind a single strip around the bottom two-thirds of the can.

Step 3: Fold up or crush the bottom third of the strip of newspaper against the base of the can to form the pot's bottom. Slide the pot off the can, and fill it with moistened seed mix.

Step 4: Set filled pots in a tray with an inch or so of water for them to soak up, then sow your seeds.

Step 5: When the seedlings are ready to go into the garden, plant them, pot and all!

A Toothy Tip

Tiny seeds are the dickens to plant, especially if you want only a few seeds per pot, so you don't have to thin out the seedlings later. Well, sink your teeth into this idea—use a toothpick to help you! Get your pots of moist seed-starting mix ready, then pour the seeds into a small dish. Wet the very tip of the toothpick, and stick it into the seeds. Then touch the tip of the toothpick to the seed-starting mix to transfer the seeds to the pot. It's that simple!

A moistened toothpick makes sowing tiny seeds a snap!

Seedling Strengthener

To get your seedlings off to a healthy, disease-free start, mist-spray them every few days with this terrific tonic.

2 cups of manure
½ cup of instant tea granules
Warm water

Put the manure and tea in an old nylon stocking, and let it steep in 5 gallons of water for several days. Dilute the mixture with 4 parts of warm water (for example, 4 cups of water for every cup of mix) before using. ✻

Super Sprouting— the Baker Way

Here's a nifty trick for jump-starting large seeds, such as sunflowers (*Helianthus annuus*) and scarlet runner beans (*Phaseolus coccineus*)! Moisten a paper towel, and spread out the seeds on one side of it. Fold the other half of the towel over the seeds, then fold it in half again. Before placing the whole package in a plastic bag, write the name of the plant on a label and tuck it in the paper towel. Set the bag in a warm place (70°F or so).

Every two or three days, unfold the towel, and carefully transfer any seeds that have sprouted to pots filled with moist seed-starting mix. After that, grow 'em like you would any other seedlings.

Sphagnum Bags 'Em!

Unlike garden-sown seeds, indoor-sown seeds don't have to deal with pesky pests, hungry critters, and bad weather. But they still can have disease problems—especially a fungal disease called damping-off, which rots seedlings right at the soil line. To stop these funky fungi before they start, simply sprinkle sphagnum moss (available at garden centers) over the entire surface of each pot, either before or right after you sow your seeds.

Jerry's TIMELY TIPS

"Want to keep your seedlings short and sturdy? Set up a small fan at the lowest setting to blow across their tops. The moving air will keep your baby flowers low and bushy—and it'll put a stop to disease problems, too!"

Cutting Remarks

Need new flowers in a jiffy? You can't do better than to take cuttings! Just snip off a few shoots, treat 'em right, and in a few weeks, you've got as many new plants as you need, *all for free.* So don't delay—read on for my sure-fire tips to taking cuttings, the problem-free, Jerry Baker way!

Be a Cut-Up!

New to the cutting craze? Just follow these four simple steps for no-hassle cuttings:

Step 1: Be prepared. Clean sand, or a half-and-half mixture of vermiculite and potting soil, is perfect for rooting cuttings. Add just enough water to make the mix evenly moist (but not soggy), and use it to fill 3- to 6-inch plastic pots *before* you go out to collect your cuttings.

Step 2: Start snipping! Gather cuttings in the morning, when plants are full of moisture. Snip off stem tips 4 to 6 inches below their topmost leaves, then stick 'em in a jar of water or a plastic bag so they won't wilt.

> **GRANDMA PUTT'S**
> *Handy Hints*
>
> When she took cuttings, Grandma Putt always made it a point to pinch off any flowers and flower buds before she stuck the stems into their pots. She knew this simple step would speed up the rooting process, because the stem could send its energy toward new roots, instead of blooms.

Step 3: Trim 'em up right. Snip off the leaves on the lower half of the stem. Cut the bottom of the stem right below a leaf joint (where leaves were attached). Insert each stem halfway into the sand or soil, spacing the cuttings so their leaves don't touch.

Step 4: Hold in the humidity. To keep cuttings from wilting before they root, put their pots in an old aquarium, or under a tent made

The best time to take cuttings is early to midsummer, when tender new growth has had a chance to toughen up a little. To see if a stem is ready, bend it over. If it snaps off cleanly, then it's perfect cutting material. Pass on any stems that bend, but don't break.

of large, clear plastic bags, to hold in the humidity. Keep them in a warm, bright place, and expect new roots to form in 3 to 6 weeks.

Best Bets for Cutting Success

Want to start your cutting career with something super-easy? Here's a Baker's dozen of annual and perennial flowers that root quick as a wink—*guaranteed*:

Asters (*Aster*)

Bee balm (*Monarda didyma*)

Catmints (*Nepeta*)

Chrysanthemums (*Chrysanthemum*)

Coleus (*Solenostemon scutellarioides*)

Dahlias (*Dahlia*)

Garden phlox (*Phlox paniculata*)

Geraniums (*Pelargonium*)

Impatiens (*Impatiens walleriana*)

Obedient plant (*Physostegia virginiana*)

Sedums (*Sedum*)

Wax begonia (*Begonia semperflorens*)

Taking cuttings is easy—simply snip off a shoot tip, dip the end in rooting hormone, stick it in moist potting soil, and cover it with a plastic bag until new growth starts!

Whip Up Some Willow Water

Treating new cuttings with a rooting hormone is a great way to get new roots in a hurry. But you don't have to shell out your hard-earned dough to buy this wonderful stuff at your local garden center. If you have access to any kind of willow (*Salix*) tree, you can make your own, right at home!

Simply snip off a few twigs, cut them up into 1-inch pieces, and soak them in a quart of water for a few days. Strain out the twigs, and use the brew to water your cuttings. Willows contain a natural rooting hormone called IBA; store-bought rooting powders contain a synthetic version of the same stuff!

Warm Thoughts

The secret to growing big, healthy cuttings every time? Keep their toes warm! You see, keeping the tops of the cuttings on the cool side (65°F or so) slows down water loss from the leaves. That's important, because cuttings don't have roots to drink up any more water if they get thirsty—they'll just wilt. But warm *soil* gets cuttings to grow roots fast—really fast—and that means big plants in a jiffy.

The easiest way to give cuttings bottom heat is to buy a heat mat, the kind sold for seed-starting. Set pots of cuttings in shallow trays, and set the trays on the heat mat. Then just plug it in, and get growing!

Just Say Whoa to Wilting

Keeping your cuttings full of moisture can be a real

To the Rescue!

If your cuttings wilt, rot, or just don't root, don't give up! Try again, keeping the following tips in mind:

Cuttings wilt. Next time, keep the rooting medium evenly moist, and the humidity high. Set the pots of cuttings in good light, but out of direct sun, so they don't overheat.

Cuttings rot. Use a fresh growing medium for each batch of cuttings; don't reuse old soil. Make sure pots of cuttings aren't sitting in water. Pick off any leaves that drop off.

Cuttings don't root. Collect cuttings quickly, so they don't have a chance to wilt before you plant them. Keep the air temperature between 65° and 75°F. Use a heat mat to warm up the soil.

challenge, especially on big-leaved plants, like coleus. To reduce moisture loss on cuttings that have extra-large leaves, use scissors to cut off half of each leaf. Then stick the cuttings in moist medium as usual.

The Root of the Matter

Rooting time for various plants varies widely—from just a few days for annuals to six weeks or more for flowering shrubs—but on average, you can expect cuttings of most flowers to be well rooted in about a month.

Here are some clues to look for:

❀ New shoot growth

❀ Slight resistance when you tug gently on the cutting

❀ Visible roots peeking out of the pot's drainage holes

Movin' On Up!

Once your flower cuttings are well rooted, it's time to give 'em some elbow room. Carefully knock 'em out of their pots and move 'em to individual containers (2- by 2-inch pots are perfect) filled with light, well-drained potting mix. Once the plants are settled into these pots (after a month or so), you can move 'em into larger pots, or right out to your garden.

FLOWER POWER TONICS

Repotting Booster Tonic

When your rooted cuttings are ready for transplanting, a dose of this terrific tonic'll help 'em adjust to their new homes in a jiffy.

½ tsp. of all-purpose plant food
½ tsp. of Vitamin B_1 Plant Starter
½ cup of weak tea water*
1 gal. of warm water

Mix all of the ingredients together, and gently pour the tonic through the soil of your repotted plants. Allow pots to drain for 15 minutes or so, then pour off any excess in the tray, and treat your trees and shrubs to the leftovers!

*Soak a used tea bag in a gallon of warm water and 1 teaspoon of liquid dish soap until the water is light brown. ❀

Divide to Multiply!

If you need big, blooming-size perennials in a hurry, dividing is definitely the way to go. In just a few minutes, you can turn one clump into two, four, or even more brand-new plants. Best of all, dividing crowded, overgrown clumps is an easy way to keep diseases at bay, so you'll be doing your plants—and yourself—a big favor at the same time!

Timing Is Everything

The best time to divide your plants is when they're *not* actively growing. For most perennials, that means early to midfall, but there are a few exceptions:

❀ Wait until spring to divide fall-flowering perennials (otherwise, you'll cut short their end-of-the-season show).

❀ Divide early spring bloomers right after their flowers fade, so they'll have all year to get settled in again.

❀ Wait until bulbs' top growth has turned yellow before you separate them.

Ready, Set, Divide!

Dividing can be stressful on plants, but when you're prepared with some of ol' Jer's garden smarts, you can help them get through it with flying colors. A day or two before you plan to divide, give the ground around the clumps a good soaking. Cut back any top growth, too—down to about 6 inches above the ground. This'll help the plants soak up and hold moisture, so they'll be less likely to wilt before they settle into their new homes.

> ### GRANDMA PUTT'S
> ## Handy Hints
>
> Instead of dividing all of her perennials at one time, Grandma Putt made it a point to do a few of them each year. That way, she always had a nice-looking garden with plenty of flowers, instead of having to start from scratch with new divisions every few years.

Best Bets for Division

Still a little nervous about trying divisions for the first time? Give any of these 10 forgiving flowers a try! They're so simple to work with that you can pull them apart with only your fingers—no tools needed:

Asters (*Aster*)

Catmints (*Nepeta*)

Daylilies (*Hemerocallis*)

Hostas (*Hosta*)

Lungworts (*Pulmonaria*)

Mountain bluet
   (*Centaurea montana*)

Phlox (*Phlox*)

Sedums (*Sedum*)

Spotted deadnettle
   (*Lamium maculatum*)

Sundrops (*Oenothera*)

FLOWER POWER TONICS

Perfect Potting Mix

If you've got a lot of divisions to pot up, you'll need plenty of potting soil. So mix up a big batch of this simple blend, and keep it handy!

1 part topsoil
1 part peat moss
1 part vermiculite
1 part compost

Mix all of the ingredients together and use for potting up all kinds of perennials and bulbs. ✳

The Long and Short of Division

If you need just a few new plants, cutting clumps into thirds or quarters is the best way to go. The large pieces will have plenty of buds and shoots, so they can go right back in the garden, and they'll fill out in a flash!

What if you want as many new plants as possible? Sure, you can do divisions here, too—you'll just need to give 'em a little extra TLC. Have some pots in various sizes, plus a good supply of moist potting soil, on hand when you dig up the clump. Pull or cut apart the clump into small sections (just remember that each piece needs at least one bud and some roots). Pot up the pieces, then set 'em in a shady, north-facing area, and keep 'em evenly moist. Once they're growing vigorously again, they're ready to go back to the garden!

Don't Suffer—Use Sulfur!

When dividing plants with fleshy roots or rhizomes—like daylilies (*Hemerocallis*) and hostas—dust the cuts with powdered sulfur after you cut them apart. (You can find it for sale at your local garden center.) This amazing stuff is just the ticket to keep root-rotting fungi from attacking your new divisions!

Problem-Solvin' Tips for Trouble-Free Divisions

New perennial divisions will dry out quick as a wink if you let 'em—and that means they won't put down new roots and grow like they should. To give 'em the TLC they need, remember these six quick tips:

❀ Divide plants on an overcast or rainy day, if possible.

❀ If it's sunny, shade new plants with cardboard boxes or burlap for a few days until they recover.

❀ Don't leave divisions lying in the sun, for even a minute! Wrap 'em in wet newspaper, or set 'em in the shade.

❀ Replant divisions as soon as you can. Prepare and moisten the soil in new beds and borders *before* you divide, and water immediately after replanting.

❀ If you can't replant immediately, pot up the divisions, or set 'em in the shade, and pack damp mulch or compost around their roots.

❀ Keep the soil around new divisions evenly moist, but not wet. Waterlogged soil leads to rot.

FLOWER POWER TONICS

Start-Up Snack

Give your just-divided perennials the following fertilizer tonic to get 'em growin' like gangbusters!

1 can of beer
1 cup of all-purpose plant food
¼ cup of ammonia

Mix the ingredients together, and pour them into a 20 gallon hose-end sprayer. Fill the balance of the sprayer jar with water. Thoroughly spray on newly divided plants. Repeat one week later. ❀

Bonus Bulbs

To divide crowded clumps of daffodils, tulips, and other spring-blooming bulbs, you need to be patient and wait until the leaves turn yellow in early to midsummer. Dig around the outside of the clumps, and lift 'em out of the soil. Separate the bulbs, and re-plant right away, at about the same depth they were growing before.

Super-Simple Layering

Layering is a fun way to make new plants without diggin' up a whole clump of flowers for division. All you do is trick a stem into taking root while it's still attached to its parent, *then* dig it out and move it to a new spot—with no muss and no fuss! Spring and early summer are the best times to give layering a try. Just follow these four simple steps:

Step 1: Choose a flexible shoot, and loosen the soil beneath it.

Step 2: Gently bend the shoot downward, and bury it in the loos-ened soil. Leave just the last few inches of shoot tip exposed. Hold the stem in place with a wire pin or a rock if it won't stay down.

Step 3: Water regularly through the summer.

Step 4: In late summer or early fall, scratch away some of the soil to check for roots. If they're still small, rebury the stem. Once the new roots are a few inches long, snip off the shoot where it's still attached to the original plant, and transplant it wherever you want it to grow. It's that easy!

Layering's a snap—bend down a branch, snip it off once it's rooted, and you've got a brand-new plant for free!

Best Bets
for Layering

Ready to give layering a try? Here are eight great candidates to get you off to a problem-free start:

Artemisias (*Artemisia*)

Candytuft (*Iberis sempervirens*)

Catmints (*Nepeta*)

Chrysanthemums
(*Chrysanthemum*)

Lavender (*Lavandula angustifolia*)

Periwinkles (*Vinca*)

Sweet William (*Dianthus barbatus*)

Thread-leaved coreopsis (*Coreopsis verticillata*)

PENNY WISE

If you think layering works well on perennials, you should try it on your favorite flowering shrubs! It's a super-easy way to make more of your favorite azaleas, forsythias, hydrangeas, lilacs, rhododendrons, viburnums, and weigelas—not to mention roses! Layering works wonders for vines such as clematis and wisteria, too. Just remember—shrubs can take a year or two to put down roots, so leave them in place for at least one full year before checking for roots.

Baby Those Babies!

Whether you've grown them from seeds, cuttings, or divisions, all of your new plants will appreciate a little extra TLC. So let's take a few minutes to talk about how to get those youngsters off on the right root—and bypass pesky problems—so they're on to a rip-roaring burst of bloom as quick as a wink!

Easy Does It!

Transplanting is a shocking experience for just about every plant, whether it's going from a pot to the garden or from one flowerbed to another. The more you do to lessen the stress, the sooner it'll get growin' again! Here are four easy ways to help ease the way:

❀ Water plants thoroughly a day or two before transplanting. Moisten the soil in the new planting spot, too!

❀ Transplant on a cloudy or drizzly day, if possible; otherwise, shade plants with burlap, bushel baskets, or cardboard boxes if it's sunny.

❀ Give each plant a good drink once it's in its new home.

❀ Check transplants daily for the first week, and water as needed to keep them evenly moist.

Check, Please!

Don't rush to get your youngsters in the ground before they're well established. Roots peeking out the bottom of the pots are a good sign that plants are ready to go. If you don't see any root tips, gently slide plants out of their pots to check how many roots have formed, and how far they've spread out. When in doubt, give your babies an extra week or two of coddling, either indoors or in a shady, protected spot outdoors, before setting them out in your garden. They'll be glad you did!

Ring Around the Transplants

Once you get a transplant settled into the garden, use your finger to draw a ring around it in the soil. This shallow basin'll help catch water and fertilizer and direct it right to the roots!

FLOWER POWER TONICS

Seedling Starter Tonic

Give your seedlings a break on moving day by serving 'em a sip of my starter tonic. This helps them recover quickly from the transplanting shock.

1 tbsp. of fish emulsion
1 tbsp. of ammonia
1 tbsp. of Murphy's Oil Soap
1 tsp. of instant tea granules
1 qt. of warm water

Mix all of the ingredients in the warm water. Pour into a hand-held mist sprayer, and mist the young plants several times a day until they're back on their feet and growing again. ❀

New-Plant Day Care

It's easy to lose track of baby plants out in the garden, especially if you're growin' perennials or shrubs that take a few years to fill in from seeds or cuttings. To get 'em up and growing on the fast track—and make caring for them a breeze—give 'em their own special nursery bed!

Set it up just like a vegetable garden—with rich, well-worked soil, and plants arranged in rows for easy weedin' and waterin'. Pick a spot in sun or shade, depending on what you're growing. Move the plants to your beds and borders after a season or two, once they're big and strong enough to fend for themselves.

FLOWER POWER TONICS

Flower Power Prep Mix

Here's a flower power mixture that'll really energize your beds and produce a bounty of bright, beautiful blooms.

4 cups of bonemeal
2 cups of gypsum
2 cups of Epsom salts
1 cup of wood ashes
1 cup of lime
4 tbsp. of medicated baby powder
1 tbsp. of baking powder

Combine all of these ingredients in a bucket, and work the mixture into the soil before you plant to get all your flowers off to a rip-roarin' start! ❋

PART 3

FAVORITE
FLOWERS~
A to Z

From spring to fall, Grandma Putt's garden absolutely overflowed with flowers. Sure, we spent time out there every chance we got, but it really never seemed like work; in fact, the flowers pretty much took care of themselves. You see, Grandma Putt filled each flowerbed with plants that were all happy in about the same conditions. It stands to reason that this made them a snap to take care of—they all needed the same things to thrive!

Giving plants exactly what they like has another big advantage: They grow more strongly and bloom like crazy. But best of all, *vigorous plants shrug off pest and disease problems that not-so-happy plants can't cope with.* And that, my friends, is the real secret to a problem-free flower garden—put the right plant in the right place, and you can count on getting great results every time! To help you on your way, I've gathered everything you need to know to be a great garden matchmaker. Simply flip to the entry on each flower you want to grow, and you'll get the whole scoop—how much sun and what kind of soil it needs to thrive, plus some bonus tips to help you get the plants off to a great start and keep them happy throughout the year.

Ageratum • *Ageratum houstonianum*

The fluffy flower clusters of ageratums look just like bits of cotton candy in the garden! These no-fuss annual favorites bloom from midsummer to frost in shades of lavender, blue, pink, or white.

Ageratum

Ageratum houstonianum

 GROW IT!

Full sun to light shade
Rich, moist, well-drained soil
Dwarf types grow 6 to 8 inches tall; full-size ones are 18 to 24 inches
Warm-weather annual

 PLANT IT!

Perfect for pairing with perennials and shrubs
Dwarf types are ideal edging plants
Attracts butterflies galore
Wonderful in window boxes and containers

 GETTING STARTED

Sow seeds indoors, six to eight weeks before your last spring frost date. They need light to sprout, so don't cover them; just press them into the soil surface. Set pots in a warm (70°F) place until seedlings appear, then grow them in cooler conditions (55° to 60°F). Ageratums hate to be cold, so don't move them outdoors until after the last frost date.

PROBLEM SOLVED!

Full-size ageratums make great cut flowers, but their longer stems tend to sprawl. To keep them standing tall, pinch off their stem tips two or three times during early summer for bushier growth. Or plant dwarf ageratums, which don't need pinching.

A Bit of Sunscreen, Please

If your ageratums tend to wilt, have scorched-looking leaves, or die out altogether in summer, the culprit is probably a combination of hot weather and drought. To prevent problems, keep the soil evenly moist with mulch and regular watering. Where summer temperatures regularly go over 90°F, a site in light shade is ideal!

For flowery fireworks in purple, lavender, white, or yellow, look no further than the amazing alliums. They'll do a bang-up job brightening your spring and summer gardens!

 GROW IT!

Full sun
Rich to poor, well-drained soil
3 inches to 3 feet tall
Hardy perennial bulbs
   (Zones 3 to 9)

 PLANT IT!

Superb with shrubs
Perfect partners for bushy
   annuals and perennials
Let low-growers come up
   through groundcovers
   for spring color

Allium
Allium

 GETTING STARTED

Some alliums are sold as bulbs in fall; others are potted and sold as perennials in spring. Confusing, huh? Actually, all alliums have bulbs, but only some can be sold dry with hardy bulbs, like daffodils. Plant these types in fall, at a depth of three times the diameter of the bulb.

The alliums with thin, fleshy bulbs—like chives (*Allium schoenoprasum*)—are sold as potted perennials. Plant these just like other perennials, in either spring or fall.

Don't Hold Back!

Alliums are guaranteed to look lonely if they're planted one here and one there. It's much better to set them out in bold clumps. Six to 12 bulbs in one area is a great start for larger alliums, such as giant onion (*A. giganteum*) and star-of-Persia (*A. christophii*). Plant smaller alliums in even bigger bunches for the best show.

FLOWER FUN!

Alliums aren't just pretty—they're downright handy to have around!

● Break up chive blossoms into salads or mix them with softened butter for a touch of color and a burst of flavor.

● Let the seedheads of large alliums dry right in the garden, then use them in dried arrangements. Spray-paint them for extra color!

● Pour enough boiling water over 1 cup of packed chive leaves to cover them; let cool, strain, and spray to repel flower pests. This also helps prevent scab on apple trees.

Alyssum, Sweet • *Lobularia maritima*

Need an excellent edging plant? How about a fabulous filler for your flowerbed? Well, look no further: Sweet alyssum is just what the doctor (Dr. Baker, that is) ordered! These sweet-smelling flowers are normally bright white, but you can also find them in shades of pink, rose, purple, and lilac.

Sweet alyssum
Lobularia maritima

 GROW IT!

Full sun to partial shade
Average, well-drained soil
Dwarf types grow 3 to 8 inches
    tall; full-size selections grow
    10 to 12 inches tall
Tolerates dry conditions but blooms
    best with regular watering
Self-sows
Cool-weather annual

 PLANT IT!

Great for the front of
    a bed or border
Charming in containers
Cute coming up
    between stones in
    walkways or in
    cracks in paving
Super for seaside gardens

 GETTING STARTED

Sweet alyssum simply couldn't be any easier to grow from seeds. Just scatter them right in the garden, anywhere you want plants. Sow in spring several weeks before your last frost date, or even in fall for flowers the following year! Just press the seeds onto the soil surface (don't cover them), since they need light to germinate.

Are your alyssum plants looking a little droopy during the dog days? Whack the plants back by about half with hedge shears, then water regularly. Sounds drastic, but it really gets 'em going again. You'll have new flowers in a jiffy!

Quick Cover-Up

If you need a cheap, nearly instant groundcover to fill in around tulips, hyacinths, or other spring bulbs, think sweet alyssum! Start with plants from the garden center, and pop 'em in anywhere. They'll fill the space in a flash and crowd out weeds in the process. Sweet alyssum is also a perfect partner for pansies, primroses (*Primula*), and newly planted perennials.

Anemones • *Anemone*

Anemones have dainty-looking blooms, but don't be fooled—they're tough as nails in the garden. Some are sold as perennials, while other kinds—those with woody tubers—are sold as bulbs. They come in many heights and colors, but they all share a showy crown of yellow stamens in the center of each bloom.

 GROW IT!

Spring-Blooming Anemones:
Partial shade
Light, rich, evenly moist soil
6 to 18 inches tall
Hardy perennials and bulbs
   (Zones 3 to 8)

Summer to Fall-Flowering Anemones:
Full sun or partial shade
Rich, well-drained, evenly moist soil
3 to 5 feet tall
Hardy perennials (Zones 4 to 8)

 PLANT IT!

Combine spring-
   bloomers with
   hostas, ferns,
   and astilbes
Plant fall-flowering
   anemones with
   perennials like asters
Enjoy them as cut
   flowers—especially
   the tall fall bloomers

Snowdrop anemone
Anemone sylvestris

 GETTING STARTED

The woody tubers of spring-blooming anemones look a lot like chunks of bark. To get them growing, soak them in warm water overnight before planting them about 2 inches deep and 4 inches apart. Can't tell which end is up? You're not alone! Just set the tubers on their sides, and they'll figure it out for themselves!

Plant potted anemones just like any other perennial, in spring or fall. They thrive for years without needing to be divided. If you want new plants, dig up small ones from the outside edges of the clumps in spring.

Careful Picking Pays!

If you're an anemone aficionado, you can have them in bloom at both ends of the gardening season! Spring-blooming anemones are either perennials or bulbs, and are generally best for the shade garden. Fall-flowering anemones are favorites for sunny beds and borders where the soil stays moist. In areas with hot summers, give them a site with afternoon shade for longer-lasting blooms.

Jerry's TIMELY TIPS

"Florist's or poppy anemones (A. coronaria) have stunning scarlet, violet, or white blooms that are eye-catching in arrangements. You'll often see their woody tubers sold in fall garden-center bulb displays, but beware—these plants aren't hardy in most areas! You can plant them outdoors in fall only in Zones 8 to 10. In the North, pot them up in fall and overwinter them in a cool, frost-free place, or wait and plant them out in spring."

Easy Early Anemones

Glorify your spring and early-summer garden with a sprinkling of these elegant anemones:

❀ **Grecian windflower** (*A. blanda*): White, pink, or blue. Bulb. Zones 4 to 8.

❀ **Meadow anemone** (*A. canadensis*): White. Very vigorous perennial. Zones 3 to 7.

❀ **Snowdrop anemone** (*A. sylvestris*): White. Vigorous perennial. Zones 3 to 8.

❀ **Wood anemone** (*A. nemorosa*): White, pale pink, or lavender. Bulb. Zones 4 to 8.

Fall Anemone Fling

Looking for showy flowers to liven up your fall garden? Anemones are the answer! Chinese anemone (*A. hupehensis*), Japanese anemone (*A. x hybrida*), and grape-leaved anemone (*A. tomentosa*) all come in shades of pink and white and are hardy from Zones 4 to 8. They're particularly pretty when paired with asters, goldenrods (*Solidago*), monkshoods (*Aconitum*), and Russian sage (*Perovskia atriplicifolia*).

Compatible Companions

Fall-blooming anemones don't get growing until late spring, so they're perfect partners for spring bulbs like daffodils or ornamental onions (*Allium*). The bulbs steal the show in spring, then when the anemones come up, their leaves will hide the yellowing bulb foliage.

Annuals

To my mind, a flower garden just isn't a flower garden without at least a few annuals. My Grandma Putt grew these versatile beauties in all colors of the rainbow, and we stuck 'em in any place we found an empty patch of ground. With the help of her sure-fire formulas, Grandma's flower-filled annual beds were the talk of the town—and yours can be, too!

No Strings Attached!

Need a garden in a hurry? Annuals are a great way to go! The results are almost immediate, but there's no long-term commitment, so you can change colors, heights, and styles every year if you want. They're also cheaper than perennials, so you can fill up your flowerbeds with these temporary treasures, while you save up for more permanent plantings.

Paper daisy
Acroclinium

So exactly what is an annual, anyway? Ask a botanist, and he'll tell you that annuals are plants that sprout, grow, flower, set seeds, and die in a single season. Gardeners have a somewhat different definition: any plant that you have to sow or set out anew each year. Annuals come in two general types: cool-weather and warm-weather.

Cool-weather annuals. You'll also hear these called hardy or half-hardy annuals, depending on how much frost they'll take. All thrive in cool conditions and generally are planted out in early spring. Most stop blooming, or at least slow down, when the weather heats up. Examples: pansies and pot marigolds (*Calendula officinalis*).

Warm-weather annuals. Also called tender annuals, these thrive in hot summer weather and bloom from early summer to frost. They hate the cold, so don't be in a hurry to set them out in spring; wait until after the last spring frost date. Examples: sunflowers (*Helianthus annuus*) and zinnias.

Perennial Partners

Now, perennial flowers have a lot going for them, but there are some times when they can really use a little help from their annual cousins. Here are four fun ways to put annuals to work in your perennial plantings:

❀ Depend on them for season-long color while perennials come into and go out of bloom.

❀ Fill in around small, newly planted perennials with annuals, and your garden will look lush right from the get-go.

Joseph's coat
Amaranthus tricolor

❀ Tuck annuals into bare spots in any garden to keep weeds from getting a roothold.

❀ Hide the yellowing foliage of early-blooming perennials and bulbs by adding warm-weather annuals for color all summer—and beyond!

Super-Duper Bed-Builders

Here's a terrific tip I learned from Grandma Putt: If you've got crummy soil, don't sweat it—let annuals do your work for you! Dig a 1-inch layer of compost into the soil as best you can the first spring, then plant your annuals. Dig some more compost into the soil in fall when you put the garden to bed for the winter. Repeat the following season. By the end of the second year, the combination of digging, compost, and annual roots will leave you with loose, rich soil that's just perfect for perennials!

Giants in a Jiffy!

Need a quick privacy screen? Don't waste time waiting for shrubs to grow up! These substantial annuals make an eye-high boundary that'll give you all the shelter you need in just a few weeks. All of the following top out at 5 to 6 feet tall:

Cannas (*Canna*)

Castor bean (*Ricinus communis*)

Chenille plant (*Acalypha hispida*)

Dahlias (*Dahlia*)

Flowering tobacco (*Nicotiana sylvestris*)

Kiss-me-over-the-garden-gate
    (*Persicaria orientale*)

Love-lies-bleeding (*Amaranthus caudatus*)

Mexican sunflower (*Tithonia rotundifolia*)

Spider flower (*Cleome hassleriana*)

Sunflowers (*Helianthus annuus*)

Sunset hibiscus (*Abelmoschus manihot*)

Coleus
Solenostemon

Swan River daisy
Brachyscome

Get Color Crazy!

Want to jazz up your yard with a new color scheme? Wondering if drifts of pink and yellow flowers would be nice accents for your perennial bed? Ready to take a chance on a color-theme garden in hot pinks, screaming reds, or soft yellows and blues? Annuals come in just about

Annuals don't need a lot of elbow room, but they do need a bit of space to spread out for good growth. Make planting them a breeze by using this rule of thumb: Space them at half their mature height. (If they grow 12 inches tall, for example, plant them 6 inches apart.) How easy can you get?

any color you can imagine, so go ahead and test out your ideas right in the ground. If you like the look, great—replace the annuals with perennials in the same color range. Want to try again? Change the design every year if you like. It's fun to keep your neighbors guessing what you'll come up with next!

Browallia
Browallia

More Annual Options

Annuals look just super planted by themselves and even better mixed with perennials, bulbs, and other plants in beds and borders. But don't stop there—here are three more great ideas for adding annual magic to your yard!

Get edgy. Grow rows of ground-hugging annuals along walkways or shrub borders to add a neat and colorful finishing touch.

Plant a pattern. Use a broomstick to draw a design on the soil—an American flag, maybe, or a daisy flower, or even your name! Then fill the pattern with different annuals that are the same height to create a carpet of many colors.

Go container crazy. Fill window boxes, hanging baskets, and all kinds of containers with annuals for summer-long color anywhere.

Tailor-Made for Shade

Most annuals are sun-worshipers, but there are annuals for shady spaces, too! Wax begonias and impatiens (*Impatiens walleriana*) are the most obvious options. If you're in the market for something different, try browallia or bush violet (*Browallia speciosa*), edging lobelia (*Lobelia erinus*), garden balsam (*Impatiens balsamina*), Persian violet (*Exacum affine*), or wishbone flower (*Torenia fournieri*). If colorful foliage is your focus, consider coleus or polka-dot plant (*Hypoestes phyllostachya*).

Keep Your Cool

Chinese houses
Collinsia

Ready to get your pansies, larkspurs (*Consolida*), and other cool-weather annuals growing? The simplest route is to sow the seeds outside, right where you want the plants to grow. Most people plant in early spring, as soon as the soil is thawed out enough to dig in, but I'll share a little secret I learned from Grandma Putt: Fall sowing is really the way to go! The seedlings that appear the following spring are extra-sturdy and start blooming weeks sooner than spring-sown ones.

Prefer to start seeds indoors? Keep these chilly cuties in a cool spot, between 50° and 65°F. In most areas, you can move them out to your garden on or before the last spring frost date. If your summers are hot and dry, try setting them out in fall instead—you'll have flowers to enjoy all winter long!

Waiting Works Wonders

I know it's exciting to get your garden started in spring, but if you're growing marigolds, ornamental peppers (*Capsicum annuum*), and other warm-weather annuals, you definitely don't want to jump the gun. Chilly nights and soggy, cold soil are a sure way to send these heat-lovers to an early grave.

Most warm-weather annuals need a head start to get blooming by midsummer, so sow them indoors in early spring. Fast-growing plants like zinnias and sunflowers are an exception; they'll sprout up quick from seed sown right in the garden after the last frost date, once the weather has settled and the soil has warmed up. This is also the ideal time to move indoor-grown seedlings out to your garden.

Jerry's TIMELY TIPS

"My best piece of advice about annuals? Start small! Believe you me, a small bed that's easy to control will make you much happier than a gigantic one that's overrun by weeds come July. You can always enlarge the garden once you've figured out how much time you have to spend."

FLOWER POWER TONICS

Flower Defender

Once your annuals are up and growing, protect them from pests with this potent brew.

1 cup of liquid dish soap
1 cup of tobacco tea*
1 cup of antiseptic mouthwash
¼ cup of Tabasco® sauce
Warm water

Mix the dish soap, tobacco tea, mouthwash, and Tabasco sauce in a 20 gallon hose-end sprayer, filling the balance of the sprayer jar with warm water. Then bathe all of your early bloomers with this super bug-busting elixir to keep 'em growing.

*Place three fingers of chewing tobacco in an old nylon stocking and soak it in a gallon of hot water until the mixture is dark brown. ❃

Snow-on-the mountain

Euphorbia variegata

Weed Wars

Baby annuals—seedlings or transplants—need protection against fast-growing weeds if they're going to grow up big and strong. To keep fast-growing weeds from getting the upper hand, don't put it off 'til tomorrow: Pull 'em as soon as you spot 'em. Can't tell the good guys from the bad? Start a few seedlings of each kind of annual flower in labeled pots indoors. That way, you'll have samples for comparison!

Stolen Seedlings

Whoa—where did all my seedlings go? If patches of young annuals disappear completely overnight, the culprit is likely to be either rabbits, slugs, or snails. Look closely at the soil, and if you see a bunch of slimy trails over the spot, your seedlings got slugged. To learn more about these pesky pests and how to stop 'em in their tracks, turn to "A Rogues Gallery," starting on page 310.

Timber!

If you find clusters of seedlings flopped over onto the soil, suspect cutworms or damping-off. A close look at the base of the stems will tell you exactly what you're dealing with.

Cutworms. These dastardly enemies of seedlings and young transplants strike at night, cutting through stems at ground level. Sometimes they eat whole seedlings, but usually they just let the stems fall where they may. Prevent damage next time by cutting 1- to 2-inch-tall rings from those cardboard tubes inside paper towel or toilet tissue rolls. Slip a collar over each seedling at transplanting time and push it into the soil a bit to keep the critters from slithering underneath.

Damping-off. These funky fungi attack the base of the stems. Afflicted seedlings turn black at the base, then just keel over. This problem's most common in wet weather, so wait until the soil has dried out a bit before sowing again.

Strawflower
Helichrysum

Got Good Growth?

If not, then it's time for you to do some detective work! Stunted, slow-growing annuals might just need some fertilizer, like a dose of my All-Season Green-Up Tonic. No better in a few days? Then check the soil pH. If the soil is on the acidic side (below 6.5), scatter some lime around the plants and water thoroughly.

If you're growing warm-weather annuals—like impatiens and sunflowers—remember that they need heat to grow well. If you put them out too early in spring, they'll just sit still until the weather warms up. Protect them this year with upside-down boxes or buckets when tempera-

FLOWER POWER TONICS

All-Season Green-Up Tonic

If your flowering plants are looking a bit peaked, give them a taste of this sweet snack. They'll green up in a jiffy!

1 can of beer
1 cup of ammonia
½ cup of liquid dish soap
½ cup of liquid lawn food
½ cup of molasses or corn syrup

Mix all of the ingredients together in a large bucket, then pour into a 20 gallon hose-end sprayer, and apply to your plants every three weeks during the growing season. ✽

Heliotrope
Heliotropium

tures dip below 50°F—and don't jump the gun when you plant next season!

Look Before You Feed!

Annuals with yellowed leaves may simply need a snack, but before you reach for the fertilizer, rule out other possible problems first:

❀ Webbing on stems and under leaves, and yellow-speckled leaves? Spider mites are sucking the sap right out of your annuals! Blast them off plants with a strong spray of water from the hose.

❀ Whiteflies are the culprit if clouds of tiny white bugs fly up when you brush the foliage. Spraying with insecticidal soap or my Flower Defender tonic (see page 146) should send these pests packing in a hurry!

❀ If your plants also have deformed flowers, suspect aster yellows disease. You may also see leafhoppers or aphids, which spread this disease. Infected plants *can't* be cured, so pull 'em up, and toss 'em in the trash.

Overstuffed Annuals

Lots of foliage, but few flowers? Most annuals enjoy rich soil, but it's possible for them to get too much of a good thing! Hold off on high-nitrogen fertilizers, and avoid working any fresh farm animal manures into the soil just before you get to planting.

GRANDMA PUTT'S
Handy Hints

Whenever an early frost threatened to end the gardening season before its time, Grandma Putt and I got busy. We'd rush out at dusk with sheets and cardboard boxes to cover frost-tender annuals. Once the temperature came back up in the morning, off the covers would come. Since early fall frosts are often followed by a long, mild Indian summer, a few nights of protection usually meant several weeks of more color from our annuals!

Climbing the Walls

Want high-flying color, but have only pennies to spend? Try some of these out-of-the-ordinary annual vines. All are a snap to grow from seeds, thrive in warm weather, and bloom from midsummer to frost. Train them on trellises, let them festoon your fences, spiral them up strings, or even let them spread over sturdy shrubs!

Balloon vine (*Cardiospermum halicacabum*): Tiny greenish flowers turn into inflated, balloon-like pods.

Cardinal climber (*Ipomoea* x *multifida*): Scarlet trumpets against rich green leaves.

Cup-and-saucer vine (*Cobaea scandens*): Cup-shaped purple flowers on leafy green "saucers."

Cypress vine (*Ipomoea quamoclit*): Rich red, starry-faced trumpets and very lacy leaves.

Hyacinth bean (*Lablab purpureus*): Pink flowers ripen into glossy purple pods.

Moonflower (*Ipomoea alba*): Perfectly perfumed white blooms that open in the evening.

FLOWER POWER TONICS

Scat Cat Solution

Cats can be great pets, but they can also be real pests if they dig in your garden—and they seem to just love the loose, fluffy soil of annual beds. Try this spicy solution to keep them away from your prized plantings.

5 tbsp. of flour
4 tbsp. of powdered mustard
3 tbsp. of cayenne pepper
2 tbsp. of chili powder
2 qts. of warm water

Mix all of the ingredients together. Sprinkle the solution around the areas you want to protect to keep kitty at bay. ❀

Lantana
Lantana

Edging lobelia
Lobelia erinus

Asters • *Aster and Callistephus chinensis*

These easy-to-grow beauties bear cheerful, daisy-like flowers in a veritable rainbow of colors, including purple, lavender, blue, pink, ruby-red, and white. Aster appreciators have two types to choose from: annual China asters (*Callistephus chinensis*) and perennial asters (*Aster*).

Blue wood aster

Aster cordifolius

 GROW IT!

Perennial Asters (*Aster*):
Full sun
Rich, well-drained, evenly moist soil
Dwarf types grow 1 to 2 feet tall;
    full-size plants reach 3 to 6 feet
Hardy perennials (Zones 3 to 8)

**China Asters
(*Callistephus chinensis*):**
Full sun to partial shade
Rich, well-drained, evenly moist soil
Neutral to alkaline pH
Dwarf types grow 8 to 12 inches
    tall; full-size plants reach
    1 to 3 feet tall
Cool-weather annual

 PLANT IT!

Perennial Asters (*Aster*):
Essential for adding
    fall color to beds
    and borders
Great for sunny wild-
    flower gardens
Some kinds are ideal
    for adding color to
    shade gardens

**China Asters
(*Callistephus chinensis*):**
Taller-growing types make
    outstanding cut flowers
Excellent for adding
    early color to
    mixed plantings

A few diseases attack China asters, but it's easy to avoid most of them—just don't plant them in the same spot two years in a row. This trick prevents soil-dwelling fungus altogether. Pull up and toss any plants that wilt or look diseased. Disease-resistant cultivars are also available.

 GETTING STARTED

China asters are a snap to grow from seeds, so plant them every two weeks through the spring to keep the color comin'! Sow seeds outdoors where you want the plants to grow, anytime after the last spring frost date. (For extra-early flowers, start a batch inside six to eight weeks before the last frost date, too!) China aster plants flower for about a month. After that, they don't rebloom, so just pull 'em up.

Look for perennial asters sold as plants at garden centers, or get a start from a gardening friend. The plants are amazingly easy to divide in spring!

Shady Characters

Spruce up your late-season shade garden with the lacy-looking flowers of these shade-loving perennial asters! All are native wildflowers, hardy in Zones 4 to 8, and they bloom from mid- to late summer into fall.

Blue wood aster (*A. cordifolius*): Lavender to white flowers.

Large-leaved aster (*A. macrophyllus*): White to pale lavender flowers.

White wood aster (*A. divaricatus*): Starry white flowers.

A Seedy Solution

If perennial asters wilt, even when the soil is moist, aster wilt may be the culprit. To save the plant, take cuttings of stem tips for rooting, but dig and destroy all the rest of it—including the roots, where this fungus disease resides.

Perennial asters set loads of seeds, but most of the fancy cultivars grown in gardens don't come true (in other words, they won't look identical to the plants they came from). To prevent plants from setting seeds, cut them to the ground after they've finished flowering.

Fall Fireworks

Use these simple tricks to make sure your perennial asters give a spectacular performance each and every fall:

❀ Cut back plants by one-third, once or twice from late spring to early July, to encourage bushy growth.

❀ Keep plants well-watered from midsummer onward.

❀ Divide clumps every two or three years in spring.

❀ Combine asters with other fall flowers, such as goldenrods (*Solidago*), as well as ornamental grasses.

Astilbes • *Astilbe*

If you're looking to add some sparkle to a shady corner, astilbes are hard to beat! Even if they didn't flower, they'd be worth growing just for their glossy, fern-like leaves. But I'm happy to say that these dependable perennials *do* bloom—and beautifully, too!—with feathery plumes in shades of red, pink, lilac-pink, and white from late spring well into summer.

Astilbe
Astilbe

 GROW IT!

Partial shade, or morning sun
   and afternoon shade
Rich, well-drained, constantly
   moist soil
6 inches to 4 feet tall
Feed in spring, then mulch
   with compost
Hardy perennials (Zones 4 to 8)

 PLANT IT!

Super for shade gardens
Perfect along the edges
   of streams or ponds
Dried flower heads
   add fall and winter
   garden interest
Cut flowers are pretty
   in bouquets

GETTING STARTED

It's a snap to fill your garden with astilbes—for just pennies a plant! When you're shopping at the garden center, look for a pot that's really packed with plants, then divide it as soon as you get home. Plant out those divisions, give 'em some special TLC during the summer—extra waterin' and lots of compost mulch—and they'll be big enough to divide again the following spring. From one pot, you can easily end up with a dozen or more new plants in just one year!

Site Smarts

Astilbes are long-lived, easy-care perennials, and all they ask in return is a steady supply of water. If the leaves of your astilbes have brown, crispy edges by summertime, the soil isn't moist enough to suit their

GRANDMA PUTT'S
Handy Hints

Grandma Putt kept her astilbes in A-1 shape by dividing the clumps every four to six years or so. She knew it was time whenever she saw the woody crowns (the part where the roots meet the shoots) peeking out of the ground in summer or fall. We'd lift and divide the clumps the following spring.

tastes. To keep astilbes blooming, dig lots of organic matter into the soil at planting time, mulch them generously with compost, and water them regularly in dry weather.

Easy-Care Combos

Astilbes are handsome enough to stand alone, but they also look great paired with other plants that appreciate shade and a steady supply of moisture. Here's a Baker's half-dozen of perfect perennial partners to choose from:

Hostas (*Hosta*)

Lady's mantle (*Alchemilla*)

Lungworts (*Pulmonaria*)

Meadow rue (*Thalictrum*)

Siberian iris (*Iris sibirica*)

Solomon's seal (*Polygonatum*)

A Shady Cover-Up

Most astilbes stay right where you put 'em, but here's a little gem that likes to spread the fun around! Dwarf Chinese astilbe (*A. chinensis* var. *pumila*) makes low-growing carpets of deep green leaves, dotted with purplish pink flower plumes up to 1 foot tall from mid- to late summer. Spaced about a foot apart, a half-dozen clumps'll make a great-looking groundcover. Or mix 'em up with other compact groundcovers like candytuft (*Iberis sempervirens*), foamflowers (*Tiarella*), and small hostas, for dots of cool color in the summer shade.

Jerry's TIMELY TIPS

"I never met an astilbe I didn't like, but to me, the best of the bunch by far is star astilbe (Astilbe simplicifolia). *This 12- to 18-inch-tall beauty bears extra-glossy, lacy leaves that sparkle even in the shadiest of sites. They make a great contrast to companions with big, broad leaves, like hostas. As a bonus, star astilbe sends up airy clusters of tiny, powderpuff-pink blooms from mid- to late summer. You won't catch many other shade perennials putting on such a great show during the dog days!"*

Baby's Breath • *Gypsophila paniculata*

To my mind, a bouquet of summer flowers just isn't finished without a few sprigs of baby's breath! In the garden, baby's breath has the same effect—like a cloud of airy white or pale pink blooms filling in around annual and perennial companions from midsummer to fall.

Baby's breath
Gypsophila paniculata

 GROW IT!

Full sun or very light shade
Rich, moist, very
    well-drained soil
Neutral to alkaline pH
2 to 4 feet tall
Hardy perennial
    (Zones 3 to 9)

 PLANT IT!

Ideal for hiding the yellowing
    foliage of spring bulbs
Fills in spaces between sum-
    mer-blooming perennials
A must-have cut flower!
Handsome, long-lasting
    dried flower

 GETTING STARTED

Baby's breath can survive in slightly acid soil (about pH 6.5), but plants really won't be happy there, and they'll probably fade away in a few years. For robust, long-lived plants, the soil pH needs to be neutral to alkaline (7.0 to 7.5), so test and adjust *before* you plant! Remember, too, to select a planting site where you won't have to move or divide the clump later on. Baby's breath has wide-spreading, fleshy roots that easily break, so it likes to be left alone once you get it in your garden.

A Breath of Fresh Air

Compact cultivars of baby's breath—like 18-inch-tall 'Pink Fairy' and 12- to 18-inch-tall 'Viette's Dwarf'—are just the ticket for small gardens. Plus, they never need staking! Taller cultivars, like 'Bristol Fairy', 'Perfecta', and

FLOWER FUN!

Don't be shy about gathering baby's breath flowers for bouquets—pick 'em early, and pick 'em often! The more you cut, the more blooms the plants will make. Cut each stem when about half of its flowers are open. In fresh arrangements, the blooms will last about a week. Or fasten several stems together with a rubber band, and hang them upside down in a warm, airy place. Tuck them into arrangements with other dried flowers to enjoy their beauty all winter long!

'Snowflake', are better for long-stemmed cut flowers, but they tend to sprawl without some support. Help them hold their heads up high by sticking some twiggy prunings in the ground around the clumps as soon as the new shoots appear in spring.

Bye, Bye, Baby!

If your baby's breath plants don't survive the winter, suspect crown rot—a disease caused by a combination of wet soil plus bacteria and fungi that rot the roots. Well-drained soil is a must for baby's breath, especially in winter, so keep it away from low areas where water tends to puddle after a rain. Digging deeply and adding lots of organic matter at planting time also help to ensure good drainage.

> ## To the Rescue!
>
> Is acid soil making it tough for you to keep baby's breath going? In that case, you need to try *creeping* baby's breath (*G. repens*). This mat-forming, 4- to 8-inch-tall perennial thrives in acid or alkaline soil, blooms from early to midsummer, and is hardy in Zones 4 to 8. Shear off the spent blooms in mid- to late summer, and it'll give you a second show of flowers in time for fall. What more could you ask for?

Annual Bonus

Love perennial baby's breath, but can't find the perfect site for it? Don't give up—try *annual* baby's breath (*G. elegans*) instead! It's a cinch to grow this easy-but-elegant annual: Just sow the seeds where you want them to grow. Scatter some more seeds around every two weeks until midsummer, and you'll enjoy a steady supply of beautiful blooms all season long!

Bachelor's Buttons • *Centaurea cyanus*

Sure, flowers come in all kinds of amazing colors, but just *try* to find a really true-blue bloom—it's not easy! Luckily, one of the best blue flowers around is also one of the simplest to grow. Besides the classic, brilliant blue form, the shaggy-petaled, daisy-like flowers of bachelor's buttons come in pink and white, too.

Bachelor's buttons
Centaurea cyanus

 GROW IT!

Full sun
Well-drained, moist soil
12 to 30 inches tall
Best for spring or fall color in
   areas with warm summers
Cool-weather annual

 PLANT IT!

Great for mixing with perennials,
   bulbs, and other annuals in
   beds and borders
An old-fashioned favorite, tailor-
   made for cottage gardens
Eye-catching as a cut flower

 GETTING STARTED

To get bachelor's buttons started, simply scratch up the soil with a rake, and sow seeds outdoors right where you want the plants to grow. They don't mind the cold, so you can start sowing in early spring—or even in fall for extra-early color the following year. To keep the color coming all summer, sow more seeds every two to three weeks until midsummer. You can also start these old-fashioned favorites indoors, but keep in mind that they're none too happy about being transplanted. Sow the seeds in individual pots six to eight weeks before your last frost date, then set the pots in the fridge for a week before germinating them in a bright, warm place (65° to 70°F).

Jerry's TIMELY TIPS

"For true-blue blooms on a problem-free perennial, plant mountain bluet (Centaurea montana). *This 18- to 30-inch-tall bachelor's buttons look-alike thrives in full sun and average, well-drained soil in Zones 3 to 8. They spread fast, so divide them every two or three years."*

Winter Blues

Bachelor's buttons are great in the garden, but don't let the fun stop there! Snip some just as the blooms open, pick off the leaves, and hang the stems in small bunches in a warm, dry place. Their bright blue blooms really liven up dried-flower bouquets!

Balloon Flowers • *Platycodon grandiflorus*

Here's a perennial that's perfect for the youngsters—and the young-at-heart! Balloon flowers get their name from the puffy, balloon-like flower buds that open into bell-shaped purple-blue, pink, or white blossoms. These trouble-free, long-lived lovelies normally bloom from early to midsummer, but they'll keep sending up flowers well into fall if you snip off the spent ones!

 GROW IT!

Full sun or light shade (afternoon shade in hot climates)
Average, well-drained soil
1 to 3 feet tall
Hardy perennial
(Zones 3 to 8)

 PLANT IT!

Enjoy anywhere you need easy-care summer color
Try dwarf cultivars as an edging for beds and borders
Showy in fall, too—the leaves turn bright yellow and orange!

Balloon flower
Platycodon grandiflorus

 GETTING STARTED

Buy young plants, or grow your own; it's easy! Just sow the seeds outdoors in spring, right where you want the plants to grow, and you'll have flowers the following year.

Low-Flying Balloon Flowers

Standard-size balloon flowers often need staking—especially if they're growing in soil that's too rich or in part shade. If you don't want to bother with a support system, try these lower-growers instead:

Balloon flowers are slow to wake up after their long winter's nap, so it's easy to forget they're around when you start digging in spring. Be sure to mark the clumps with labels, stakes, or a ring of pebbles, so you won't cut into them by accident.

❀ **'Double Blue':** 18 to 24 inches tall; double, lilac-blue flowers.

❀ **'Mariesii':** 12 to 18 inches tall; purple-blue.

❀ **'Sentimental Blue':** 12 inches; lilac-blue.

❀ **'Shell Pink':** 24 inches; pale pink.

Bee Balm • *Monarda didyma*

Also known as bergamot and Oswego tea, this sturdy native wildflower boasts fragrant leaves and showy, shaggy-looking flower clusters in shades of scarlet, maroon, pink, purple, and white. But bee balm is more than just a pretty plant—it's a must-have if you're hoping to attract hummingbirds to your yard!

Bee balm

Monarda didyma

 GROW IT!

Full sun or light shade
Rich, moist, well-drained soil
3 to 5 feet tall
Hardy perennial (Zones 4 to 8)

 GETTING STARTED

Buy young plants in spring, or get a division from a friend's plant. Once you have bee balm, you'll have plenty to share! To keep it from taking over your garden, combine it with equally vigorous plants, and plan on dividing the clumps every two to three years.

 PLANT IT!

Wonderful in sunny wildflower gardens
Perfect partner for other summer perennials in beds and borders
Marvelous in masses

FLOWER FUN!

Bee balm has many uses. Here's a few:

● Harvest and dry bee balm leaves, then use them to make a citrusy-tasting tea.

● Put individual fresh blooms in salads to add eye-catching color!

● To keep pesky gnats from sneaking through your window screens, put 3 cups of fresh bee balm flowers and/or leaves in a bowl, and pour 3 cups of boiling water over them. Cover and let sit for 30 minutes. Strain, then spray the liquid on your window screens (from the inside).

Mildew Mashers

Bee balm leaves blotched with ugly white patches are a sure sign of powdery mildew. To keep these funky fungi away, pick a planting site with good air circulation (not up against a wall, for instance), and make sure the soil stays constantly moist. Or, start with mildew-resistant cultivars, like red-flowered 'Jacob Cline', pink 'Marshall's Delight', lilac-purple 'Prairie Night', and rosy pink 'Petite Delight'. If mildew still shows up, cut plants to the ground for a crop of new foliage.

Begonias • *Begonia*

Ask for begonias at your local garden center, and you're liable to find yourself looking at packs of annuals, bags of bulbs, pots of perennials—and even houseplants! They look different from a distance, but all begonias have a few things in common: wing-shaped or rounded leaves; thick, juicy stems; and clusters of flowers that range from small and dainty to showy and simply enormous (7 inches plus!). Blooms come in shades of pink, white, red, orange, or yellow.

 GROW IT!

Annual Begonias:
Partial shade to shade (sun is okay if the soil stays moist)
Average, well-drained soil
8 to 12 inches tall
Warm-weather annual or tender perennial

Tuberous Begonias:
Partial shade
Rich, loose, well-drained soil
6 to 24 inches tall
Best in areas with cool (60° to 65°F) nights; need shelter from wind
Tender bulb (tuber)

 PLANT IT!

Annual Begonias:
Ideal as edgings or low hedges
Mix with shade-loving perennials
Plant over hardy spring bulbs to hide fading foliage
Great for containers

Tuberous Begonias:
Enjoy as color accents in shady beds with rich, moist soil
Perfect for pots and hanging baskets

Tuberous begonia
Begonia

 GETTING STARTED

Starting **annual begonias** (also called wax begonias) from seed is a little tricky, so unless you need several dozen, it's best to buy them. Look for short, bushy plants that have just one or two open blooms, so you can make sure you're getting the color you want.

When shopping for **tuberous begonias,** take some time to inspect them carefully before buying. Here are some things to look for:

- The tubers should be hard and solid, not shriveled or deformed.
- Reject any with cuts, soft patches, or moist spots.
- It's okay if there are some small, pink buds on the tops of the tubers, but avoid any that have already sprouted.

The secret to getting the very best begonia tubers? Shop early—within a week after they appear in stores. Or, for an even better selection, buy through mail-order suppliers.

Get Those Begonias Be-Goin'!

Want to enjoy tuberous begonia blooms weeks before everyone else on your block? Start them indoors, 8 to 10 weeks before your last spring frost date. Fill a flat (a shallow plastic tray sold in garden centers) with loose, slightly moist potting mix, set the tubers on top, then barely cover them with mix. Put them in a bright area out of direct sun, and keep them moist until they start growing. When the shoots are about 2 inches long, move each tuber to its own 4- or 5-inch pot.

Don't let fall frosts call a halt to your beautiful annual begonias! Dig whole plants in late summer or early fall, cut 'em back about halfway, and pot 'em up. Set potted begonias in a sunny east- or west-facing window, and they'll bloom all winter long. Come spring, plant your potted buddies back out in the garden!

Which End Up?

If the shoots haven't sprouted yet, it can be tough to tell which side of a begonia tuber should point skyward. Here's the secret: The shoots come from the concave (pressed-in) side, and the roots grow out of the rounded side. So normally, you'll plant tubers with the rounded side down. But here's a great trick I learned from Grandma Putt: If your tubers aren't showing any buds at planting time, turn them topsy-turvy, and plant them bottoms up! Keep them in warm (70°F), humid conditions for about a week, then flip them over and plant them shoot-side up. That'll get them off to a super-fast start!

A Pinch in Time'll Boost the Bloom

Most tuberous begonias produce clusters of three flowers: one male flower flanked by two females. The female flowers have a swollen seed capsule right behind the petals, while the male doesn't. When the blooms are still small buds, pinch off the two female flowers. All the growing energy in that stem will go into making one huge bloom!

The Trouble with Begonias

In the right site, tuberous begonias are relatively trouble-free. But in case trouble brews, here are some symptoms to look for, and the trick to setting things right!

Tubers or roots rotted; blackened stem bases. The soil is too wet. If you spot the signs right away, use a sharp knife to cut away the diseased parts of tubers. Dust the cuts with sulfur, then replant in loose, rich, well-drained soil. Dig and discard badly diseased plants, along with the soil right around their roots.

Flower buds drop off. Soil that goes from wet to dry and back again causes this problem; so can sudden hot or cold spells. Just be patient—the plants will recover and will grow more buds.

Stunted plants with yellowed or wilted leaves. Nematodes (microscopic worm-like critters) may be the culprit here. It's best to discard infected tubers. Plant new ones in a new area.

Feedin' and Waterin'

Annual begonias are about as easy-care as you can get—just give 'em a drink now and then, when the soil gets dry. Tuberous begonias, on the other hand, take a bit more

Jerry's TIMELY TIPS

"Tuberous begonias have brittle stems that'll snap right off in a strong gust of wind—or even under the weight of their own big blooms! To keep 'em standing tall, insert two or three short stakes around each tuber when you plant them out in the garden. Instead of using string, which can cut into the stems, tie 'em up with soft, fluffy yarn or strips of panty hose."

TLC to produce those amazing blooms. They like moist, cool soil, so mulch generously with chopped leaves or compost. Water often during dry spells, but let the soil surface dry out slightly between waterings, because soil that stays *too* wet leads to root rot. And to keep the flowers coming all season long, feed all your begonias every two to three weeks with Compost Tea or my All-Season Green-Up Tonic (see page 147).

Perennial Favorite

If you're lucky enough to have a shady site with moist soil, here's a real gem for you! Unlike most begonias, which shrivel away at the slightest touch of frost, hardy begonia (*Begonia grandis* subsp. *evansiana*) can survive the winter outdoors as far north as Zone 6—or even in Zone 5, if you give it a sheltered site and a thick blanket of leaves. Each year, you'll enjoy the 30-inch-tall clumps of wing-shaped leaves topped with arching clusters of pink or white flowers from late summer through fall. Just plant 'em once, and you'll never have to fuss with 'em again!

FL❋WER POWER TONICS

Compost Tea

This simple solution is super for feeding tuberous begonias—plus all kinds of other flowers, too! Put several shovelsful of compost or manure into a large trash can, and fill the can to the top with water. Allow the mixture to sit for a day or two, stirring it several times each day. To use, dilute with water until it is light brown. Give each plant about a cup of this tea every two or three weeks, and your feeding worries will be over! ❋

Bellflowers • *Campanula*

Ring in the arrival of summer by filling your garden with a bounty of bellflowers! There are dozens of different ones to try: from low-growing groundcovers to upright clumps that grow up to 5 feet tall, with blue, purple, lilac, violet, or white flowers. Most are perennials, but a popular, old-fashioned biennial belongs here, too—Canterbury bells (*C. medium*). And while bell-shaped blooms are the norm, you'll find bellflowers with cupped, saucer-shaped, and even starry blossoms.

 ## GROW IT!

Full sun to partial shade; afternoon shade is a plus in warm areas
Most need rich, well-drained, evenly moist soil
3 inches to 5 feet tall, depending on the species
Best where summer temperatures drop below 70°F at night
Hardy perennials (Zones 3 to 8)

 ## PLANT IT!

Ground-hugging bell-flowers make great edging plants
Taller types make terrific cut flowers
Mix all kinds of bell-flowers into beds and borders for early summer color

Carpathian harebell

Campanula carpatica

 ## GETTING STARTED

It's a snap to grow a garden full of bell-flowers from seeds—cuttings, too! Sow the dust-like seeds indoors in pots. Press 'em into the surface of the growing mix, but don't cover 'em up; they need light to sprout. For full-size plants in a hurry, start from stem cuttings taken in spring, before bloom. Snip off shoots at the base of the plant, and root 'em in a 50-50 mix of perlite and vermiculite.

Bells for Beds and Borders

If you haven't grown bellflowers before, you're in for a real treat. Get

To keep your bellflowers ringin', give 'em a spring snack of well-rotted manure, compost, or a general flower fertilizer (like 5-10-5). Water deeply during dry spells, too. Most'll bloom again if you take off the faded flowers, so once the main flush of flowers has finished, snip off spent stems or shear 'em off, just above the leaves.

Canterbury bells
Campanula media

started with this trio of trouble-free, summer bloomers!

Clustered bellflower (*C. glomerata*): 1 to 2 feet tall; vigorous spreader. Zones 3 to 8.

Milky bellflower (*C. lactiflora*): 3 to 5 feet tall; clump-forming; self-sows. Zones 3 to 7.

Peach-leaved bellflower (*C. persicifolia*): 1 to 3 feet tall; slow-spreading clumper; self-sows. Zones 3 to 7.

Three Steps to Beautiful Bells

Canterbury bells (*C. medium*) were one of Grandma Putt's favorite flowers, and I wouldn't be without 'em either! It's possible to grow these old-fashioned charmers as annuals (start the seeds indoors six to eight weeks before your last frost date), but they'll give a bigger and better show if you treat them like biennials. Here's how:

Step 1: Sow seeds outdoors in early summer, in pots or a nursery bed. They'll sprout and grow into leafy clumps.

Step 2: Cover the plants with evergreen boughs for the winter. (They're hardy in Zones 5 to 8, by the way.)

I'm not kidding when I tell you bellflowers are practically problem-free! About the only pests that attack 'em are slugs and snails, which leave slimy trails and chewed-up leaves. Stop these pests in their tracks by trapping them in shallow dishes of grape juice or beer nestled into the soil.

Step 3: In spring, transplant 'em to the garden where you want 'em to bloom.

Blanket Flower • *Gaillardia x grandiflora*

Talk about flower power! This hardworking perennial offers nonstop, knock-your-socks-off blooms from midsummer well into fall, in stunning shades of red, orange, rust, maroon, and yellow.

 GROW IT!

Full sun
Average, moist,
   well-drained soil
Drought- and salt-tolerant
Hardy perennial
   (Zones 3 to 8)

 PLANT IT!

Super in seaside gardens
Wonderful for sunny
   wildflower plantings
Outstanding with other long-
   blooming perennials, like
   yarrows (*Achillea*) and
   daylilies (*Hemerocallis*)

Blanket flower
Gaillardia

 GETTING STARTED

If you're nervous about growing plants from seeds, give blanket flowers a try! You're practically guaranteed success with these fast-starters. The seeds need light to sprout, so don't cover 'em; just press 'em into the surface of the growing mix. They grow so fast, you can get blooms the first year if you start 'em indoors six to eight weeks before your last frost date. Keep blanket flowers vigorous by dividing 'em every two or three years in spring or fall.

Don't Be a Wet Blanket

Blanket flowers grow just fine in sandy or poor, dry soil, but heavy, wet clay is another story! Wet soil, especially in winter, means rotted roots and certain death. Really rich soil—or too much fertilizer—also leads to short-lived plants that tend to flop over. So, to get the best from your blanket flowers, set 'em out in that hot, dry site where nothing else seems to thrive—then stand back and enjoy the show!

FLOWER FUN!

To use blanket flowers in fresh bouquets, cut them once the petals have opened fully. Cut off lower leaves and use a knife to split the bottom ¾ inch of the stem. Add a splash of citrus cola (nondiet) to the water to extend the life of the flowers. The dried flower heads are also pretty in winter flower arrangements.

Bleeding Hearts • *Dicentra*

Trying to grow a flower-filled garden in a shady site can be enough to break your heart. But don't despair—just plant bleeding hearts! Their graceful, arching sprays of heart-shaped flowers, held over mounds of fern-like leaves, add a touch of elegance to any shade planting. Flowers mostly come in shades of pink, cherry red, and white.

Bleeding heart
Dicentra spectabilis

 GROW IT!

Light to full shade
Moist, rich, well-drained
    soil; avoid soggy sites
12 to 30 inches tall
Water in dry weather
Hardy perennials
    (Zones 3 to 9)

 PLANT IT!

Tailor-made for shady gardens
Super for late spring and
    early summer color in
    beds and borders
Perfect partners for hostas,
    ferns, columbines (*Aquilegia*),
    and spring bulbs

 GETTING STARTED

Bleeding heart seed is tough to sprout unless it's fresh from the plant, so you're best off buying potted plants. Handle carefully to avoid breaking the brittle roots when you set 'em in the garden.

Just Leave 'Em Be

When you're planting bleeding hearts, work plenty of compost into the soil to make it loose and rich. They don't like to be disturbed after planting, so put some effort into making the site just right *before* you set them out, and they'll thank you with years of trouble-free flowers! If you *do* have to move a clump, dig it up in early spring or in late summer, after the foliage has died down.

GRANDMA PUTT'S
Handy Hints

The star attraction of Grandma Putt's shady flowerbed was a huge clump of common bleeding heart (*D. spectabilis*). Its dangling pink hearts were glorious in early summer, but once hot weather arrived, Grandma Putt knew its annual disappearing act wasn't far away. About the time the leaves turned completely yellow, she'd plant impatiens or begonias around it to fill the bleeding heart's space for the rest of the summer.

Bugleweeds • *Ajuga*

If you need a groundcover that's pretty as well as practical, look no further than the bugleweeds! Their good-looking, leafy rosettes spread quickly to fill space fast, and their short flower spikes of blue, pink, or white blooms make a cheerful carpet in the spring garden.

Bugleweed
Ajuga

 GROW IT!

Sun or shade, but
  best in partial shade
Well-drained, average
  to rich soil
6 to 10 inches tall
Hardy perennials
  (Zones 3 to 8)

 PLANT IT!

Great as an easy-to-grow
  groundcover
A super space-filler around larger
  plants, like hostas and ferns
Plant over spring bulbs to
  support the bulb blooms
  and keep them clean

 GETTING STARTED

If you know anyone who already grows bugleweed, you have a ready source of new plants—most folks are happy to share! Otherwise, pick up a few potted plants at the garden center. Look for densely packed pots, then divide 'em before planting the individual rosettes about 6 inches apart in spring or fall.

The Bugle Doctor

Patches of dead or rotted bugleweed plants are a sure sign of crown rot. Rake up and throw away infected plants. Transplant healthy plants to a better site, or loosen the soil to improve drainage on the existing one. Dust plants with powdered sulfur to keep these funky fungi from coming back.

Jerry's TIMELY TIPS

"Common bugleweed (A. reptans) can creep into lawn grass like lightning, and it's tough to get rid of without harming the turf, too. So be smart and keep 'em apart from the start—install edging strips around new bugleweed plantings! Check the edge every few weeks, and trim off any wayward bugleweed plants that are trying to sneak out."

Lots of flowers can get by with hardly any care, but for low-maintenance beauty, bulbs have to be the winners—hands down! Hardy bulbs are easy to plant, and they'll come back bigger and better every year, with hardly any help from you. Tender bulbs take a little extra effort—you'll need to dig them up in the fall if you want to keep them from year to year—but when you consider the show they put on, those few minutes of work each year are more than worthwhile!

Achimenes
Achimenes

Tuber, or Not Tuber?

Gardeners use *bulb* as a catchall term for a variety of underground features that store food for plants. Of course, you can grow all of these without knowing exactly what they are. But understanding the differences can be a big help when you want to divide or multiply 'em!

Bulb. A true bulb is made up of fleshy scales attached to a basal plate that produces the roots. Onions, daffodils, and tulips are all true bulbs.

Corm. This is a swollen, solid, bulb-like stem, with growth points (called eyes) on the upper side. Crocuses and gladiolus grow from corms.

Tuber. A tuber is a fleshy, rounded underground stem, with "eyes" scattered all over its surface. Potatoes are tubers; so are caladiums and tuberous begonias.

Tuberous roots. These are swollen, fleshy sections of roots. They make

FLOWER POWER TONICS

Bulb Breakfast

Don't spend a fortune buying special bagged fertilizer for your bulbs. Just whip up a batch of this marvelous mix.

10 lbs. of compost
5 lbs. of bonemeal
2 lbs. of bloodmeal
1 lb. of Epsom salts

Blend all of the ingredients together in a wheelbarrow. Before setting out your bulbs, work this hearty breakfast into every 100 square feet of soil in your bulb beds and borders. ❀

shoot- and flower-producing buds only at the end of the root nearest the crown (the point where all the roots come together). Dahlias and daylilies (*Hemerocallis*) grow from tuberous roots.

Timing Is Everything

The earlier you get daffodils, tulips, and other hardy bulbs in the ground, the more time they'll have to grow roots before the cold winter weather arrives. And since longer roots make for stronger plants, it just makes sense to get those bulbs in the ground right away—especially in cold climates! Here's a simple schedule to help you plan your bulb-planting sessions:

Zones 2 to 4—September.

Zones 5 to 7—October or November.

Zones 8 and 9—November or December.

Peruvian lily
Alstromeria

Fall Into Spring

Want a spectacular show of flowers in spring? Plan ahead, and plant spring-flowering bulbs in fall. They like full sun best, but they'll do all right just about anywhere, as long as the soil's not soggy. Spring bulbs are ideal for planting under deciduous trees, because the bulbs get lots of light while they're busy growing in spring, and they couldn't care less that the site's shaded while they're on their summer vacation.

Jerry's TIMELY TIPS

"Everybody loves the fabulous flowers of daffodils, tulips, and other spring bulbs, but the yellowing foliage that follows in early summer is another matter. Don't even think of cutting off the leaves before they're completely yellow—they need to make food for next year's flowers! Instead, pair bulbs with later-rising perennial buddies like hostas, or buy a bunch of annuals and tuck them in around the declining bulb foliage; they'll fill the space in no time at all!"

Crown imperial
Fritillaria imperialis

Naked ladies
Amaryllis belladonna

Autumn crocus
Colchicum autumnale

Snowdrop
Galanthus nivalis

Send 'Em to the Back of the Class

Most times, you want to put short flowers near the front of your beds and borders, and tall ones toward the back. But when it comes to planting small bulbs, I want you to break that rule and set those little guys where the big fellers normally go. By the time the perennials come up, those little bulbs'll be done for the season, and big, bushy perennials will do a bang-up job of hiding the yucky bulb foliage.

Topsy-Turvy Bulbs

Have you ever held a bulb in your hand, turning it this way and that, trying to figure out which is the top and which is the bottom? With some bulbs, it's anyone's guess, but for most, there's a definite difference. The top of the bulb comes to a point, while at

---

FLOWER POWER TONICS

Bulb Bath

To keep all your bulbs bug-free, treat 'em to a nice, warm bath right before planting. Here's what you'll need.

2 tsp. of baby shampoo
1 tsp. of antiseptic mouthwash
¼ tsp. of instant tea granules
2 gal. of warm water

Mix all of the ingredients in a bucket, then carefully place your bulbs into the mixture. Stir gently, then remove the bulbs one at a time and plant them. When you're done, don't throw the bath water out with the babies; give your trees and shrubs a little taste, too! ❋

---

the base, there's usually some sign of roots, or the flat plate that the roots grow out of. Setting a bulb upside down won't kill it, but the new shoot'll have to put more energy into righting itself, and that can weaken the bulb.

Please Fence 'Em In

You carefully planted a bunch of bulbs yesterday, and today, they're scattered all over your yard! Don't blame your dogs, or the kids down the street—squirrels are probably the culprits. It's not the bulbs themselves that these pesky critters are after; it's the loose, fluffy soil that seems to draw them like a magnet.

To keep squirrels from up-ending your bulbs, lay chicken wire over the area immediately after planting, and cover it with mulch. Remove the wire any time the following year; squirrels don't seem to bother established bulbs.

Lay 'Em in Layers to Boom the Bloom!

Don't think that limited gardening space means you have to give up on a bounty of bulbs. Here's a great way to get two, three, or even four times the flowers from the same amount of garden space, or even one large flowerpot—just plant 'em in layers!

Simply dig a hole about 10 inches deep, then set large bulbs, like lilies or giant onions (*Allium giganteum*) in the

PENNY WISE

Most tender bulbs—gladiolus, tuberous begonias, and the like—don't cost much, so you might decide to treat them like annuals and just buy new ones each year. But it's not hard to keep 'em from year to year, and you'll save yourself a few bucks in the process. As soon as their leaves start to turn color in fall, dig 'em up, and set 'em in a shady spot to dry off for a few days. Pack 'em in paper bags or in boxes of dry peat moss or vermiculite, and keep 'em in a cool (40° to 45°F), dry place until spring.

Quamash
Camassia esculenta

bottom. Replace enough soil to barely cover those bulbs, then set in slightly smaller bulbs, such as daffodils or tulips. Add more soil, then maybe some grape hyacinths (*Muscari*) or dwarf daffodils; cover them, too. If you still have room, finish up with a layer of small bulbs, such as crocuses. In spring, scatter seeds of sweet alyssum (*Lobularia maritima*) or some other low-growing annual over the area, and you'll have a bounty of beauty!

FLOWER POWER TONICS

Bulb Booster

Give your bulb beds a boost each year with a taste of this terrific tonic!

2 lbs. of bonemeal
2 lbs. of wood ashes
1 lb. of Epsom salts

Sprinkle this mixture on top of flowerbeds where bulbs are growing in early spring, just as the foliage starts to peek out of the ground. ✤

Go Wild!

Bored with planting bulbs in beds and borders? Then it's time to get creative! Here are four fun ideas for brightening your life with bulbs:

✤ Grow them in container gardens for movable spots of color on a deck or patio. Potted bulbs also make great fillers for bare spots in spring and summer flower gardens!

✤ Plant dwarf daffodils, reticulated iris (*Iris reticulata*), and other small

Amaryllis
Amaryllis vittata hybrida

Checkered lily
Fritillaria meleagris

Crocosmia
Montbretia crocosmiiflora

Elephant's ears	**Freesia**	**Spanish bluebells**	**Italian arum**
Colocasia esculenta	*Freesia*	*Scilla campanulata*	*Arum italicum*

bulbs where they'll come up through a low-growing groundcover, like bugleweeds (*Ajuga*). The groundcover's leaves will help hold up the bulb flowers when spring breezes blow. Plus, they'll keep soil from splashing up on the flowers when April showers fall!

❀ Tuck some extra gladiolus or lily bulbs in a corner of your vegetable garden for use in summer bouquets. That way, you can cut them to your heart's content without ruining the colorful display in your yard.

❀ Set out crocuses, Siberian squill (*Scilla siberica*), and other small bulbs right in your lawn. They'll provide delightful drifts of spring color, and when they're done, you can just mow their tops off!

Get Down with Bulbs

Spring-blooming bulbs are super for sprucing up the space around the base of mature shrubs, where the grass tends to be sparse and scrawny. They'll get all the sun they need in spring, then go dormant by the time the shrubs leaf out for summer.

GRANDMA PUTT'S
Handy Hints

After a day spent grubbing around in the garden planting bulbs, your fingernails can get mighty grimy. When I was a youngster, Grandma Putt used to get tired of nagging me to scrub my nails, so she had me try this trick: Before heading out to the garden, I lightly scratched my fingernails over a bar of soap. Come clean-up time, the dirt and soap would wash right out!

Butterfly Bush • *Buddleia davidii*

The amazing, lilac-like flower clusters of these free-flowering shrubs do more than look great all summer long—their lilac, purple, pink, and white blooms also attract butterflies like there's no tomorrow! South of Zone 6, they are stout shrubs, but in the North, they're killed to the ground each winter, so they grow more like perennials.

Butterfly bush
Buddleia davidii

 ## GROW IT!

Full sun
Moist, rich soil is best; good
    drainage is a must
5 to 8 feet tall in the North; 10
    or 15 feet tall in the South
Hardy shrub (Zones 5 through 9)

 ## PLANT IT!

A beautiful backdrop for
    flowerbeds and borders
Fantastic for foundation
    plantings
Perfect partners for tall
    perennials and
    ornamental grasses

 ## GETTING STARTED

Unlike most shrubs, butterfly bushes grow fast from seeds. If you start them indoors in mid- to late winter, you might even get flowers the first year. Of course, if you need only one plant, you're better off buying the smallest potted butterfly bush you can find; it'll fill in quick!

 For a great show all summer long, trim the spent flower clusters off your butterfly bush every few days. Make the cuts just above a set of leaves, and the plant will thank you by sending up two new spikes to replace each one you cut off. I'd say that's time well spent!

A Snip in Time

Butterfly bushes make flowers on their new stems, so you'll want to cut 'em back hard each spring. In cold climates, the top growth'll probably die off in winter anyway, so just cut it right to the ground. In the South, trim the stems back to about a foot above the ground. After pruning, give each plant a shovelful of compost to get 'em growin' like gangbusters!

Candytuft • *Iberis sempervirens*

This old-fashioned favorite gives you the best of both worlds: the showy flowers of a perennial, with the year-round interest of an evergreen shrub—all wrapped up in an easy-care, ankle-high package! You'll enjoy the dense mounds of deep green leaves season after season, with the added bonus of brilliant white blooms early each spring.

 GROW IT!

Full sun or very light shade
Average soil; good drainage
   is a must
6 to 12 inches tall
Hardy perennial (Zones 3 to 9)

 PLANT IT!

A perfect partner for spring-
   blooming bulbs
Excellent for edging beds,
   borders, and walkways
Great as a groundcover

Candytuft
Iberis sempervirens

 GETTING STARTED

It's amazingly easy to propagate perennial candytuft, so buy just one plant, or get a start from a friend. Divide the clump in spring, take cuttings in early summer, or dig up individual rooted stems from spring to fall. You'll have as much as you need in no time at all!

A Lot Off the Top

To keep candytuft clumps bushy, cut 'em back by one-third as soon as they're done flowering. That'll get rid of the spent flower clusters, plus encourage dense, branching regrowth. Every two or three years, give 'em an even closer shave—cut 'em back by about two-thirds after they bloom—for lots of vigorous new shoots.

To the Rescue!

For cut flowers that just don't quit, give annual candytufts a try. Rocket candytuft (*I. amara*) sends up white to lilac-white flowers in summer, while globe candytuft (*I. umbellata*) produces fragrant, white, pink, lilac, purple, or red flowers. Simply sow seeds outdoors after danger of frost. To keep the blooms coming all summer, sow again every two weeks until warm weather arrives.

Canna • *Canna x generalis*

If you like your blooms big and bold, then you need to grow some cannas in your garden! These tropical-looking lovelies bloom all summer long in can't-miss colors like shocking orange, fire-engine red, flaming yellow, and hot pink. The leaves are worth a second look, too—bright green, blue-green, deep red, or even tiger-striped!

Dwarf canna
Canna

 ## GROW IT!

Full sun
Rich, moist, but well-drained soil
Dwarf types grow 2 to 3 feet
   tall; standard sizes are
   5 to 6 feet tall
Tender rhizomes (perennial
   in Zones 8 to 11; overwinter
   indoors elsewhere)

 ## PLANT IT!

A great choice for
   bold color in beds
   and borders
A mass planting makes
   an eye-catching
   landscape accent
Dwarf cannas are top-
   notch container plants

 ## GETTING STARTED

In the South, cannas planted outside in spring give a good show by summertime. To get them bloomin' early north of Zones 7, give 'em a head start indoors. About five weeks before your last spring frost date, pot up the rhizomes in soil-less potting mix. Set the rhizomes with the pointed growing tips up, and just barely cover them with mix. Keep them warm (about 75°F) and just barely moist until they begin growing. After that, move them to a sunny site, keep them evenly moist, and feed weekly with a diluted houseplant fertilizer. Move the plants to the garden after all danger of frost has passed and the soil has warmed up—about the time you would normally set out tomato and pepper plants.

To keep your favorite cannas from year to year, dig up the clumps after light frost has blackened the leaves, and cut the tops back to 6 inches. Leave soil on the roots, and set clumps in boxes of barely damp vermiculite or peat moss. Store them in a cool (40° to 50°F), dry place. Sprinkle them very lightly with water every few weeks to keep the roots from shriveling.

Canna Get Your Attention?

Want even more bang for your gardening buck? Then get yourself any or all of the amazing cannas that have fabulous foliage to go with their beautiful blooms! You'll enjoy them from spring to frost, 'cause their leaves look great even when the flowers aren't around. Here are three of my favorites:

'Pretoria': Orange-yellow flowers; yellow-striped leaves.

'Red King Humbert': Rich red blooms; bronze-purple leaves.

'Durban': Red flowers; leaves striped with orange, yellow, red, *and* green!

Making Cents with Cannas

No doubt about it: Cannas are some of the best bulbs for summer flowers and foliage. But buying new plants of high-quality cultivars each year can really break the bank—they can cost $10, $15, or even more for a single rhizome! Fortunately, there's no need to buy your favorite cannas more than once. In early spring, chop each rhizome into pieces with at least two growing points on each, then pot up the pieces and grow them indoors until the weather warms up. After a few years of chopping and potting, you'll have as many "new" plants as you could ever use from that one rhizome—plus plenty to trade with your gardening buddies!

Landscape Lingo

If you're buying cannas from a catalog—or reading their labels at a garden center—be sure to look for the term *self-cleaning.* No, this doesn't mean they'll do your laundry for you; it means the flowers drop off the plants all by themselves. They'll stay tidy-looking throughout the season with no deadheading—and that translates into time savings for you!

Catmint • *Nepeta faassenii*

You want pretty flowers? You want tough, trouble-free plants? Then you want catmint! This dependable perennial makes tidy mounds of scented, gray-green leaves that look good all season long, plus airy spikes of tiny lavender, violet, or white flowers in the summer.

 GROW IT!

Full sun or light shade
Average, well-drained soil
18 to 36 inches tall
Thrives in dry soil;
    damp soil causes
    crown rot and death
Hardy perennial
    (Zones 3 to 8)

PLANT IT!

Catmints make perfect edging
    plants for beds and borders
For a stunning show, pair 'em
    with bright summer bloomers
    such as yarrows (*Achillea*), sun-
    drops (*Oenothera*), and yuccas
Grow 'em in masses for a great-
    looking groundcover

Catmint
Nepeta

Jerry's TIMELY TIPS

"Catnip (N. cataria) is one member of this clan you may want to keep out of your garden. Cats love it, and you probably don't want to encourage your neighbor's kitties to roll around in your flowerbeds! Catnip tends to seed around, too, so you can end up with lots of unwanted seedlings— and that means more weeding work for you."

GETTING STARTED

Look for potted catmints at your local garden center. They're available most of the growing season, but spring and fall are the best times to get 'em in the ground. Work a few handfuls of compost into each planting hole, but hold off on any other fertilizer; too-rich soil makes catmints flop over.

Whack 'Em Back!

Believe you me, catmints are just about the easiest-care perennials you'll ever find! Forget watering and feeding, and don't worry about dividing 'em unless they get too big or slow down on flowering. The one bit of attention they do appreciate is a simple summer haircut. Once the first flush of flowers has faded, cut each clump back by one-half to two-thirds. They'll bounce right back with new foliage and flowers, and they'll bloom 'til frost!

Chrysanthemum • *Chrysanthemum x morifolium*

It's hard to imagine fall without a garden full of chrysanthemums! These beauties come in all the colors of autumn leaves and then some: yellow, bronze, purple, pink, red, and white. More often than not, they're grown as annuals, and most people pop 'em in the garden in late summer to last through frost. But with a little know-how on your part, mums make great perennials, too!

 GROW IT!

Full sun
Rich, well-drained soil
1 to 4 feet tall
Hardy perennial
   (Zones 4 or 5 to 9)

 PLANT IT!

Add to containers for instant
   spots of color
Use to replace faded annuals in fall
Combine with fall-flowering asters
   and ornamental grasses
Plant in masses in front of shrub
   borders or along walkways

Chrysanthemum
Chrysanthemum

 GETTING STARTED

What's the secret to success when growing mums as perennials? Well, first, make sure you buy hardy cultivars. Believe it or not, many of the mums you see for sale in fall aren't cold-hardy enough to survive a northern winter! Talk to other gardeners in your area to find out which cultivars they've had good luck with. (Maybe they'll even share a few starts with you!) Or buy from mail-order sources that offer mums known to be hardy in your climate.

   The other secret to long-lived mums? Set 'em out in *spring!* Fall planting doesn't leave much time for the plants to get their roots down—and that can spell certain death to all but the hardiest cultivars.

FL✹WER POWER TONICS

Magic Mum Booster

Whenever Grandma Putt set out new mums in spring, she'd give 'em a little extra TLC. She'd fill the hole with plenty of compost, and then follow that up with a handful of this mix to get those mums growin' up right!

2 lbs. of dry oatmeal
2 lbs. of crushed dry dog food
½ cup of sugar
1 handful of human hair

Mix all of these ingredients in a 5-gallon bucket. Work a handful of this mix into the base of each hole before planting. Mums love this mix, as do many other perennials—so why not give all your new plantings a taste? ✳

Mum Pest Patrol

Mums are generally tough, trouble-free plants, but here are a few problems to watch out for:

Twisted, stunted, or yellowed growth. Look for aphids or spider mites clustered on shoot tips or on the undersides of leaves. Blast these critters off the plants with a strong spray of water from the hose.

Greenish yellow leaves or distorted growth. If you don't see pests, the problem is probably a virus. Pull up infected plants and toss 'em in the trash before leafhoppers and other insects spread the virus to nearby plants.

Yellow-brown spots or blotches on leaves. Microscopic, worm-like critters called foliar nematodes are the culprit. Throw away infested plants, and the soil right around their roots, too. Start with new, cutting-grown plants, and plant them in a new site.

To the Rescue!

If you've popped a potted florist mum in the garden, only to be disappointed because it never seems to bloom, you're not alone! While all mums start forming flower buds at about the same time, different cultivars take different amounts of time to actually come into flower. Typical florist mums take longer to bloom than most garden mums, so the flower buds often are killed by freezing weather before they open. In areas with short summers, stick to mums rated as early-season bloomers. If hard freezes don't come until October or November in your region, try a mix of early-, midseason-, and late-blooming mums to spread out the color!

Lights Out!

Mums don't set flower buds at just any old time. They need short days and a long period of darkness at night for the process to begin. Normally, nights are long enough, and days short enough, for flower buds to start forming by late July. But if you plant them under a lamppost or streetlight where they get light for part or all of the night, they may never flower!

Give 'Em a Pinch

The key to keeping mums nice and bushy is givin' them a good pinch every now and then. When the plants are about 6 inches tall, pinch or cut 'em back halfway. Repeat a month later, and again in another month if you have time. Don't pinch after August 1 in the North or August 15 in the South.

Spread the Wealth

Keeping mum clumps from getting crowded will go a long way to keeping pests and disease at bay! Every two or three years, dig up the clumps in spring and divide them. Replant the green, outer portions of the clump, and toss the woody, brown center into your compost pile.

Jerry's TIMELY TIPS

"When cold weather finally calls a halt to your chrysanthemums, don't be in a hurry to cut them down. Cut off the dead flowers if you want, but leave the stems standing until early spring; they'll help protect the crown from cold temperatures."

Clematis • *Clematis*

These fabulous flowering vines cover lampposts and mailboxes across the country with showy blooms in shades of red, pink, yellow, purple, blue, and white. The flowers can be starry or bell-shaped and single, semi-double, or double, from 1 inch wide up to an amazing 8 inches across. Best of all, we can enjoy these rainbow beauties from midspring all the way into fall!

Clematis

Clematis texensis

GROW IT!

Full sun to partial shade (light afternoon shade is ideal)
Average, well-drained soil
Height depends on the size of the support
Hardy perennial vines (Zones 3 to 9)

PLANT IT!

Train on lampposts, mail-boxes, wood or metal pillars, or trellises
Grow over nonflowering shrubs like privet
Pair with roses and other summer-flowering shrubs

GRANDMA PUTT'S
Handy Hints

Grandma Putt had an easy way to figure out where to set out a new clematis clump. She always looked for a site where the vines could have their "heads in the sun and feet in the shade." You see, clematis like cool soil, but bloom best with plenty of sun, so give 'em a site where low-growing shrubs or bushy perennials will shade the roots. A place on the north, or shady, side of a low wall or rock also fits the bill!

GETTING STARTED

Put a few extra minutes into preparing a great planting site, and you'll get years of beautiful clematis blooms in return. Just follow these four simple steps:

Step 1: Dig a deep, wide planting hole. The size'll vary depending on how big your clematis plant is, but a hole about 1 foot deep and 18 inches across should be about right.

Step 2: Add a few shovelsful of compost to the hole, mix it in with the soil, and then set your plant in the center.

Step 3: Take away some of the soil in the hole, or add more if needed, so the roots are at the right height. You want the crown (where the shoots join the roots) about 3 inches below the soil surface. That way, if clematis wilt kills off the vines above ground, new shoots can come up from the buried base of the plant!

Step 4: Fill the hole with the soil you removed, water thoroughly, then cover the soil with about 3 inches of chopped leaves or another mulch to keep the roots cool and moist.

Climbing the Walls

Clematis have a different climbing strategy than most vines. Instead of twining their stems around a structure, like wisteria does, they wrap their leaf stems around something about finger thickness or smaller. Plastic netting around a post or downspout, or a string hanging down from a wall, will help them clamber up in no time. Want the vines to cover a trellis or a sheet of lattice? Make sure those structures are made from wood or metal pieces less than an inch across.

Confused about clematis pruning? You're not alone! The trick is to know what kind of clematis you have. Here's how:

Early-blooming clematis. These flower in early spring to early summer. They get along fine without needing annual pruning, but if vines are getting messy-looking, trim them right after they flower. Examples: Alpine clematis (*C. alpina*) and anemone clematis (*C. montana*).

Early large-flowered hybrids. These bloom from late spring into early summer and may rebloom in late summer. They don't need heavy annual pruning—just a spring shape-up before they start growin'. Cut out any dead or damaged growth, and cut off the vine tips, just above any pair of plump, healthy buds. Examples: 'Barbara Jackman', 'General Sikorski', 'Niobe', and 'The President'.

Late-flowering clematis. These bloom from summer to early fall. Cut 'em back each year in early spring, to 8 to 12 inches above ground, just above a healthy pair of buds. Examples: 'Ernest Markham', 'Jackmanii', 'Polish Spirit', and sweet autumn clematis (*C. terniflora*).

Cockscomb • *Celosia argentea*

If you're looking for flowers that really earn their keep, cockscombs are just the ticket! These sun-lovers send up showy blooms that fill your garden with color month after month. But even better, they're a snap to dry, so you can enjoy their bright colors in your home all through the dull days of winter, too!

Cockscomb
Celosia argentea

 GROW IT!

Full sun or very light shade
Rich, moist, but well-drained soil
Dwarf forms grow 6 to 8
   inches tall; standard sizes
   reach 2 to 3 feet tall
Thrives in heat and humidity
Warm-weather annual

 PLANT IT!

Eye-catching in beds
   and borders
Dwarf types are great
   as fillers to follow
   spring bulbs
Taller types are top-
   notch cut flowers

 GETTING STARTED

To get your cockscomb plants off to a fast start, sow the seeds indoors six to eight weeks before your last spring frost date. Plant in peat pots so you won't have to disturb the roots at transplanting time, and cover the seeds with about 1/4 inch of growing mix. Move the plants to your garden two weeks after the last spring frost date, once you're sure the weather is going to stay warm.

Something to Crow About

The blooms of some cockscombs look like feathery plumes, while others supposedly resemble a rooster's comb. (To me, they look a whole lot more like Day-Glo cauliflowers!) For something really different, try wheat celosia (*C. spicata*). It thrives in the same conditions, and its dense, cream-and-pink spikes look super in dried bouquets.

FLOWER FUN!

If you want cockscombs for fresh or dried arrangements, grow a dozen or so plants in a corner of your vegetable garden. That way, you can cut all you want without spoiling your pretty flower gardens! Harvest blooms just as they fully open. To dry them, snip off their leaves, then hang the stems upside down in small bunches in a warm, dry place.

Columbines • *Aquilegia*

Columbine blooms are so dainty, you might think the plants are equally delicate—and nothing could be further from the truth! These old-fashioned favorites are a snap to grow from seed, and they'll delight you each summer with elegant and intricate flowers in a rainbow of colors.

GROW IT!

Full sun or partial shade (afternoon shade in hot climates)
Average, well-drained soil
Dwarf types grow 10 to 12 inches tall; standard sizes reach 2 to 3 feet tall
Fairly drought-tolerant, but bloom best with steady moisture
Hardy perennials (Zones 3 to 8)

PLANT IT!

Perfect partners for other early summer perennials, such as irises and peonies
Ideal for adding bright color to shady spots
All colors attract hummingbirds

Columbine
Aquilegia hybrid

GETTING STARTED

One packet of seeds can give you enough columbines to fill a whole bed or border. Sow outdoors in pots, or even right in the garden, from early spring to early summer. Do not cover the seed; light speeds their sprouting.

Wild columbine
Aquilegia canadensis

Keep the Color Comin'

Columbine plants tend to die out after three or four years, so plan on sowing a few new seeds each year. Better yet, let your plants go to seed, then scatter those seeds around. Full-grown plants have deep taproots and don't like to be moved, but it's easy to transplant self-sown seedlings while they're still small.

To the Rescue!

Winding, white tunnels on columbine leaves are a sure sign of leaf miners. Sprays can't get at 'em, since the little critters are *inside* the leaves. If you see only a few infected leaves, pick them off; otherwise, cut badly infested plants right to the ground. (Trust me, they'll produce new, healthy leaves in short order!) Either way, toss the infested leaves and stems in the trash—don't compost them—to get rid of the pests.

Coneflower, Purple • *Echinacea purpurea*

Despite the name *purple coneflower,* the blooms of this perennial aren't purple at all—they're actually pink, rose, purplish pink, or white. But who cares? Gardeners, butterflies, and birds all flock to these beautiful, tough-as-nails wildflowers.

Purple coneflower
Echinacea purpurea

 GROW IT!

Full sun
Well-drained, average soil
2 to 5 feet tall
Heat- and drought-tolerant
Hardy perennial (Zones 3 to 9)

 PLANT IT!

Outstanding for summer
   color in beds and borders
Great with ornamental grasses
Wonderful in sunny
   wildflower gardens

 GETTING STARTED

Buy small plants, or grow your own from seeds; it's easy! Simply sow in pots in fall and leave them outside for the winter, or set the pots in your fridge for a month before moving them to a warm, bright place to sprout.

FLOWER FUN!

Here's one plant you may know better by its botanical name: echinacea. Yup, it's the same stuff sold in health food stores to help boost your immune system! To make your own, in early fall, dig up plants that are at least two years old, and cut off the roots. Wash and dry them, then chop them up. Spread the pieces on a cookie sheet and dry them in your oven. To make a tincture, combine 1½ ounces of the dried root with ¾ cup each of vodka and distilled water. Place the ingredients in a jar, screw the lid on tight, and give it a shake. Store in a cool, dark place for two weeks; then it's ready to use!

Bloomin' Bonus

Once they're in the garden, purple coneflowers pretty much take care of themselves. They don't mind drought, but they'll make a lot more flowers if you water them regularly. Snipping off the spent blooms will also help keep the flowers comin'. Just be sure to let a few blooms mature on the plant—birds love to feed on the seeds, and you'll get some self-sown seedlings, too!

Abundant clumps of coreopsis give any garden a sun-splashed look all summer long. Most are perennials, and the single or double daisy-like flowers usually come in shades of yellow or gold. One popular species—*C. rosea*—has pink blooms, and another—called calliopsis (*C. tinctoria*)—is an annual native to the Great Plains.

 ## GROW IT!

Full sun
Average to rich,
   well-drained soil
1 to 3 feet tall
Heat- and drought-tolerant
Hardy perennials
   (Zones 3 to 9) or
   warm-weather annual

 ## PLANT IT!

Pair with other sun-lovers,
   like daylilies (*Hemerocallis*)
   and yarrows (*Achillea*),
   in beds and borders
Lovely, long-lasting cut flowers
Great for sunny
   wildflower gardens

Coreopsis
Coreopsis

 ## GETTING STARTED

If you only want one or two clumps, or you need a particular color, buy small starter plants. But since you can never have enough of these bright beauties, I suggest growing them from seed! Simply sow indoors six to eight weeks before your last frost date, or right in your garden in early summer.

Give 'Em a Trim

Are your coreopsis plants looking a little ragged? Cut them to the ground in midsummer, and they'll quickly send up tidy new clumps of fresh green leaves. Dividing the clumps every two or three years in early summer will also help keep them in top-notch form.

Jerry's TIMELY TIPS

"For loads of flowers without a lot of fussing, grow thread-leaved coreopsis (C. verticillata). Pale yellow 'Moonbeam' is most popular, because it blooms from early summer right through fall—even if you don't bother taking off the spent flowers."

Here are two easy-as-pie annuals that no garden should be without! *C. sulphureus* and *C. bipinnatus*—both commonly called cosmos—thrive in any sunny spot, and their show-stopping, daisy-like flowers are absolutely beautiful in bouquets.

Cosmos
Cosmos bipinnatus

 GROW IT!

Full sun
Poor to average, evenly moist, but well-drained soil
Dwarf types grow 18 to 24 inches tall; standard sizes reach 3 to 5 feet tall
Warm-weather annuals

 PLANT IT!

Fantastic fillers around newly planted perennials
Top-notch cut flowers
A beacon for butterflies!

 GETTING STARTED

Cosmos are a snap to grow from seeds. Just scatter them outdoors after all danger of frost has passed, right where you want the plants to grow. Keep a sprinkling can handy, and water daily until seedlings appear. For earlier blooms, start a batch indoors, too. Sow four to six weeks before the last spring frost date, and put pots in the fridge for two weeks, since a bit of chilling speeds them along. After that, germinate in a warm place (about 70°F).

To Stake, or Not to Stake

Tall-growing cosmos often need support, so if staking isn't your thing, stick with dwarf cultivars. *C. bipinnatus* 'Sonata' and 'Versailles Mix' produce flowers in a range of pinks, reds, and white. For hot-color combos, plant *C. sulphureus* 'Klondike' or 'Ladybird Mix' to get dazzling oranges, reds, and yellows.

GRANDMA PUTT'S
Handy Hints

Once Grandma Putt had cosmos in her garden, she never bought seeds a second time. Every summer, she'd use yarn to mark plants with flowers in her favorite colors. Once they'd set seeds, she'd collect 'em, crumble the seedheads into a bowl, then scatter the seeds and chaff back in the garden. Not particular about which colors you get? Then let your plants scatter their seeds on their own!

Crocuses • *Crocus*

Nothin' says "Spring's here!" like the cheerful yellow, white, purple, and lavender blooms of crocuses. Inexpensive to buy and easy to plant, crocus corms are small enough to tuck in just about anywhere. So no more excuses—plan on planting a bunch of these cuties in your garden this fall.

Crocus
Crocus

 GROW IT!

Full sun
Poor to average,
   well-drained soil
3 to 6 inches tall
Hardy corms
   (Zones 3 to 8)

 PLANT IT!

Scatter among perennial
   clumps in beds and borders
Plant in grassy areas for a
   pretty spring meadow effect
Tuck into groundcover
   plantings for early color

 GETTING STARTED

Buy spring-flowering crocuses in fall. They look best in groups of at least a dozen corms, so buy as many as you can afford if you want the best show come spring. Plant them 3 to 4 inches deep, and about 3 inches apart.

Record-Early Blooms

For the first crocuses on your block each year, pick a site against a south-facing wall, where the soil will be warmed by the winter sun. Then fill that spot with the very earliest-blooming crocuses, including snow crocus (*Crocus chrysanthus*), cloth-of-gold crocus (*C. angustifolius*), and *C. tommasinianus*. To extend the crocus season through mid-spring, include some later-blooming Scotch crocuses (*C. biflorus*) and Dutch crocuses (*C. vernus*), too.

Jerry's TIMELY TIPS

"Believe it or not, you can grow the world's costliest spice right in your backyard! I'm talking about saffron crocus (C. sativus). The small red parts (called stigmata) in the center of each bloom are the source of saffron—a spice used to add yellow coloring and delicate flavoring to foods.

Plant the corms as soon as you get them in late summer for blooms in fall. When they flower, pick the red stigmata, dry them, and store in an airtight glass jar for later use."

Daffodils • *Narcissus*

Dependable daffodils fill spring gardens with drifts of yellow, gold, orange, white, and even pink blooms. The most common kinds bear one flower per stem, with a cup or trumpet surrounded by six petals. But if you're in the mood for something different, you can also find double-flowered forms, as well as cultivars that produce clusters of flowers!

Daffodil
Narcissus

 GROW IT!

Full sun to partial shade
Poor to rich, well-drained soil
A spot under deciduous
 trees that's sunny in
 spring is ideal
Hardy bulbs (Zones 4 to 9)

 PLANT IT!

Tuck daffodil bulbs into
 groundcover plantings
Pair with perennials in
 sun or shade
Plant drifts of daffodils along
 shrub borders or walkways

 GETTING STARTED

Buy bulbs in late summer or fall. Plant them two to three times as deep as the bulb is tall. (For most daffs, that means you'll want the tip of the bulb 4 to 6 inches below the soil surface.) And take my advice: Daffodils look *much* prettier planted in groups, rather than scattered here and there or lined up in single rows!

 **PENNY WISE**

When you're shopping for daffodils, use bulb size for an easy price comparison. "Landscape-size" or "single-nose" bulbs are three years old and produce one flower stem the first year. They're inexpensive and usually a good buy. "Bedding-size" or "double-nose" bulbs are four years old and produce two flower stems. "Exhibition-size" or "triple-nose" bulbs are five years old. These are the most expensive, but each bulb will produce three or more flower stems—that's three times the flower power of a "single-nose"!

Daffodil Divisions Multiply Your Options!

With so many delightful daffodils to choose from, how do you decide which ones to grow? Well, to make life a little easier, experts have organized the thousands of cultivars into about a dozen different divisions. You'll often see these divisions described in catalogs and on garden center displays. Just pick a couple of cultivars from several different divisions, and you're *guaranteed* to get a nice variety of flower shapes, sizes, and colors!

And the Show Goes On...

Want to enjoy the daffodil season for as long as possible? Choose cultivars from divisions that bloom at slightly different times to keep the show going for several weeks!

Early spring: Cyclamineus, Triandrus, and Trumpet daffodils.

Early to midspring: Small-cupped, large-cupped, and Tazetta daffodils.

Midspring: Double, Poeticus, and Jonquilla daffodils.

Clay Soil Solutions

Daffodils are among the easiest bulbs to grow—as long as you *don't* plant them in soggy soil. So, if your soil tends to puddle up for more than a few hours after a rain, dig deep holes at planting time. Setting the bulbs an inch or two closer to the surface than usual can help, too. An even easier solution is to grow your daffodils on slopes or in raised beds, so they'll sit high and dry!

FLOWER FUN!

For long-lasting bouquets, pick daffodils when they're about half open. Make a 1-inch-long slit up through the base of each stem, then stand the flowers in water up to their necks for several hours before putting them with other flowers in an arrangement. Why bother with this extra step? Because daffodil stems are full of sticky sap that clogs the stems of other flowers. Treating them this way prevents the problem and lengthens the vase life of *all* the flowers in your bouquet.

Dahlias • *Dahlia*

For color that just won't quit, dahlias are the answer! These sturdy plants come in an astounding range of flower sizes, colors, and forms, from dainty, 2-inch miniatures to dinner-plate-size doubles that are 10 inches or more across! Blooms come in all colors except true blue, and the plants flower continuously from midsummer to frost.

Dahlia
Dahlia

 GROW IT!

Full sun
Rich, well-drained,
   evenly moist soil
Dwarf types grow 12 to 18
   inches tall; standard kinds
   reach 5 to 6 feet tall
Tender perennials (Zones 8 to
   10) or warm-weather annuals

 PLANT IT!

Enjoy dwarf types as edging
   plants in sunny beds and
   borders, or in containers
Plant full-size dahlias
   toward the back of
   perennial borders
Grow rows of dahlias
   in vegetable gardens
   for cut flowers

 GETTING STARTED

Buy dahlias in spring as bare roots or potted plants. Or grow a garden full of dahlias from a single packet of seeds! Sow the seeds indoors four to six weeks before your last spring frost date. Transplant seedlings to individual pots, and pinch off the shoot tips when the young plants are 4 to 6 inches tall. Move them out to your garden after all danger of frost has passed.

While they're usually grouped with lilies, gladiolus, and other summer bulbs, dahlias actually grow from **tuberous roots**—swollen roots that have buds only where they join together (at the crown). When you buy or divide clumps of dahlias, make sure that each plump root has a piece of the crown at one end. Otherwise, it won't have any buds—and you won't get any plants!

Dahlia Dilemma

Most dahlia flowers will face the sun—that means south and west. With a little planning, you can use this trick to your advantage! On the north and east sides of your house, plant dahlias out toward the edge of your property, so the blooms will face toward you. On the south and west sides, keep plants next to the house so they face into your yard.

Plant 'Em Again, Sam!

Dahlias couldn't be any easier to carry over from year to year! Here's how to do it:

Step 1: Dig up the clumps after the first fall frost, and cut the stems back to 6 inches above the roots.

Step 2: Shake off any loose soil, then set the clumps upside down to dry out for a few hours.

Step 3: Store the clumps of roots in boxes of barely moist vermiculite or sand, in a cool (36° to 45°F), dry spot.

Step 4: Divide the clumps in spring, and dust the cuts with sulfur to prevent rot.

Step 5: Pot up the pieces and keep them in a warm, bright place to get a head start on the season, or plant them directly in your garden after the last frost date.

FLOWER FUN!

If you're aiming to get the biggest dahlia blooms on the block, give your plants a good pinch now and then! Look for the largest bud on each stalk, then pinch out (or snip off) the buds that appear on either side of it. Pinch out any side shoots that come off the main stalk, too!

Put 'Em to the Stake!

There's just no getting around it: If you want full-size dahlias to stay upright, you need to stake 'em. Smart gardeners put in the stakes at planting time, so they don't end up skewering the roots when they try to stick 'em in later on. And don't bother with short, thin stakes; dahlia plants in full bloom get mighty heavy! So use 6- to 7-foot-tall stakes, and drive 'em 18 inches into the ground. Use yarn or strips of panty hose to tie the stems to the stakes.

Daisies

What's prettier than a patch of daisies? Nothin', if you ask me! Best of all, these beauties are among the easiest flowers you'll ever grow. The best-known daisies have white flowers with yellow centers, but they come in a bunch of other colors, too, including pink, yellow, red, bronze, and orange.

Painted daisy
Tanacetum coccineum

 GROW IT!

Full sun
Average to rich,
    well-drained soil
2 to 6 feet tall
Hardy perennials
    (Zones 3 to 5
    through 8 or 9)

 PLANT IT!

Combine summer daisies with
    other colorful perennials,
    such as catmints (*Nepeta*)
    and yarrows (*Achillea*)
Fall daisies make perfect partners
    for asters, goldenrods (*Solidago*),
    and ornamental grasses
All daisies make top-notch
    cut flowers

GETTING STARTED

Buy young plants of your favorite daisies, and set 'em in the garden in spring or early summer. They're also easy to grow from seeds; simply sow indoors in late winter or early spring. Daisies need dividing in spring or fall every two to four years, so you only need a few plants to start with; after a few years, you'll have plenty!

Spring Fling

Hey, daisy lovers—you don't have to wait for summer and fall to get your flower fix! Leopard's banes (*Doronicum*) bloom in early to mid-spring, with sunny yellow petals surrounding a golden center. Give 'em sun in the North, part shade in the

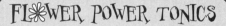

Homegrown Daisy Spray

If you grow painted daisy (*Tanacetum coccineum*)—also called pyrethrum daisy—you have the makings for a great homemade pest spray. Here's how to make it.

⅛ cup of 70% isopropyl alcohol
1 cup of packed, fresh painted
    daisy flower heads

Pour the alcohol over the flower heads and let sit overnight. Strain out the flowers, then store the extract in a labeled and sealed container. When you need it, mix the extract with three quarts of water to make a spray that controls a wide range of garden pests.

South, and rich, moist, well-drained soil everywhere. These trouble-free beauties'll reward you with their cheerful yellow daisies each and every spring!

Sweet and Petite

If you hate staking (and who doesn't?), plant some of these dwarf daisies. They'll stay up-right with no help from you!

Leopard's bane (*Doronicum*): 'Little Leo' (12 to 14 inches tall).

Oxeye (*Heliopsis helianthoides*): 'Ballerina', 'Incomparabilis, and 'Summer Sun' (all are 2 to 3 feet tall).

Shasta daisies (*Leucanthemum* x *superbum*): 'Little Miss Muffet', 'Silver Princess', 'Snowcap', and 'Snow Lady' (all are 1 to 2 feet tall).

Sneezeweed (*Helenium autumnale*): 'Butterpat', 'Coppelia', 'Crimson Beauty', and 'Moerheim Beauty' (all are 2 to 3 feet tall).

PROBLEM SOLVED!

Please pick the daisies? That's right, folks! Cutting a few blooms every few days for bouquets—or simply snipping off the dead ones—encourages your plants to keep producing flower buds. More important, it also keeps them from dropping so many seeds. Sure, a few seedlings can be fun, but daisies can really overdo it! Regular dead-heading, plus pulling up any unwanted seedlings that do appear, will keep your daisies from taking over your beds and borders.

Weedy Wildflower

With its classic white-and-yellow blooms, oxeye daisy (*Leucanthemum vulgare*) may look innocent, but watch out—this vigorous perennial can spread far and wide! Give it a place where its spreading ways won't bother you— maybe in a meadow garden, or along a row of shrubs—or confine it in a large pot or planter. Either way, dig and divide plants every two to three years to keep 'em healthy.

Oxeye daisy
Leucanthemum vulgare

Daylilies • *Hemerocallis*

Big flowers, bright colors, and a cast-iron constitution—daylilies have it all! These dependable perennials produce clumps of grass-like leaves and clusters of showy, trumpet-shaped blooms that come in just about every color except true blue. As the name suggests, each flower opens for only a day. But good-quality hybrids produce lots of buds on each plant, so they can easily light up the mid-summer garden for a month or more.

Daylily
Hemerocallis

 GROW IT!

Full sun or light shade
Average to rich, moist,
    well-drained soil
Dwarf types grow 18 to 24
    inches tall; standard cultivars
    reach 2 to 6 feet tall
Tolerate poor soil and drought,
    but do not bloom as well
Hardy perennials (Zones 3 to 9)

 PLANT IT!

Enjoy mass plantings in
    front of hedges and
    shrub borders
Grow them as out-of-the-
    ordinary groundcovers
Try them on a steep,
    hard-to-mow slope
Dwarf daylilies grow
    great in containers

 GETTING STARTED

There are literally thousands of named daylilies to choose from, so narrow down your choices based on the flower form, bloom color, and height that you need. My advice? Buy plants in bloom! That's not something I normally recommend, but it's simply smart with daylilies; you'll see exactly what you're getting. Plus, these plants are tough enough to tolerate transplanting even in full flower!

More for Your Money

Need a whole bunch of daylilies to cover a slope or fill an empty spot in your yard? Instead of buying individual plants, check mail-order nursery catalogs for daylily collections, which are often great bargains. For the best bloomers on the block, stick to collec-

FLOWER FUN!

Believe it or not, daylily flowers are edible! Toss a few buds into a Chinese- or Thai-style stir-fry, or add them fresh from the garden to salads and soups. They taste just like green beans!

tions of top-notch named or labeled plants, and stay away from inexpensive "hybridizers' mixes," which often consist of rejected seedlings that have ho-hum flowers.

Divide and Conquer

While fussy gardeners divide their daylilies every three years like clockwork, many clumps'll do just fine if left alone for as many as 10 years—or even longer! You'll know your daylilies need dividing when they start flowering less than before, or if they outgrow their space in the garden. Early spring and early fall are the ideal times to divide, but you can actually dig 'em any time the ground isn't frozen. Cut the top growth back to 3 inches, dig up the clumps, and then divide 'em into pieces with three or four shoots each.

Landscape Lingo

Here are a few terms that are handy to know when you're shopping for daylilies:

Ever-blooming. Ever-bloomers flower non-stop all summer long! ('Stella de Oro' is a popular ever-bloomer.)

Miniature. Any daylily with flowers that are less than 3 inches across. ("Miniature" refers to the size of the blooms, *not* the plant!)

Reblooming. These daylilies produce a main flush of bloom in midsummer, followed by additional spikes later in the season. Also called *remontant* or *recurrent*.

Tetraploid. These hybrids have larger flowers with thicker petals than those of common (*diploid*) daylilies.

Faded Flower Funk

Daylily flowers look like damp tissue paper the day after they bloom, so pick 'em off regularly to keep your plants looking their best. Of course, if you have a whole bunch of daylilies, this can get to be a real time-consuming chore. In that case, just go out once a week or so, and snap off any seedpods that are forming. Once all the flowers on a stem have opened up, snip off that stem close to the leaves.

Deadnettles • *Lamium*

These groundcovers sure don't have the prettiest name, but believe me—they're as pretty as a picture in a shady garden! The low-growing plants produce small clusters of two-lipped flowers in spring, but their main claim to fame is the attractive bright green or yellow-green leaves that are splashed with silver.

Deadnettle
Lamium

 GROW IT!

Partial to full shade
Average to rich, moist,
   well-drained soil
8 to 12 inches tall
Grows in full sun with
   constantly moist soil
Hardy perennial
   (Zones 3 or 4 to 8)

 PLANT IT!

Great as groundcovers
   for shady sites
Perfect partners for other
   vigorous, shade-loving
   perennials, like lungworts
   (*Pulmonaria*) and hellebores
Excellent as edging plants
   along beds and borders

 GETTING STARTED

Start with one (or a few) purchased plants. Once you have 'em, it's easy to make more by taking cuttings in summer or dividing the clumps in spring or fall. Division is also a good way to control clumps that have outgrown their space.

Jerry's TIMELY TIPS

"If your deadnettles start looking ragged by midsummer, give 'em a trim! Cut them back by about half with grass shears or hedge clippers, and they'll bounce back with fresh new growth before you know it!"

Grand Groundcovers

For an extra-pretty patch of beautiful blooms and lovely leaves, plant one of these top-notch cultivars of spotted deadnettle (*L. maculatum*):

'Beacon Silver': Green-edged, silver leaves with pink flowers.

'Beedham's White': Silver-splashed, yellow-green leaves and white flowers.

'White Nancy': Green-edged silver leaves with white flowers.

Delphiniums • *Delphinium*

No doubt about it—delphiniums are the stars of the early-summer flower garden! Their stately spikes of flowers tower above low mounds of maple-like leaves. Blooms come in shades ranging from sky blue to dark royal blue, plus violet, lavender, pink, and white. Delphiniums thrive where summers are cool and can be tough to grow elsewhere—but they're worth a bit of extra effort!

 GROW IT!

Full sun to partial shade
Rich, well-drained soil
3 to 6 feet tall
Soil with neutral to
    alkaline pH is best
Hardy perennials (Zones 3 to 7)

 PLANT IT!

Plant them along the back of
    perennial borders
Group in drifts of three or five
    plants for the best show
Perfect partners for poppies
    (*Papaver*), peonies, and phlox
Fabulous cut flowers!

Delphinium
Delphinium

 GETTING STARTED

Start with purchased plants, or grow your own from seed. Sow 'em indoors in late winter, then set the pots in your refrigerator for two weeks before moving them to a cool, bright place to sprout. Handle the young plants with care at transplanting time, because it's easy to break their brittle roots.

Take Your Pick

Stumped by all the different delphiniums you have to choose from? Here are some tips to help you tell 'em apart:

❀ Belladonna Group Hybrids are the shortest delphs—from 3 to 4 feet tall—and have loosely branched flower spikes. They also live longer and are more heat-tolerant than most other hybrid delphiniums. 'Blue Fountains' can even grow in Zone 8!

❀ Elatum Group Hybrids are 4 to 6 feet

To the Rescue!

Delphiniums appreciate evenly moist soil, but they hate wet feet! To avoid soggy soil, which leads to crown rot and dead plants, make slightly raised mounds of soil right in your flowerbeds, then plant delphiniums in them. Or, grow your delphiniums in a raised bed. After planting, grade the soil right around each plant with a rake or hoe so that it slopes away from the stems.

Delphiniums, continued

Love delphiniums, but don't have time for the extra care they need? Plant annual larkspur (*Consolida ajacis*) instead! Larkspur has tall, spiky blooms that come in all the colors that delphiniums do, and it flowers from May or June through July in areas with cool summers. Where summers are steamy, larkspur blooms in spring and early summer, then dies out when Mother Nature turns up the heat.

tall and produce dense spikes of flowers.

❀ Pacific Hybrids, also sold as Pacific Giants, look like Elatum Group Hybrids, but they don't live very long. Plan on setting out new plants every year or two.

Secure Stem Staking

Staking is a fact of life if you want to keep your delphinium flowers from snapping off in a stiff breeze. Choose bamboo poles or plastic-dipped steel stakes that are about as tall as your plants are in full bloom. Set them out in late spring, when plants are about 1 foot tall. Push the bottom foot of each stake into the ground, then tie the stems to the stakes with soft yarn or strips of panty hose. That'll keep those beautiful blooms straight and tall!

Dandy Delphiniums

Growing great perennial delphiniums is a snap in areas with cool summers, like the Pacific Northwest. Elsewhere, follow these four tips for top-notch delphiniums:

❀ Where summers are hot, give plants a site with morning sun and dappled afternoon shade.

❀ Mulch in spring to keep the soil moist and cool.

❀ Feed with 5-10-5 fertilizer in spring when stems are 3 inches tall; repeat when blooms appear.

❀ Water deeply once a week through the summer.

Dianthus • *Dianthus*

If you're looking for a perennial with lots of flowers but little need for fussing, dianthus are just the ticket! These old-fashioned favorites come in all shades of pink, plus white, maroon, and ruby-red, plus many combinations of two or more colors. They're also known as pinks, but not because of their most common color—it's because the ragged tips of the petals look like they've been trimmed with pinking shears!

 GROW IT!

Full sun

Dry to evenly moist, well-drained soil

Alkaline to neutral soil pH is best, but plants tolerate slightly acid soil

6 to 24 inches tall

Partial shade during the hottest part of the day protects plants from high heat in warm climates

Hardy perennials (Zones 3 to 9)

 PLANT IT!

Perfect edging plants for beds, borders, and pathways

Many dianthus make great additions to rock gardens

Enjoy their eye-catching colors with other early-summer perennials, such as bellflowers (*Campanula*) and columbines (*Aquilegia*)

Cottage pink
Dianthus plumarius

 GETTING STARTED

To add pinks to your garden, either buy plants or start from seeds. Simply sow the seeds indoors or out in midspring, and just barely cover 'em up; they'll sprout in about three weeks. After a few years, you might find self-sown seedlings, which are easy to move with a trowel!

Hands Off!

For a delightful dianthus that couldn't be easier to grow, try sweet William (*D. barbatus*). Sow the seeds in summer, and you'll have loads of flowers the following year, from late spring to early summer. And here's the secret to keeping the color com-

Having trouble keeping your dianthus in the pink? Try mulching 'em with gravel (limestone chips are great) or small stones to improve drainage around the crown. And to stop the soil from getting too acidic, scatter some wood ashes around the plants each year.

GRANDMA PUTT'S
Handy Hints

To keep her perennial pinks bloomin' their fool heads off, Grandma Putt kept pinchin' off the faded flowers. When an entire clump stopped sending up new blooms, she'd chop all the stems back by about two-thirds with a pair of hedge shears. Sounds harsh, I know—but dianthus don't mind! They'll spring right back with a new flush of foliage that lasts well into fall.

ing: *Don't pinch off the spent blooms!* Let 'em drop their seeds in the garden, and you'll enjoy a bounty of blooms each year with no more work on your part.

Scents-ual Shopping

When it comes to fragrant flowers, not all dianthus are created equal! If you want the best-smelling blooms, check out cheddar pinks (*D. gratianopolitanus*). They have spicy-scented, single or double flowers in late spring above 4- to 12-inch-tall, mat-forming plants. Cottage pinks (*D. plumarius*), sometimes called border pinks, usually have fragrant flowers also. They bloom from spring to early summer on mounding, 1- to 2-foot plants. To make sure you're getting great-smelling plants of either dianthus, buy 'em when they're blooming, so you can sniff 'em before you shell out your hard-earned cash!

How Dry I Am!

Dry soil doesn't faze dianthus plants one bit. In fact, frequent watering and mulching with moisture-holding organic materials (like compost and chopped leaves) are a sure recipe for dead dianthus. Talk about killin' 'em with kindness!

Delightful Dianthus—the Baker Way

To keep your dianthus plants healthy and happy, plan on digging the clumps up and dividing 'em every two to three years or so. Otherwise, the clumps tend to die out in the center—leaving you with a straggly bunch of floppy flowers.

Forget-Me-Nots • *Myosotis*

When you're planning a flower garden for spring color, don't forget forget-me-nots! These tiny treasures are simply smothered with clusters of blue, violet, pink, or white flowers in mid- to late spring—just perfect for pairing with late daffodils and early tulips.

 GROW IT!

Full sun or light shade
Moist, but well-
    drained soil
6 to 12 inches tall
Biennials or short-lived
    perennials (Zones
    5 to 9)

 PLANT IT!

Grow forget-me-nots
    in shady sites or
    cottage gardens
Mix 'em up with
    spring bulbs for a
    spectacular show
Excellent as edging
    plants for the front
    of beds and borders

Forget-me-not
Myosotis

 GETTING STARTED

To get forget-me-nots started in your garden, either buy a few plants or grow 'em yourself. Starting from seeds couldn't be any easier—simply scatter 'em where you want the plants to grow! Early spring sowings may give blooms the first year; later sowings (through late summer) will flower the following spring.

Don't Gloss Over Bugloss!

If you can't get enough of forget-me-nots' sky-blue blooms, you need to add some Siberian bugloss (*Brunnera macro-phylla*) to your garden! Don't be fooled by the goofy-sounding name; this perennial is a real beauty, with mounds of rich green, heart-shaped leaves sprinkled with blue blooms from mid- to late spring. Siberian bugloss thrives in partial to full shade and rich, evenly moist soil in Zones 3 to 8.

PROBLEM SOLVED!

Forget-me-nots aren't shy when it comes to makin' babies—they'll produce seedlings in abundance! To keep 'em from taking over your garden, pull up most of the plants after they've flowered. Leave just a few to set seed for next year's flowers.

Four-O'Clocks • *Mirabilis jalapa*

This plant is so smart, it can even tell time! Its flowers open in late afternoon and die by the next morning (or later, if the weather is cloudy). Also called marvel of Peru, this amazing annual adds hundreds of fragrant, trumpet-shaped blooms to your garden from midsummer to frost. Four-o'clocks flowers come in pink, red, magenta, yellow, and white, and are often striped with more than one color.

Four-o'clocks
Mirabilis jalapa

 GROW IT!

Full sun to
    partial shade
Average, well-
    drained soil
2 to 3 feet tall
Warm-weather annual
    or tender perennial

 PLANT IT!

Tuck a few into beds and borders for
    dependable midsummer to fall bloom
Plant near patios and porches to
    enjoy the fragrant flowers
Four-o'clocks are top-notch
    container plants!
The flowers attract hummingbirds
    and moths

 GETTING STARTED

Four-o'clocks are easy to grow from seeds! Sow the seeds outdoors on your last spring frost date, or get a head start by sowing 'em indoors, six to eight weeks before the last frost date. Press the seeds onto the soil surface, but don't cover them, because they need light to sprout.

PENNY WISE

Once you have four-o'clocks growing in your garden, you may never need to buy seeds or plants again! They'll drop a fair amount of seeds by the end of the growing season, so there's a good chance you'll find some self-sown seedlings next spring. It's easy to move these little guys anywhere you want 'em while they're still small.

Time to Store the Four-O'Clocks!

For bigger plants and even more flowers, save your favorite four-o'clocks from year to year. After the first fall frost, cut the stems back to about 6 inches, then dig up the woody, tuberous roots after the first light frost in fall. Store 'em in cardboard boxes filled with barely damp vermiculite, peat moss, or sand in a cool (40° to 50°F), dry place. Replant in spring.

Foxgloves • *Digitalis*

There's nothin' like a big patch of foxgloves to add a touch of old-time charm to your garden! These classic favorites produce a handsome clump of leaves topped by showy bloom spikes in shades of pink, purple, or white in early summer.

 GROW IT!

Full sun or partial shade
Average to rich, evenly
    moist, well-drained soil
2 to 5 feet tall
Afternoon shade is best
    where summers are hot
Biennials or short-lived
    perennials (Zones 4 to 8)

 PLANT IT!

Pair up foxgloves with other
    early-summer bloomers, such
    as bleeding hearts (*Dicentra*)
    and bellflowers (*Campanula*)
Plant 'em on the edge of shade
    gardens, with hostas and ferns
Fabulous combined with roses
    in cottage gardens

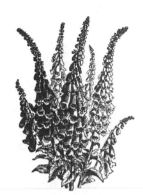

Foxglove
Digitalis

 GETTING STARTED

You can buy foxglove plants, but they're a snap to grow from seeds, too! Sow in pots six to eight weeks before the plants need to go into the garden. That means sowing seeds outdoors in midsummer if you plan to set out your plants in early fall, or indoors, in early spring, for seedlings to plant out in early summer.

Perennial Parade

When you think of foxgloves, the flower that most often comes to mind is common foxglove (*Digitalis purpurea*). This biennial usually dies after flowering in its second year, but it may last another year or two with deadheading. For more dependably perennial plants, try strawberry foxglove (*D.* x *mertonensis*), with pinkish, rose-pink, or white blooms; or yellow foxgloves (*D. grandiflora* and *D. lutea*), with pale yellow flowers. All are hardy in Zones 3 to 8.

Jerry's TIMELY TIPS

"Once your foxgloves are done flowering, take a minute to cut off most of the stalks. Snip each stem just above the foliage. But remember to leave a few spikes to set seed, so you'll always have a few seedlings coming along to replace older plants as they die out."

Foxtail Lilies • *Eremurus*

Also called desert candles, these bulbs'll add eye-poppin' clusters of starry-shaped flowers to your spring and early-summer garden. While the individual pink, yellow, or white flowers are tiny, the flower spikes sure aren't—each foxtail-like spike contains literally hundreds of blooms!

Foxtail lily
Eremurus

 GROW IT!

Full sun
Rich, well-drained soil
1 to 4 feet tall
Hardy perennial bulbs
(Zones 5 to 8)

 PLANT IT!

Grow foxtail lilies in groups of three
or more for maximum impact
Pair them with other dramatic summer
perennials, such as irises and yuccas
Fantastic as cut flowers (*if* you can
bear to cut them!)

 GETTING STARTED

Proper planting is a *must* for fabulous foxtail lilies! Plant in fall, and dig a wide, deep hole. To give them perfect drainage (they can't stand wet, heavy clay soil), add some loose soil back in, then top it with a 1- to 2-inch-thick layer of coarse sand. Place the starfish-like roots on top of the sand. Handle 'em with care, because they're brittle and break easily. Settle the roots so that they're 4 to 6 inches beneath the surface, then cover them with soil.

 The tall flower spikes can get snapped off in a strong breeze, so it's best to plant your foxtail lilies where they're protected from wind. If you don't have a sheltered spot, plan on staking them!

Outfox Jack Frost

Spring frost can really zap foxtail lilies, so plan a protection racket. In late fall, after the ground has frozen, cover the plants with 3 to 4 inches of compost, sand, or sawdust. If the spring shoots show above this layer while frosts are still possible, protect the new growth with evergreen branches or large cardboard boxes overnight. Once all danger of frost has passed, carefully pull away the protective mulch layer, too.

Gayfeathers • *Liatris*

Whether you call 'em gayfeathers, blazing stars, or just plain old liatris, these native wildflowers are real show-stoppers! Their claim to fame is their feather-like flower spikes, which are covered with fuzzy flower heads in pinkish purple or white. But they do more than attract your eye—gayfeathers are magnets for birds and butterflies, too!

 ### GROW IT!

Full sun
Average to rich,
    well-drained soil
1 to 6 feet tall
Established plants are
    drought tolerant
Hardy perennials or bulbs
    (Zones 2 or 3 to 8 or 9)

 ### PLANT IT!

Enjoy gayfeathers in wildflower gardens or sunny beds and borders
Grow 'em in groups of three or more for a spectacular show
Perfect partners for ornamental grasses, purple coneflowers (*Echinacea purpurea*), and Shasta daisies (*Leucanthemum* x *superbum*)

Tall gayfeather
Liatris scariosa

 ### GETTING STARTED

To get gayfeathers going in your garden, purchase potted plants in spring, or buy 'em as corms or tuberous roots with other bulbs in fall or spring. Plant corms 2½ inches deep; set tuberous roots 4 to 6 inches deep.

Leave 'Em Be

Gayfeathers rank right near the top of my favorite perennials—and you'll love 'em too, once you try 'em! You can count on gayfeathers to come back year after year with no help from you: no extra fertilizer, no special watering, and no division, either! In fact, the only reason you'd ever need to dig 'em up is if they outgrow their space; in that case, just divide the clumps in early spring or fall.

FLOWER FUN!

Gayfeathers are a beauty in the garden—and even better in bouquets! To help the flowers last as long as possible in arrangements, try this trick: Make a 1-inch cut up through the base of the stem, remove any leaves that'll be under water, and stand the stems in a deep container of water overnight before arranging. To keep your flowers looking fresh, cut the spent blooms off at the tops of the spikes.

Hardy geraniums, also commonly called cranesbills, produce masses of pretty flowers in shades of pink, magenta, purple, violet, and white.

Spotted geranium
Geranium maculatum

 GROW IT!

Full sun or partial shade
Rich and evenly moist, but well-drained soil
6 inches to 3 or 4 feet tall
Where summers are hot, give plants shade during the hottest part of the day
Hardy perennials (Zones 3 or 4 to 8)

 PLANT IT!

Compact geraniums look super near the front of beds and borders
Bigger geraniums make great groundcovers under shrubs
Compatible companions include bellflowers (*Campanula*), columbines (*Aquilegia*), and coral bells (*Heuchera*)

GETTING STARTED

You're best off buying plants to get started. Good drainage is a must, so dig the soil at least 12 inches deep at planting time.

Jer's Top Five Geraniums for Fall

PROBLEM SOLVED!

Need a groundcover that's pretty as well as practical? Plant hardy geraniums! Endres cranesbill (*G. endressii*), bigroot geranium (*G. macrorrhizum*), and *G. x oxonianum* are all vigorous enough to make thick, weed-suppressing mats in a jiffy. Bigroot geranium tolerates heat and drought, too!

I'll be honest with you, folks—I never met a hardy geranium I didn't like! They come in such a wide variety of colors and sizes that it's easy to find one (or more) that's just perfect for any garden. For an added bonus, look for the kinds that have particularly colorful fall foliage. Here are five of my favorites for fall color:

Armenian cranesbill (*G. psilostemon*)

Bloody cranesbill (*G. sanguineum*)

Dalmatian cranesbill (*G. dalmaticum*)

Lilac cranesbill (*G. himalayense*)

Showy geranium (*G. x magnificum*)

Geraniums, Zonal • *Pelargonium*

Nothin' says "It's summertime!" like the bright blooms of these classic flower garden favorites. They're a breeze to grow, and they'll produce their rounded clusters of scarlet, pink, or white flowers all the way from spring to frost. And if you bring your plants indoors in fall, they'll bloom all winter long, too!

 GROW IT!

Full sun to light shade
Rich, well-drained soil
1 to 3 feet tall
Neutral to slightly alkaline
    pH is best
Annuals or tender perennials
    (Zone 10)

 PLANT IT!

Pair 'em with other colorful
    annuals and perennials in
    beds and borders
Wonderful for containers
    and window boxes
Hummingbirds like the
    flowers, too!

Geranium
Pelargonium

 GETTING STARTED

Add zonal geraniums to your garden by buying plants or starting seeds. Seed-grown geraniums need a long head start, so get those seeds planted 14 to 16 weeks before your last spring frost date, and keep 'em warm (about 70°F). Whether you buy them or grow your own, wait until all danger of frost has passed before you set them outside.

Cutting Cutup

For lots of plants in a jiffy, take cuttings of your zonal geraniums! You can take the cuttings as soon as you buy the plants in spring. Or wait until late summer to take cuttings of your favorites, then enjoy 'em as houseplants for the winter and set 'em back out in your garden next spring.

To root cuttings, take 4-inch pieces of stem, and remove all but the top three leaves on each. Let the cuttings

PENNY WISE

Don't spend a bundle buying new geranium plants each spring! It's easy to save your favorites from year to year; just dig up the plants before the first fall frost and pot 'em up. Keep 'em barely moist in a cool (50° to 55°F), bright room over winter. When spring returns, cut the stems back by half to two-thirds to encourage bushy new growth.

dry for four to six hours to seal the stem ends, dust the ends with rooting powder, and then stick 'em in pots filled with clean sand. Water, then keep the cuttings slightly dry while they root.

Landscape Lingo

Sure, common zonal geraniums are great, but they're just the tip of the iceberg! Look for these more unusual types, too:

Ivy-leaved geraniums. Trailing stems that reach 3 to 4 feet long, plus ivy-like leaves—that's what you'll get with these beauties! They have single or double pink, lilac, or white flowers, too. They look wonderful trailing out of window boxes.

Regal or Martha Washington geraniums. One- to 4-foot tall plants with rounded green leaves and eye-catching single flowers in shades of red, purple, pink, white, maroon, and orange.

Stellar geraniums. These bear clusters of single, star-shaped flowers in a range of colors. 'Bird Dancer', with green-and-purple leaves and starry pink flowers, is one of my favorites!

Container Culture

While geraniums growing in the ground need practically no care, pot-grown plants take a bit of pampering to look their best. Water 'em every few days, and feed regularly, either with a very weak solution each time you water or with full-strength flowering plant fertilizer (5-10-5 is fine) every two weeks. And don't forget to pinch off the dead flowers as soon as you see 'em, to keep your plants in tip-top shape!

These Geraniums Just Make Scents!

A geranium that smells like a rose— or an apple, or an orange? You'd better believe it! Scented geraniums don't offer much in the way of flowers, but they come in an amazing array of leaf scents and sizes. Most of 'em have names that describe their fragrance: apple geranium (*P. odoratissimum*), peppermint geranium (*P. tomentosum*), and rose geranium (*P. graveolens*), to name just a few! You'll usually find scented geraniums sold with herbs, rather than with regular geraniums. They're nice in pots on a table or next to a bench, so you can reach 'em to rub the leaves and take a good whiff!

Gladiolus • *Gladiolus*

It's hard to believe that these big, bold bloomers are so amazingly easy to grow! Each corm sends up a sturdy stalk topped with funnel-shaped blooms with satiny petals. Gladiolus—known as glads to their friends—come in all colors but true blue and black, so you're sure to find at least one that's just perfect for your garden!

 GROW IT!

Full sun
Light, rich, evenly moist soil
2 to 4 feet tall
Tender corms (hardy in
    Zones 7 or 8 to 10)

 PLANT IT!

Enjoy as accents among
    annuals and perennials
    in beds and borders
Plant extra glads in your
    vegetable garden to cut
    for summer bouquets

Gladiolus
Gladiolus

GETTING STARTED

You'll usually find the corms of common glads for sale in spring. Set the largest corms (those over 1 inch in diameter) about 6 inches deep; the smallest ones (less than ½ inch across) about 3 inches deep; and the medium-sized corms 4 to 5 inches deep. To extend the bloom show, plant only a handful to start, then another batch two weeks later. Keep planting at two-week intervals from midspring through midsummer, and you'll enjoy fantastic flowers all summer long!

Winter Care for Great Glads

The common, large-flowered glads (*G.* x *hortulanus*) can survive winter temperatures as low as 0°F, as long as they're under a cozy 3- to 6-inch-deep blanket of mulch, like partially rotted leaves. But

To the Rescue!

The major pests of glads are tiny insects called thrips, which cause off-color streaking on petals and silvery markings on the leaves. If your glads have been bothered by thrips, give them some extra TLC when you get 'em ready for winter storage. After you dig 'em up and knock off the loose soil, place 'em in paper bags along with 2 tablespoons of mothball crystals for every 100 corms. Fold over and clip the top of each bag, then keep 'em at about 70°F for three to four weeks. Remove the corms and store as described in "Winter Care for Great Glads" at left.

most folks dig up their glads whenever the foliage begins to turn color in fall, or when it has been killed by frost.

After digging, cut off the leaves and set the corms in a warm, dry place for a few hours. Next, break off and toss the withered old corm at the base of each plump new corm. Dust the good corms with powdered sulfur to stop funky fungi and bad bacteria from getting started during storage. All that's left to do now is store the corms in a cool (40° to 50°F), dry place for the winter.

 If you like the spiky blooms of glads, but aren't happy about having to plant them each year, give hardy gladiolus (*G. communis* subsp. *byzantinus*) a try. Each of its corms produces a graceful spike of 10 to 20, magenta-pink flowers in late spring and early summer. Best of all, they grow only 2 to 3 feet tall (shorter than the usual 4-foot-tall common glads), so they never need staking! Hardy glads can survive winters outdoors in Zones 5 to 10.

Thanks for Your Support

When you spot your glads poking up through the soil, give 'em a boost with a dose of 5-10-5 fertilizer (1 cup per 25 feet of row), then water thoroughly to wash the fertilizer into the soil. Soon after that, when the shoots are about a foot high, it's time to think about providing some sort of support—remember, those blooming spikes get mighty tall! Either stake 'em, or mound up 4 to 6 inches of soil around the base of each stem.

Groundcovers

Wish your garden would work for you, instead of the other way around? That's not as crazy as it sounds, and here's how to do it—just plant lots of groundcovers! Great groundcovers look super even in tough growing conditions, and they fill in spaces in sun or shade with ease. And once you get 'em going, they need next-to-no care. So get busy, and see where groundcovers can go to work for you!

The Savvy Landscaper

Snow-in-summer
Cerastium

Sure, groundcovers look great, but they're more than pretty faces; they'll also take a big bite out of the time you spend on boring chores like mowing and weeding! Here are seven super ideas to get you started:

❀ Plant groundcovers under and around shrubs to crowd out weeds.

❀ Create islands of groundcovers around trees to make mowing easier.

❀ Replace areas of lawn grass with groundcovers to reduce mowing.

❀ Create easy-care, garden-like beds with patches of mixed groundcovers.

❀ Eliminate hard-to-mow spots, such as odd corners, by replacing lawn with groundcovers.

❀ Cover steep slopes with groundcovers.

PENNY WISE

There are two smart shopping strategies when it comes to buying groundcovers. One option is to buy a bunch of small potted plants or a tray of rooted cuttings. These tend to be pretty cheap, but the small plants'll take a while to fill in. Your other option is to look for midsummer or fall sales, then buy pots of overgrown groundcovers at bargain-basement prices. Divide the crowded clumps when you get 'em home, and you'll have lots of good-sized starts for just a few bucks!

❀ Reduce overall maintenance, such as weeding and watering, with drifts of low-maintenance groundcovers.

Cover Your Bases—on a Budget

You don't have to bust your budget—or your back—to get growing with groundcovers. Fast-spreading plants, like bishop's weed (*Aegopodium podagraria*), might look like a bargain, but think twice before you depend on them for an easy-care groundcover. They fill up space quickly (which is good), but they keep on expanding forever, and you're left pulling 'em up or cutting 'em back again and again and again (and that's *not* good)!

Instead, start with a few plants—a half dozen or so—and plant only part of the bed you want to fill. After that, it's simply a matter of multiplying the plants you already have. Take cuttings two or three times each summer, or divide the plants each year, and use the new plants to fill more of the space. You'll have a handsome patch of groundcover in no time!

Need an easy, problem-free way to keep groundcovers from creeping where you don't want 'em? Plant 'em where existing barriers do most of the controlling for you! For example, plant groundcovers between the sidewalk and the street, and you've got 'em trapped. All you need to do is trim along the edges once in a while. Or plant 'em in a bed surrounded by lawn, so when you mow the grass, you'll trim off any wandering groundcover shoots, too.

Mix 'Em Up!

Don't think for a second that you need to settle on just one groundcover for your garden. Why not fill an area with patches of two or more different kinds? Planting several groundcovers together has a couple of advantages. First, they'll likely bloom at different times, so you'll get a longer season of color. And second, if a disease or other problem strikes one type of plant, the others will still be there, ready to fill in!

Cover-Ups for Sun

Have plenty of room for easy-care, sun-loving groundcovers? Here's a dozen delightful groundcovers for sun:

Bellflowers (*Campanula portenschlagiana* and *C. poscharskyana*)

Candytuft (*Iberis sempervirens*)

Creeping baby's breath (*Gypsophila repens*)

Daylilies (*Hemerocallis*)

Green-and-gold (*Chrysogonum virginianum*)

Hardy geraniums (*Geranium*)

Lamb's ears (*Stachys byzantina*)

Moss phlox (*Phlox subulata*)

Orange coneflower (*Rudbeckia fulgida*)

Plumbago (*Ceratostigma plumbaginoides*)

Sedums (*Sedum*)

Snow-in-summer (*Cerastium tomentosum*)

PROBLEM SOLVED!

Smashed plants, compacted soil, and yellowed leaves are all signs that people and/or pets have made a pathway through your groundcover plantings. What's the solution? Make that pathway official! Widen the existing path, and spread a layer of mulch over it. Or, for a more decorative solution, install stepping stones. That'll keep any wandering feet on the straight and narrow!

Herbs to the Rescue

Sure, everyone loves herbs in herb-and-flower gardens, but here's a way to surprise your visitors: Plant herbs as groundcovers! Catmints (*Nepeta*), lavenders (*Lavandula*), oregano (*Origanum vulgare*), and thymes (*Thymus*) are all tough, no-nonsense plants that can cover the ground with ease. Just give them full sun and well-drained soil. Then enjoy!

Groundcovers, continued

Lily-of-the-valley
Convallaria majalis

Shady Characters

Have shady areas you'd like to cover up with no-nonsense groundcovers? Here's my top-10 list of great choices for shade:

Bugleweed (*Ajuga reptans*)

Deadnettles (*Lamium*)

Hostas (*Hosta*)

Lenten rose (*Helleborus* x *hybridus*)

Lesser periwinkle (*Vinca minor*)

Lily-of-the-valley (*Convallaria majalis*)

Lilyturfs (*Liriope*)

Pachysandras (*Pachysandra*)

Sweet woodruff (*Galium odoratum*)

Wild gingers (*Asarum*)

Weekly Weeder

Newly planted patches of groundcovers need a little help to get off to a great start. Here's a quick list of three things you can do to speed them along:

❋ Water thoroughly after planting, then spread a 1- to 2-inch-deep layer of mulch between the plants.

❋ Plan on a regular weeding session once a week for the first year.

❋ To fill in bare patches, loosen the soil, then move wandering stems into that area and fasten them down with U-shaped pieces of wire.

Bad-News Bullies

Vigorous groundcovers may seem like a blessing the first year or two, because they fill in so fast. After that, though, they'll try to take over your whole garden, if you're not careful! Here are a few invasive groundcovers you might want to think twice about before planting:

Bishop's weed (*Aegopodium podagraria*)
Crown vetch (*Coronilla varia*)
English ivy (*Hedera helix*)
Houttuynia (*Houttuynia cordata*)

Don't Be a Pain-in-the-Grass!

Before planting groundcovers on a new site, you'll need to get rid of any weeds or lawn grass that's already growing there. If you choose to use a chemical weed killer, make sure you read the label and follow all directions carefully. Prefer a chemical-free option? Then try this:

❀ In a sunny site, cover the area with black plastic in early summer, and fasten down the edges of the plastic with U-shaped wire pins or piles of soil. Wait two months, remove the plastic, then till under the dead grass, and add compost to the soil before planting.

❀ To plant a shady site, cover it with a layer of newspaper, six to eight sheets thick. (Wetting the papers first will make them much easier to spread—and a whole lot less likely to blow away!) Top the papers with 2 to 3 inches of topsoil mixed with compost, then plant right away.

Jerry's TIMELY TIPS

"There's no getting around it—the best groundcovers like to spread their wings. Once your plantings have filled in, watch for signs that they've gotten overgrown. Fewer flowers and fewer leaves are both common signs of crowding; look for very congested, twiggy growth, too. What's the solution? Dig out some of the plants, divide 'em, and use 'em to start new patches in other parts of your yard. Back at the original patch, add some fresh soil to the bare spots. The remaining plant will fill in again, in no time!"

Neat 'n Tidy

To keep your flowering groundcovers looking their best, give 'em a good trim once a year. Cut all the plants back by about a third of their height, using hedge shears, hand pruners, or a string trimmer. Clip summer- or fall-flowering groundcovers in spring; trim spring-bloomers right after they finish flowering.

To the Rescue!

Ugh! Dead growth on groundcovers sure isn't pretty! Here's a fast, easy way to get overgrown groundcovers looking great again: Give 'em a quick trim with your lawn mower in late winter or early spring. Simply set your mower blade as high as it will go, run it over the area you want to spruce up, then rake off the trimmings and toss 'em in your compost pile. To make the area look really nice, spread a 1-inch layer of mulch over the soil, too.

Shrubby Covers

Flowering perennials aren't the only plants that make great groundcovers! Here are eight great shrubs you can try:

Bearberry (*Arctostaphylos uva-ursi*)

Creeping juniper (*Juniperus horizontalis*)

Dwarf sweet box (*Sarcococca humilis*)

Rhododendrons and azaleas (*Rhododendron*)

Rugosa rose (*Rosa rugosa*)

Shrubby cinquefoil (*Potentilla fruticosa*)

Wintercreeper (*Euonymus fortunei*)

Yellowroot (*Xanthorhiza simplicissima*)

Just Add Color

Here's a bright idea for adding extra color to your groundcover beds—think *bulbs*! Taller daffodils work great with almost any groundcover. Shorter bulbs, like crocuses or snowdrops (*Galanthus*), will show up only on the edges of plantings, or in groundcovers that die back to the ground each winter. And don't overlook summer-blooming bulbs like magic lilies (*Lycoris squamigera*) or even fall crocuses (*Colchicum*).

For a garden that's pretty—and pretty useful, too—herbs are just the ticket! Gather your favorite herbs together in their own patch, or mix 'em up with flowering annuals, perennials, and bulbs in your beds and borders. And here's a little secret: The toughest part of growing herbs is deciding which ones to try first! Sure, the best-known herbs—parsley, sage, basil, thyme, mint, and rosemary—are super for cooking. But there are also herbs for fragrance, for crafts, for medicine—and more!

Herb Growing 101

Growing herbs couldn't be simpler. Just follow these five steps, and you'll get 'em growin' like gangbusters!

Step 1: Choose the right site. Most herbs like full sun and average to rich soil that's well drained.

Step 2: Test the soil. Take a soil sample to find out pH and nutrient levels. (For a refresher on how to do this, turn back to "pH Matters" on page 84.) Amend the soil as recommended. Add a dose of compost to your soil every year, too.

Borage
Borago officinalis

It's probably no coincidence that some of the most popular herbs are also among the easiest ones to grow. Sure, you can plant 'em in a garden with rich soil, but they'll be just as happy with a sunny spot that's hot and dry. Loosen the soil, work in a handful or two of compost, and plant away! Thyme and oregano are two perennial herbs that positively thrive in dry soil. Other herbs that can take the heat include lavenders (*Lavandula*), wormwoods (*Artemisia*), and lavender cottons (*Santolina*).

Step 3: Start with plants. Since you need only one or two plants of most herbs, start with plants, rather than seeds. Some exceptions: Dill, basil, and cilantro (coriander) are all easy to grow from seeds.

Step 4: Water wisely. Water thoroughly at planting time, but after that, let the top inch of soil dry out before watering your herbs again.

Step 5: Be a mulch manager. It's fine to mulch most herbs lightly, but keep organic mulches (like chopped leaves) several inches away from herbs with woody stems, like lavender and thyme. Too much moisture around their stems will lead to rot. Instead, try mulching these types of herbs with sand or gravel.

GRANDMA PUTT'S
Handy Hints

There's one herb Grandma Putt never planted directly into the garden—sweet bay (*Laurus nobilis*). It's a tender shrub that can't stand chilly weather, so she kept hers in a pot year-round. In summer, her sweet bay went out on the patio, but once cool weather threatened, she brought it back indoors and kept it in a cool (50° to 60°F), sunny spot for the winter.

Give Herbs the Sniff Test

Watch out—not all herbs are created equal! Seed-grown plants of tarragon and oregano may or may not smell or taste the way they're supposed to. (Some don't have any scent—or flavor—at all!) To make sure you're getting what you want, buy your herbs from a reputable nursery—and always rub and sniff a leaf before you buy.

Using Herbs the Baker Way

Confused about when to harvest, and what to do with all those great herbs you're growing? Keep things simple with the following suggestions:

Keep culinary herbs close to the house. You're more

Peppermint
Mentha piperita

likely to use herbs if you plant 'em right near your kitchen door. That way, they're just a few steps away from the cooking pot!

Harvest herbs any time of day. Fresh herbs always taste better than dried ones, no matter when you pick 'em. So, pick whenever you have the time—not by the clock or calendar!

Use fresh, then freeze. Fresh-picked herbs should be used right away. If you have more than you can use fresh, store in zipper-lock plastic bags in the fridge for a few days. Be sure to freeze the extras for winter soups and stews.

Cut Off Creepers

Warning: Mints spread far and wide if you don't watch 'em! A simple solution is to plant 'em in bottomless buckets sunk in the garden. Then cut off any roots that creep out over the edge of the bucket. Want an even easier option? Plant 'em in an out-of-the-way spot, and just let 'em go wild! When the plants grow too far, cut 'em down with your lawn mower.

Clip, Don't Tug

The key to a healthy harvest—for your herbs, that is—is using a sharp pair of scissors or garden shears to clip off leaves and stem tips. Otherwise, you're likely to damage your plants—at least the stems, and maybe the roots, too—when you tug on shoots as you try to pinch or snap them off. At best, the plants may just grow a little more slowly as they recover; at

FLOWER FUN!

Bottling herbal flavor is as easy as 1, 2, 3! All you need is some vinegar and fresh herbs, and you've got yourself the fixin's for gourmet-quality marinades and salad dressings. Just follow these three simple steps:

Step 1: Fill clean jars with white wine (or rice wine) vinegar, and add several sprigs of herbs—all of one kind, or a mix of two or three per jar. Close the jars, and set 'em on the kitchen counter or in an out-of-the-way place.

Step 2: After several weeks, open the jars and smell the vinegars. If you can detect a rich, herbal aroma, they're ready to use; otherwise, reclose the jar, and check again every week until they are ready.

Step 3: For an extra-special look, strain out the old herbs, move the vinegar to a fancier bottle, then add a new sprig or two to the vinegar.

the worst, you might pull a whole plant out of the ground! Making a clean cut with sharp shears is a much better way to go.

Basil
Ocimum basilicum

Herbs, Herbs Everywhere!

Stumped about where to add herbs to your landscape? Try these ideas:

❀ Combine lavender, basil, and other herbs with perennials and annuals in beds and borders.

❀ Plant a theme garden—perhaps a garden of medicinal herbs, herbs for potpourri, or herbs for tea.

❀ Grow a garden of herbs with fragrant leaves and flowers—and add a bench so you can sit and enjoy the aromas!

PENNY WISE

Fresh-tasting herbs in winter can be as close as your freezer! Spread freshly picked herb leaves on cookie sheets and stick 'em in the freezer. When they're frozen to a crisp, simply place the leaves in plastic bags for space-saving storage, then keep them in the freezer until you need 'em. Or try this trick: Pack fresh herb leaves into a food processor, top with a bit of olive oil, and chop away. Once the leaves are all minced up, pack the mix into ice-cube trays and freeze them. Use your frozen herb cubes right from the trays, or move 'em to plastic bags for easier storage.

❀ Plant low-growing herbs, like Roman chamomile (*Chamaemelum nobile*) and thyme, along pathways and between stepping stones, where you'll release their scent as you step on them.

❀ Edge pathways with herbs like lavender, and enjoy the perfumed foliage and flowers as you brush by them.

❀ Combine herbs in a kitchen garden with salad fixings, tomatoes, and peppers for quick-and-easy harvesting.

❀ Grow herbs in pots, planters, window boxes, and hanging baskets to add color and fragrance to decks, porches, and patios.

The Great Indoors

For a taste of summer even when there's snow on the ground, grow some herbs on a sunny windowsill during winter. In late summer or early fall, gather your indoor garden by dividing and potting up perennial herbs (oregano, tarragon, thyme, and mints are all good candidates) or taking cuttings (easy with lemon balm, marjoram, and mints, too). You can also start new plants of many annual and perennial herbs from seeds for indoor growing; try this with basil, dill, fennel, marjoram, parsley, and cilantro (also known as coriander).

Fridge Drying

Some herbs, like basil and parsley, are slow to air-dry, and they often lose their pretty green color in the process. Use this trick to dry them quick: Harvest a handful of stalks, and put 'em in brown paper lunch bags. Shut the tops of the bags with clothespins, write the herb name on the outside of each, and set the bags in the fridge. Check on the herbs in a few days; they're ready when they're crispy to the touch. You can thank your fridge's dehumidifying action for this quick and easy miracle. Best of all, you can store the dried herbs—bags and all—right in the fridge until you need 'em!

FLOWER POWER TONICS

Herb Garden Potpourri

For a potpourri that smells good enough to eat, give this magical mix a try.

2 cups of thyme shoots, dried
1 cup of rosemary leaves, dried
1 cup of mint leaves, dried
1/2 cup of lavender flowers, dried
1/4 cup of cloves, whole
2 tbsp. of orrisroot, powdered

Combine all the ingredients in a large bowl. Mix with your hands (they'll smell great afterward). Put the mixed potpourri in closed glass jars for storage, or sew into fabric sachets and use to freshen up closets and drawers.

Sage
Salvia officinalis

Herbs for Shady Spots

Stuck with a shady garden? You can still grow herbs! Here's a handful of herbs that'll grow just fine in partial to full shade:

Bee balm (*Monarda didyma*)

Catnip (*Nepeta cataria*)

Chervil (*Anthriscus cerefolium*)

Cilantro/coriander (*Coriandrum sativum*)

Feverfew (*Tanacetum parthenium*)

Germander (*Teucrium chamaedrys*)

Lemon balm (*Melissa officinalis*)

English thyme
Thymus vulgaris

Lovage (*Levisticum officinale*)

Mints (*Mentha*)

Parsley (*Petroselinum crispum*)

Sweet woodruff (*Galium odoratum*)

Tarragon (*Artemisia dracunculus*)

Jerry's TIMELY TIPS

"It stands to reason that herbs with edible leaves have edible flowers, too! Toss fresh herb flowers into salads, float 'em in soups, or mix 'em in with herb leaves in pesto. Herbs with especially flavorful edible flowers include basil, borage, chives, cilantro (coriander), dill, garlic, lemon balm, mint, oregano, parsley, rosemary, sage, and thyme."

How Dry I Am

If you've never tried drying herbs at home, you won't believe how easy it really is! Just bundle a few stems of fresh herbs together with a rubber band, and hang 'em upside down until the leaves are crispy. If you're worried about dust, cut a hole in the bottom of a brown paper bag; cut a few flaps in the sides, too, for ventilation. Turn the bag over, slip it over the stems of an herb bundle so they poke through the hole in the bottom, and hang up the covered bundle. A warm, dark, airy place is perfect for drying herbs. They'll be crispy-dry in about two weeks.

Do you like plants with pretty flowers? (Of course you do!) Do you enjoy looking at interesting leaves, too? (Who doesn't?) Then you've come to the right place, folks—these pretty perennials are just perfect for you! It used to be that the sun-loving kinds with showy pink, red, and white flowers were called coral bells, and the shady ones with silvery or maroon leaves were known as heucheras or alumroots. But nowadays, it's easy to find heucheras that have beautiful blooms and fabulous foliage, all on the same plant!

 ### GROW IT!

Partial shade
Rich, evenly moist,
    well-drained soil
6 to 18 inches tall
Plants tolerate full sun to
    full shade, but an area
    with morning sun and
    afternoon shade is best
Hardy perennials
    (Zones 4 to 8)

 ### PLANT IT!

Enjoy the handsome clumps along
    paths and walkways, or use them
    as edgings for beds and borders
Grow them in groups of six or more
    plants for a dramatic show
Pair heucheras with shade-loving
    perennials such as hostas, spring
    bulbs, lungworts (*Pulmonaria*),
    and bleeding hearts (*Dicentra*)

Coral bells
Heuchera

 ### GETTING STARTED

To get the best-looking leaves, buy heuchera and coral bell plants in the colors that appeal to you. Spring is the best time for planting.

Cutting Remarks

To keep coral bells bloomin', cut off the flower stalks as the blooms fade. Use sharp scissors or garden shears for this task, and trim the stems as close to the low mound of foliage as you can.

Most heucheras don't have attractive flowers, so you can cut off

Both heucheras and coral bells have shallow roots, and that means they can't take much drought. Watering regularly during dry weather will help 'em look their best. It's a good idea to mulch 'em, too; that'll help keep the soil moist and add some nutrients at the same time!

bloom spikes as soon as they appear. Or leave a few, and see if you get any seedlings. They won't look much like the plants they came from, as far as leaf color goes, but they can be interesting—and maybe even worth keeping!

To the Rescue!

You can grow coral bells and heucheras as far north as Zone 3, if you give 'em a little extra TLC to get 'em through the winter. In late fall, after the soil has frozen, cover your plants with evergreen boughs or salt hay. Then remove the mulch in spring, when hard frost is no longer a threat.

Winter Watch

Because their roots don't go very deep, coral bells and heucheras often get pushed right up out of the soil during the winter by repeated cycles of freezing and thawing. To keep 'em snug in the ground all winter long, check your plants during mild spells in winter to see if any were pushed out of the soil. If so, loosen the soil if you can, and replant the clumps. Or, if the soil is still frozen, cover the crowns with mulch to keep 'em from drying out, then replant them in spring.

Division Decision

Once they're in the ground and growin', coral bells and heucheras don't need much fussing to stay happy and healthy. They appreciate a scattering of 5-10-5 fertilizer in spring, if you think of it, or a light mulch of rotted manure. And plan on dividing 'em every four or five years, especially if the clumps have developed crowded, woody crowns and have risen above the soil surface. Smaller-than-normal leaves, sparse flowers, and short bloom spikes are other signals that your plants need dividing. Dig up the clumps in spring, discard the old and woody parts, and replant the rest. Set the roots about 1 inch under the soil surface.

Hibiscus • *Hibiscus*

If you're searching for show-stopping blooms, look no further than hardy hibiscus! These shrub-size perennials are impossible to ignore, with huge flowers that range from 6 to 10 inches across. Each bloom opens for only a day, but plants produce clusters of flowers and stay in bloom for about six weeks in summer. As its name suggests, scarlet rose mallow (*H. coccineus*) bears red blooms, while common rose mallow (*H. moscheutos*) has pink, red, or white flowers.

 ## GROW IT!

Full sun or very
   light shade
Rich, well-drained soil
4 to 10 feet tall
Evenly moist soil is best
Hardy perennials
   (Zones 5 or 6 to 10)

 ## PLANT IT!

Enjoy these bold plants in beds
   and borders with other summer-
   blooming perennials
Plant them as accent plants against
   walls or fences, and combine
   them with shrubs
Scarlet rose mallow (*H. coccineus*)
   is great for soggy to wet sites

Rose mallow
Hibiscus moscheutos

 ## GETTING STARTED

For blooms the first year, buy plants to add these giant-size perennials to your garden. Seeds take a little longer to reach flowering size, but they're a great option if you have some patience—and room for lots of hibiscus plants! Simply sow the seeds indoors in late winter, and set out the seedlings after your last frost date.

No Need to Divide

These shrub-size plants have deep, woody roots, but they'll live happily in one spot for many years, so don't worry about dividing 'em. If you want more plants, take cuttings in late summer, and root 'em indoors. Several popular cultivars also come true from seeds, including red-flowered 'Lord Baltimore', pink 'Lady Baltimore', and the dwarf-size Disco Belle Series plants.

It's easy to dig into the crowns of hibiscus by accident in spring, because the plants don't sprout until most other plants are already up and growin'. So use labels to mark the clumps, or surround 'em with a ring of sturdy stakes as a reminder.

Hollyhock • *Alcea rosea*

Here's an easy-to-grow favorite that adds a sure-fire touch of country charm to any bed or border! Hollyhocks send up tall spikes of flowers from summer to early fall. They bloom in a rainbow of colors, including pink, red, yellow, pure white—and even an amazing maroon-black!

Hollyhock
Alcea rosea

 GROW IT!

Full sun or light, part-day shade
Average to rich,
    well-drained soil
Dwarf types grow 2 to 3 feet
    tall; standard sizes reach
    4 to 5 feet
Biennial or short-lived
    perennial (Zones 3 to 9)

 PLANT IT!

Grow single clumps as accents
    against garages, houses,
    fences, or walls
Plant hollyhocks toward the
    back of perennial borders
They make great partners for
    large ornamental grasses
    and other bold perennials

 GETTING STARTED

Buy plants, or grow your own hollyhocks from seeds. Sow the seeds indoors or out, barely covering them with soil (light encourages them to sprout). If you sow seeds indoors in late winter, the plants may bloom the first year. Or sow 'em in spring to early summer, then move the plants to their permanent spots in the garden in late summer or early fall for flowers the following summer.

FLOWER FUN!

When I was a boy, I remember the girls in the neighborhood would make dolls out of hollyhock flowers. They'd turn one bloom upside down to make a skirt, and stick a piece of wire or a toothpick through the center to make the body. They'd top that with a bud to make the head, and another bloom for the bonnet. Why, in no time, they'd have a doll that was as cute as a button!

Keep 'Em Comin' Along

For a dependable show of blockbuster blooms, pull up two-year-old plants *after* they've flowered, and replace 'em with new seedlings each year. Or, if there are particular colors you want to keep, cut off the bloom stalks when they're finished flowering to help the plants live another year.

There's no doubt about it—hostas are tailor-made for filling shady gardens! They send up summer spikes of lavender, purple, or white flowers, but it's really the leaves that are the big story: They come in shades of green, blue, or yellow, often with white or golden spots, splashes, or stripes. Plant one, or try a mix—I *guarantee* you'll love 'em all!

 GROW IT!

Light to full shade
Rich, evenly moist soil
2 inches to 4 feet tall
Hardy perennials
  (Zones 3 to 8)

 PLANT IT!

Combine hostas with shade-loving flowers, like bleeding hearts (*Dicentra*)
  and lungworts (*Pulmonaria*)
Large types make great groundcovers;
  smaller ones are excellent for
  edging beds and borders
Hostas make top-notch container plants

Hosta
Hosta

 GETTING STARTED

Add hostas to your garden by buying plants in spring or fall. Dig deeply and add plenty of organic matter to the soil to encourage wide-spreading roots and good drought tolerance.

Patience Pays

You can never really tell how big a hosta is going to get while it's still in a pot. It actually takes two to four years after planting for them to reach their full size. So, before you stick a potted hosta into any old spot, check the label to see how big your chosen plant will get when it's full grown, and make sure you give it enough room to spread out without smothering its companions.

FL*WER POWER TONICS

Quassia Slug Spray

There's no getting around it: Slugs love hostas! But don't despair—here's a magical mixer that'll really knock those slimy slitherers for a loop.

**4 oz. of quassia chips (available at
  health food stores)
1 gal. of water**

Crush, grind, or chop the chips, add them to the water in a bucket, and let steep for 12 to 24 hours. Strain through cheesecloth, then spray the liquid on hostas and other slug-prone plants, such as bellflowers (*Campanula*). This spray also helps control aphids, but will not hurt good guys like lady beetles and honeybees. ❀

To the Rescue!

If you ask slugs about it, all hostas are not created equal! Hostas with thick-textured leaves generally have fewer problems with slugs and snails than those with thin leaves. So if you're tired of slugs making Swiss cheese out of your hosta leaves, try planting the following cultivars: 'Blue Umbrellas', 'Invincible', 'Krossa Regal', 'Regal Splendor', and 'Sum and Substance', as well as *H. sieboldiana* 'Elegans' and 'Frances Williams'.

Shopping Secrets

Hostas can be expensive, so keep these smart tips in mind when you're shopping:

Compare size. Look at pot size, sure, but turn a pot on its side and see how big the plant in the pot really is. A pot with two or more plants in it is a better buy than one with just a single clump.

Think speed. Hostas grow at different rates. Fast-growing plants like 'Francee' and 'Golden Tiara' fill pots quickly, so they're always less expensive than slower-growing cultivars like 'Great Expectations'.

Pay for quality. It's worth paying a little more for top-notch cultivars. All hostas multiply, after all, and in a few years, you'll have lots of great-looking plants, rather than ordinary ones. But don't buy the very newest cultivars—they're super-expensive, and the price'll usually come down after the first few years.

No-Dig Division

Hostas rarely need dividing, unless they outgrow the space you have for them. If you just want to share some with friends, or use 'em to fill new gardens, you don't need to dig up the whole clump: Pull some soil away from one side of the plant, and look for the small suckers or crowns that are around the outside of the clump. Use a sharp spade to cut 'em off—make sure you get some roots, too—and you'll have a whole new plant without any hassle!

If you want a spring garden filled with fragrance, it's hard to beat hyacinths! Also called common or Dutch hyacinths, these easy-to-grow bulbs produce cheerful clusters of starry blooms in shades of pink, lilac, violet, yellow, and white.

GROW IT!

Full sun or partial shade
Average to rich,
    well-drained soil
8 to 12 inches tall
Hardy bulb
    (Zones 5 to 9)

PLANT IT!

Tuck hyacinths among perennials in
    beds and borders
Plant 'em in groups of a dozen or
    more for formal displays
Hyacinths look great in containers
    on a deck or patio
They're outstanding cut flowers, too!

Dutch hyacinth
Hyacinthus orientalis

GETTING STARTED

Look for hyacinth bulbs for sale in fall, with daffodils and other spring-blooming bulbs. In most areas, planting 'em 4 to 5 inches deep is fine. Hyacinths appreciate a little extra protection in cold-winter areas, so if you live in Zone 5, set the bulbs 6 or even 8 inches deep, and mulch them over the winter. Then remove the mulch in spring, after all danger of hard frost has passed.

Making Sense of Hyacinths

Ever notice that your hyacinth blooms are really full the first year, then they get looser spikes with fewer blooms in the following years? If you want to keep your blooms at their brand-new best, feed the plants with a balanced fertilizer (like 5-10-5) in spring when the leaves emerge. For formal plantings with the very biggest flowers, plant new bulbs every year, and move the old ones elsewhere.

FLOWER POWER TONICS

Bulb Soak

Get your hyacinths—and other bulbs, too—off to a great start by soaking them in this super solution before planting.

1 can of beer
2 tbsp. of liquid dish soap
¼ tsp. of instant tea granules
2 gal. of water

Mix all of the ingredients together in a large bucket, and carefully dip the bulbs in the mix before planting. ✽

Hydrangeas • *Hydrangea*

When it comes to flowering shrubs, hydrangeas are at the top of the list for pure flower power! They pick up where forsythias and other spring-flowering shrubs leave off, gracing your garden with huge clusters of pink, blue, or white blooms from early summer to fall.

Hydrangea
Hydrangea

 GROW IT!

Full sun to partial shade
Rich, well-drained,
   evenly moist soil
3 to 15 feet tall
Hardy shrubs
   (Zones 4 to 9)

 PLANT IT!

Plant hydrangeas in groups or rows
   for shrub borders or hedges
Pair them with bold perennials,
   such as large hostas and ferns
Combine them with other
   shade-loving shrubs, like
   rhododendrons and azaleas

 GETTING STARTED

Buy plants in spring or early fall. Hydrangeas generally send their roots *out,* rather than *down,* so it's important to dig a wide planting hole rather than a deep one. (It should be just about as deep as the existing root ball, but about three times the width.)

FLOWER FUN!

Hydrangeas make great cut flowers! But unlike many flowers, they do double duty: You can enjoy 'em both fresh *and* dried! Simply pick the flowers and put the stems in a vase with 2 or 3 inches of water in it. Don't replace the water when it's used up; this way, the flowers will dry right in the vase!

Pretty Pink or Baby Blue?

The popular florist's hydrangea (*H. macrophylla*), also called big-leaved hydrangea, can be a bit confusing to grow. You set out a plant with beautiful blue blooms one year, and the next, the flowers are a muddy mauve color! What's the deal?

The answer is that flower color depends on how acidic your soil is. Florists' hydrangeas produce blue to purple flowers in acidic soil (pH 5.0 to 5.5) and pink to red blooms in slightly acidic to slightly alkaline soil (pH 6.0 to 7.5). So, if you want to make sure your plant has the blues, work powdered sulfur into the soil before planting, or scratch it into the soil surface after planting. Mulching with pine needles helps keep the soil on the acidic side, too!

Pruning Puzzle

Hydrangeas aren't hard to prune—*if* you know where the flower buds are! Here's how to tell:

❀ Smooth hydrangea (*H. arborescens*) and panicle hydrangea (*H. paniculata*) bloom on new wood—growth from the current year—so prune them in late winter or early spring. Cut smooth hydrangea to within several inches of the ground to get stems that are strong enough to hold up the heavy flowers.

❀ Oak-leaved hydrangea (*H. quercifolia*) and florist's hydrangea (*H. macrophylla*) bloom on old wood—growth from the previous year—so prune them right after they flower. If you wait until fall or early spring to trim them, you'll cut off all the flower buds!

PROBLEM SOLVED!

Hey, Jer—my hydrangea bush looks great, but it never blooms! What's up? Well, my friend, you're not alone! Here's why: Florist's, or big-leaved, hydrangeas can survive the winter as far north as Zone 5, but the cold kills the top growth—and all the flower buds along with it. That means no flowers for you! If your plant fails to flower every year, dig it out and try a different kind of hydrangea. Otherwise, a little spring protection can help it get through late frosts; simply cover your plants with old sheets if a sudden cold snap threatens.

Climbing the Walls

Looking for something different to liven up your garden? Try this hydrangea—it's a climber instead of a shrub! Climbing hydrangea (*H. petiolaris*) can pull itself up to 60 feet against a wall or tree, or it can sprawl along the ground as a groundcover. Either way, it's a beauty, with flat-topped clusters of white flowers in early to midsummer. The stems have pretty, peeling, cinnamon-brown bark, too!

Want a spectacular shade garden that just won't quit? Then give impatiens a try! These trouble-free flowers bear single or double blooms in bright and soft shades of pink, rose, salmon, lilac-pink, and white. Best of all, they bloom from early summer right up to frost!

Impatiens

Impatiens

 GROW IT!

Partial to full shade (full sun to very light shade for New Guinea types)
Rich, moist, well-drained soil
6 inches to 2 feet tall
Warm-weather annuals or tender perennials

 PLANT IT!

Dwarf cultivars look fabulous as edgings for flowerbeds
Mix 'em with other shade-loving annuals and perennials to brighten up a shady area
Perfect for pots and planters on shady decks and patios

 GETTING STARTED

Most folks buy impatiens as transplants, but it's easy to grow your own, too. Start seeds indoors, 8 to 10 weeks before your last spring frost date. They need light to sprout, so don't cover them up; just press 'em lightly into the seed-starting mix. Wait for a week or two after your last frost date to set the plants outside.

PROBLEM SOLVED!

If you've had trouble with impatiens growing taller than you expected, you're not alone! They can get pretty rangy during the dogs days of summer—especially in the South. To find impatiens that stay low and bushy, check the plant tags for types described as "compact"; Impulse Series and Super Elfin Series impatiens are two good choices.

The Kindest Cut

Here's a little secret you may not know about impatiens: They're a snap to grow from cuttings. In fact, they'll even root sitting in a glass of water! Keep your favorites from year to year by taking cuttings in late summer. Pot up the rooted cuttings, and keep 'em in a warm, bright spot for the winter. Come spring, take cuttings from those impatiens, and you'll have dozens of new plants to fill your garden—for free!

Sun, shade, dry soil, soggy sites—you name it, and there's an iris that'll thrive there! As a bonus, these exotic-looking beauties come in every color of the rainbow, and then some. What more could you ask for?

 GROW IT!

Most need full sun; some
   grow in shade
Most need average to rich,
   well-drained soil
4 inches to 3 feet tall
Hardy perennials or bulbs
   (mostly Zones 4 to 9)

 PLANT IT!

Bearded and Siberian irises (*I.
   sibirica*) are classic companions
   for peonies and bellflowers
   (*Campanula*)
Dwarf perennial irises and bulb
   irises are perfect for rock gardens
All irises make terrific cut flowers

Bearded iris
Iris hybrid

 GETTING STARTED

Buy plants or bulbs to get irises going in your garden. Plant bulb-type irises in fall, and most perennial irises in spring. (Bearded irises are often sold as dormant rhizomes for mid- to late-summer planting.)

An Iris Parade

If you're an iris aficionado like I am, you want to enjoy your irises for as long as possible. So choose 'em carefully, and you can keep 'em coming from early spring through most of the summer!

   The earliest irises begin blooming from February to mid-March in the South, or March into mid-April in more northern areas. These include the perennial crested iris (*I. cristata*), plus the following bulbs: reticulated iris (*I. reticulata*), danford iris (*I. danfordiae*), *I. histrioides*, and Dutch iris. Bearded irises bloom from late spring into early summer, followed by Siberian iris and Japanese iris (*I. ensata*).

FL✲WER POWER TONICS

Get-Up-and-Grow Iris Tonic

For the most beautiful bearded irises on the block, feed your plants a dose of this magical mix.

4 parts bonemeal
6 parts hydrated lime

Mix the ingredients together and sprinkle around established plants in early spring. Your irises will get off to a flying start! ✳

The secret to keeping irises looking their best is dividing them often. Dig up and divide bearded irises every three years, in midsummer or early fall. Divide most other perennial irises in spring or early fall—every three to five years is fine. Siberian iris is the one exception: It's happiest left undisturbed, so divide your plants only if they begin to have blooming problems.

Wet 'n' Wild

Got a soggy spot that could use some color? Here are some irises just for you! Louisiana irises, yellow flag (*I. pseudacorus*), and blue flag (*I. versicolor*) all thrive in damp soil or standing water. Siberian irises can take moist to wet soil, too. And a site that's damp in spring and early summer, but dries out later in the year, is perfect for Japanese iris.

Big Bad Borers

It's just a fact of life: If you grow bearded irises, sooner or later, you'll have borers. These moth larvae hatch on the leaves in spring, and then tunnel down through the plants. Once they start snacking on the centers of the rhizomes, bacterial soft rot isn't far behind, causing smelly, slimy, rotted rhizomes. But don't let these buggers get you down—just try the three tricks below to keep the plump, pink caterpillars from irritating your irises:

Dutch iris
Iris hybrid

Pick a good spot. Give the plants full sun and well-drained soil. When you plant, make sure the upper half of each rhizome is *above* the soil surface.

Go on pest patrol. If you notice borers tunneling through the leaves, squash them between your thumb and forefinger. Also, dust the rhizomes with pyrethrin to kill any emerging larvae.

Keep 'em clean. When you divide your irises, discard any rhizomes with rot or visible larvae. Cut back and destroy old leaves at the end of the season, and rake up any debris around your plants.

Lamb's Ears • *Stachys byzantina*

The "please-touch-me," furry foliage of this dependable perennial makes it a favorite with young folks—and the young at heart! Lamb's ears have flowers, too—spikes of small, purplish pink blooms in summer—but it's really the soft, silvery leaves that steal the show.

 GROW IT!

Full sun or partial shade
Very well drained, average soil
About 6 inches tall in leaf to
    18 inches tall in bloom
In hot climates, give plants
    shade during the hottest
    part of the day
Hardy perennial (Zones 4 to 8)

 PLANT IT!

Lamb's ears are a classic
    choice for edging beds,
    borders, and paths
Pair 'em with bright blooms
    to help keep the colors
    from clashing
Plant in groups to get a
    great-looking groundcover
    on poor soil sites

 GETTING STARTED

Buy plants in spring, or beg a few starts from a friend. Lamb's ears spread by creeping roots and fill in at a pretty good clip, so divide 'em in spring if they spread too far.

Lamb's ears
Stachys byzantina

Ears Lookin' at You, Kid!

The flowers of lamb's ears aren't much to crow about, so many gardeners cut off the flower stalks as they appear. To save yourself this step, do what I do, and plant cultivars that produce few or no bloom spikes! 'Silver Carpet' has small, silvery white foliage, while 'Countess Helene von Stein' (also sold as 'Big Ears') produces large, greenish white leaves.

There's no getting around it—rotted leaves are a common problem with lamb's ears in hot, humid weather. Don't worry, though; the damage isn't permanent! Simply cut off all the top growth close to the ground, and good-looking, new growth will sprout up in a few weeks. In fact, it's smart to shear your lamb's ears back each fall if you didn't do it earlier; that'll stop the funky fungi from getting a foothold during wet winter weather.

Lavender • *Lavandula angustifolia*

Question: Is lavender an herb, a perennial, or a shrub? Actually, it's all three! This fragrant favorite blooms in early to midsummer, with spikes of small, clustered flowers, usually in shades of lavender-purple or violet. But it's not just the blooms that are perfumed; the shrubby mounds of silvery gray leaves release that same great scent when you brush by them.

Lavender
Lavandula angustifolia

 GROW IT!

Full sun
Poor to rich,
    well-drained soil
2 to 3 feet tall
Hardy shrub
    (Zones 5 to 9)

 PLANT IT!

Lavender looks perfect paired
    with other sun-loving perennials,
    like yarrows (*Achillea*) and lamb's
    ears (*Stachys byzantina*)
Compact types make terrific
    edging plants
Grow lavender in groups as
    a low hedge or groundcover

 GETTING STARTED

Buying plants is by far the easiest way to add lavender to your garden. You can plant it in spring or fall in most areas; in Zone 5, spring planting is best.

FLOWER FUN!

Besides a restful night's sleep, how about one filled with wonderful dreams? To create your own dream machine, try my secret recipe: Mix a half cup each of dried lavender, lemon balm (*Melissa officinalis*), and hops (*Humulus lupulus*), and dump 'em into a muslin bag. Pull the drawstring closed and slip the bag into your pillowcase or under your pillow. Lay your head down, and then it's sweet dreams, baby!

Soil Solutions

After years of having my lavender plants die off during the winter, I finally discovered the secret to long-lived lavender: well-drained soil! Lavenders hate having wet feet, especially in winter. Planting in raised beds is a great way to keep your lavender plants high and dry. Or make individual mounds of sandy soil right in the garden, and plant your lavenders on top!

Laid-Back Lavender

Give it the right site, and lavender is about as trouble-free as you can get. Here are the basics for growing perfect plants every time:

❀ Established plants don't need watering except during prolonged droughts.

❀ Leaf spot may attack foliage where summers are humid. Choose a site with good air circulation to help prevent problems.

❀ Keep organic mulches, like bark or chopped leaves, about a foot away from lavender plants. (Gravel, stone chips, and sand all are fine to use right around the plants.)

❀ Lavender usually doesn't need feeding. But if you want to perk up tired-looking plants, spread some compost mixed with a bit of 5-10-5 fertilizer around them in spring.

❀ Established lavenders hate being disturbed, so don't divide 'em.

PENNY WISE

Don't be too quick to set that old Christmas tree out for the trash! With a few quick snips, you can turn it into a real treasure— the perfect winter mulch for your lavender. Simply lay a few boughs over each clump, and it'll keep your plants cozy without holding in the moisture that can lead to root rot. Come spring, it's a snap to remove the boughs and let the sun shine in!

Prune for Pretty Plants

To keep lavender plants looking bushy, you've got lots of options! You can trim them lightly each year, or cut 'em back hard once every few years. And you can do it in spring, just as the plants start growing, or in summer, as you harvest the flowers.

To tidy up plants that have taken to sprawling, simply cut back the top branches, snipping them just above new, upright shoots near the center of the plant. Cut all the branches back in layers, shortening the center branches the most and the outer branches the least.

Lilacs • *Syringa*

If you get a kick out of fragrant flowers, you absolutely have to add some lilacs in your garden! These easy-to-grow shrubs really pack a wallop of a punch in the perfume department, and they're mighty pretty, too. They bloom from late spring to early summer, with eye-catching clusters of white, pink, purple, magenta, violet, and lavender-blue flowers.

Lilac
Syringa

 GROW IT!

Full sun
Average to rich, well-
    drained soil
8 to 15 feet tall
Hardy shrubs or small
    trees (Zones 3 to 7)

 PLANT IT!

Grow a row of lilacs as a hedge
Mix 'em in with shrubs that
    bloom later in the summer,
    such as hydrangeas and
    viburnums
They're fantastic as cut flowers!

 GETTING STARTED

Start with container-grown or balled-and-burlapped lilacs in spring or early fall. Here's a tip that'll save you hours of pruning later on: **Don't buy grafted lilacs.** Grafted plants send up strong suckers from their roots, so you'll have to keep after them (by either digging 'em out or cutting 'em off) or they'll soon take over. Cutting-grown (also called *own-root*) lilacs send up suckers, too, but those shoots are the same as the rest of the plant, so you don't need to worry about them crowding out the main stems.

 Powdery mildew makes lilac leaves look tired and dusty in hot, humid weather, but fortunately, it doesn't really harm the plants. A site with good air circulation helps the leaves dry quickly after a rain, making it hard for mildew to get a foothold.

Pruning Primer

Lilacs flower on old wood—in other words, last year's stems—so the best time to prune them is right *after* they flower. That'll give 'em all summer to make new buds for next year. To keep older plants growing strong, cut one or two of the oldest stems to the ground each year. If a clump really gets out of hand, you can take drastic measures and cut the whole shootin' match down to a foot or so above the ground. Don't worry; it'll grow back in no time at all.

The Lilac Doctor

There's nothing sadder than a lilac with no flowers! If your bush isn't blooming, check out the list below to find out why— then try my sure-fire tricks to getting your lilac back on track:

Too shady? Lilacs need at least six hours of sun a day to bloom well, so move your bush to a brighter site.

Poor pruning? If you prune after midsummer, you'll cut off the following year's flower buds. Get your pruning done earlier next year!

Too much food? Excess nitrogen can lead to lots of leaves but no blooms, so hold off on the fertilizer.

Too dry? Dry spells in late summer and fall can do bad things to flower buds, so water your lilacs regularly when Mother Nature doesn't do the job.

Jerry's TIMELY TIPS

"Keep your lilacs at the top of their game by taking off the flowers once they fade. Either snap 'em off between your thumb and index finger, or clip 'em off with pruning shears. That way, the plant won't waste its energy on making seeds. Just be careful not to remove the new buds at the base of each bloom; that's where next year's flowers will come from!"

No good reason an established bush isn't blooming? Try a light root pruning in early summer. Simply take a sharp spade and cut down into the soil on two sides of the plant, about a foot out from the trunk. That should get those buds coming for next year!

For big-time garden drama, look no further than lilies! These bed and border favorites bear big blooms in can't-miss colors like fiery orange, rousing red, and sunshine yellow, as well as pastel pinks, creams, and white.

Goldband lily

Lilium auratum

 ### GROW IT!

Full sun for most kinds
Rich, evenly moist, well-drained soil
2 to 8 feet tall
Select a site protected from strong winds
Hardy bulbs (Zones 2 to 5 through 7 or 8)

 ### PLANT IT!

Plant lilies in clumps, not in rows
Grow 'em behind shorter perennials that'll fill in after the lilies are done, like daylilies (*Hemerocallis*) and catmints (*Nepeta*)
Lilies are top-notch cut flowers

 ### GETTING STARTED

Look for lily bulbs in garden centers in spring or fall. (If you shop in fall, buy your bulbs early, and get 'em in the ground at least a month before the first frost so they can grow roots before the ground freezes.) Plant most bulbs 6 to 9 inches deep; small bulbs can be an inch or two closer to the soil's surface.

Landscape Lingo

Lilies grow from **scaly** or **non-tunicate** bulbs, meaning the fleshy scales aren't covered with a papery covering, like they are in daffodil bulbs. As a result, lily bulbs dry out more quickly and are also more prone to damage than tunicate bulbs. So treat your lilies with a little extra TLC!

Lilies Never Sleep

Unlike tulips and other spring bulbs, lilies aren't totally dormant when they're shipped to the store. That means you need to get 'em back in the ground as soon as possible after you get 'em home. Can't plant right away? Store the bulbs in the refrigerator or a dark, cool (40°F) place.

Shady Characters

Sure, lilies are stars in sunny gardens, but don't despair if you only have shade—

there are lovely lilies for you, too! Here's a six-pack of lilies that'll thank you for giving 'em dappled, all-day shade, or a spot with morning sun and afternoon shade:

American Turk's-cap lily
  (*L. superbum*)

Canada lily (*L. canadense*)

Henry lily (*L. henryi*)

Japanese lily (*L. speciosum*)

Leopard lily (*L. pardalinum*)

Martagon lilies (*Martagon Hybrids*)

PENNY WISE

Lilies make top-notch cut flowers, but they cost a bundle if you buy blooms from a florist. So, save yourself some dough, and grow your own! Here's a little trick that'll save you a lot of clean-up time and effort: Make sure you pick off the anthers—those pollen-covered bits that dangle on long stalks from the center of each flower. Otherwise, the pollen will drop off, and it can permanently stain fabric and furniture.

Feeding Frenzy

The secret to keeping lilies looking their very best? Give 'em plenty to eat! In early spring, late spring, and midsummer, scatter a handful of 5-10-5 fertilizer around each clump. If you have wood ashes handy, give your lilies a dose of them, too: 1 pound for every 20 square feet of lily bed in spring. That'll really get 'em shootin' up like skyrockets!

Keep 'Em High and Dry

Every time Grandma Putt sent me out to plant lilies, she'd come with me to make sure I picked a good planting spot. She had two special rules: Never plant new lily bulbs where other lilies failed to grow, and never plant 'em in soggy soil. Where the soil was on the heavy (clay) side, here's a little secret that never failed to do the job: She'd have me tilt each bulb a bit in its planting hole, so water didn't collect between the scales and cause the bulbs to rot.

Japanese lily
Lilium speciosum

Lupines • *Lupinus*

These cottage-garden favorites sure can't take the heat—they're happiest where summers are cool and rainy. But no matter where you live, lupines are worth a try; their showy flower spikes come in practically every color of the rainbow!

Lupine
Lupinus

GROW IT!

Full sun
Average to rich, moist,
    well-drained soil
2 to 5 feet tall
Hardy perennials (Zones 3 to
    8) or cool-weather annuals

PLANT IT!

Classic choices for early-
    summer color in perennial
    borders and flowerbeds
Enjoy 'em in meadows and
    sunny wildflower gardens
Grow some in a cutting garden;
    they're fantastic as cut flowers!

GETTING STARTED

Start with purchased plants or grow your own from seeds; either way, it's easy! To speed up sprouting, soak the seeds for 24 hours before planting in warm water with a touch of dish soap added. Sow 'em outdoors several weeks before your last spring frost date, or sow indoors in individual pots in a cool spot (55° to 65°F).

PROBLEM SOLVED!

Looking for even longer-lasting lupines? Try Carolina lupine (*Thermopsis villosa*)! This trouble-free perennial is tailor-made for steamy southern summers, sending up show-stopping spikes of bright yellow blooms atop 3- to 4-foot stems each summer. Or try their kissin' cousins, the baptisias: *Baptisia australis,* commonly called blue false indigo, has blue blooms, while *B. alba* has cool white spikes.

Go Loopy for Lupines!

Do you live in an area where summers are hot and steamy? Here are two tips for keeping your lupines lookin' good:

❀ To help the plants beat the heat, give 'em a site that gets some shade during the hottest part of the day.

❀ Plant lupines in fall, then pull 'em out when they're done flowering the following year.

Marvelous marigolds simply couldn't be any easier to grow! Their cheerful flowers come in shades of yellow, orange, maroon, and creamy white, adding a dazzling display of welcome color to summer beds and borders.

 ## GROW IT!

Full sun
Average, well-drained soil
6 to 36 inches tall
Plants tolerate drought, but bloom best with regular watering
Warm-weather annuals

 ## PLANT IT!

Grow marigolds in mixed plantings with other annuals or perennials
Enjoy compact cultivars as edging plants along paths and walkways
Tuck marigolds into pots and planters for months of easy-care color

Marigold
Tagetes

 ## GETTING STARTED

Pick up some transplants at your local garden center in spring, or grow your own. Sow the seeds indoors six to eight weeks before your last spring frost date, or sow them outdoors two weeks before your last spring frost date.

Summer Vacation for Marigolds

Marigolds like warm weather, but sometimes, things get a little too hot even for them! If your plants stop blooming during the dog days, don't pull 'em out: Keep 'em watered, and be patient—they'll start flowering again when cooler weather arrives. When your plants *are* blooming, pinch off the spent flowers to keep new buds coming.

Marigolds are marigolds, right? Well, not exactly. You'll find four different types at garden centers, so be a little adventurous, and give 'em all a try!

African or American marigolds (*T. erecta*): Double, 4- to 5-inch-wide flowers on 1½- to 3-foot-tall plants. Compact cultivars stay under 18 inches.

French marigolds (*T. patula*): Six- to 12-inch-tall plants with 1- to 2-inch-wide, single, semi-double, or double flowers.

Triploid marigolds: Crosses between African and French marigolds, with 1-foot-tall plants and single or double, 2- to 3-inch-wide flowers. They keep blooming in hot weather.

Signet marigolds (*T. tenuifolia*): Mounding, 9- to 12- inch plants with lacy leaves and masses of tiny, ¾-inch-wide flowers.

Morning Glories • *Ipomoea*

What a way to start the day! Morning glories certainly are glorious, with their big, showy blooms in shades of blue, purple-blue, pink, red, and white. Each flower opens for only one morning, but new buds open every day, so the show keeps going all summer long!

Morning glory
Ipomoea tricolor

 GROW IT!

Full sun
Average, well-drained, moist soil
Climbs from 6 to 12 feet
Warm-weather annuals

 PLANT IT!

Train morning glories up trellises, over deck railings, or around lampposts
Grow 'em on fences, or even over shrubs
Hummingbirds are attracted to the blooms

 GETTING STARTED

Morning glories are so simple to start from seeds, there's no reason to ever buy plants! Soaking the seeds in warm water for 24 hours before planting gets 'em off to a speedy start. In most areas, outdoor sowing—two weeks after your last frost date—is easiest. If spring in your area tends to be long and cool, start the seeds indoors in individual pots several weeks before your last frost date. Move 'em to the garden once outdoor temperatures stay above 45°F.

Support Groups for Morning Glories

Don't worry about giving your morning glories a heavy-duty structure to climb; they'll wind their way up strings attached to a fence or netting wrapped around a pole. Just make sure you have their support system in place *before* you sow the seeds.

For something a little different, grow some of these morning glory kissin' cousins!

Cardinal climber (*I. x multifida*): Small, scarlet flowers and lacy leaves.

Moonflower (*I. alba*): Fragrant, white flowers that open at night.

Spanish flag (*I. lobata*): Clusters of tube-shaped, red, orange, and yellow flowers.

Nasturtium • *Tropaeolum majus*

Help 'em climb or let 'em creep; either way, these old-fashioned favorites can't be beat for bright blooms all summer long. Their fancy flowers come in shades of red, orange, yellow, and cream. But don't think these beauties are just pretty to look at—their peppery-flavored flowers and leaves are mighty tasty, too!

 ### GROW IT!

Full sun
Poor, well-drained soil
Creeping types grow
   1 to 2 feet tall;
   climbers get to
   8 feet high
Warm-weather annual

 ### PLANT IT!

Tuck nasturtiums into
   perennial beds and
   borders as fillers
Train climbers up mailboxes
   or lampposts; they'll need
   strings or netting to climb
Use creeping types as
   edgings, or let 'em spill
   over walls

Nasturtium
Tropaeolum majus

 ### GETTING STARTED

You can buy nasturtiums as transplants, but why bother? They're a snap to grow from seeds! Once the soil has warmed up a bit, sow 'em right in the garden about a week after your last spring frost date.

Be Nasty to Nasturtiums!

If you've got lots of leaves, but not many blooms, you're bein' too nice to your nasturtiums. In rich, moist soil, the plants will look lush and leafy, but you'll get hardly any flowers—and that's no fun! So give 'em a spot with poorer soil next year—they especially like sand—and hold off on the compost and fertilizer!

FLOWER FUN!

Sure, nasturtium leaves and flowers taste great in salads, but did you know that the flower buds and seedpods are edible, too? Simply pick buds and seedpods that aren't yet ripe (they should still be soft, not hard), put 'em in a clean glass jar or bottle, and cover 'em with vinegar. In about three days, you'll have a spicy substitute for capers! They'll store well, unrefrigerated, for about a year.

Pansy • *Viola x wittrockiana*

Wherever you plant 'em, the perky faces of pansies always seem to say "howdy!" Blooms come in a boatload of colors, and while types with dark, velvety faces are most common, you can also buy solid-color pansies that are just as pretty. There's not a bad one in the bunch, so why not plant a mix? That's a sure-fire way to get the most bang for your gardening buck!

Pansy
Viola x wittrockiana

 GROW IT!

Full sun or partial shade
Rich, moist, well-drained soil
6 to 9 inches tall
In areas with hot summers, give plants partial shade, especially in the afternoon
Biennial or cool-weather annual

 PLANT IT!

Plant pansies in containers for spots of spring color on a deck or patio
Enjoy 'em as edgings along beds, borders, and paths
They're top-notch companions for spring bulbs

 GETTING STARTED

It's easy to find pansy plants for sale everywhere in spring, and in Zones 6 and south, you can often find 'em in fall, too! If you want to grow your own from seeds, sow indoors 10 to 12 weeks before your last spring frost date. Set the pots in your fridge for two weeks, then move 'em to a warmer (65° to 70°F) place to sprout.

GRANDMA PUTT'S
Handy Hints

One of the first chores I had as a boy in Grandma Putt's garden was pickin' pansies—and now I know why! The more dead flowers you cut off, the more new blooms your plants'll produce!

Don't Get Squirrely

Tired of squirrels messin' with your newly planted pansies? These pesky critters just love to nip off the best blooms, or even pull whole plants out of the soil. To protect your pansies, try this trick: Drape black plastic netting over newly planted pansies for the first week or two they're in the ground, until they get rooted into the soil a bit. You'll hardly see the netting, but it's enough to send squirrels scurryin'!

Peonies • *Paeonia*

For the show to end all shows in the early-summer garden, you want to plant peonies—*lots* of 'em! They may look delicate and finicky, but these dependable perennials are easy to grow and tough as nails. After you enjoy their huge blooms—they come in shades of pink, red, white, and even pale yellow—you'll admire the handsome, dark green leaves all summer long.

Peony
Paeonia

 GROW IT!

Full sun or very
   light shade
Average to rich,
   well-drained soil
18 to 36 inches tall
Hardy perennials
   (Zones 4 to 9)

 PLANT IT!

Grow 'em in beds and
   borders for can't-miss
   color—and fragrance,
   to boot!
Pair peonies with Siberian
   iris (*Iris sibirica*), blue
   false indigo (*Baptisia
   australis*), and other
   early-summer bloomers
They're fantastic for
   cut flowers

GETTING STARTED

Buy potted peonies in spring at your local garden center, or order bare-root peonies by mail for fall planting. If you can't set out bare-root plants as soon as they arrive, moisten them lightly and keep them in their packing material. They can wait for up to a week in a cool, dark place. If the roots look dried out, soak 'em in water for a few hours before planting.

Preplanting Pointers

Peonies rate right near the top of the no-fuss, no-muss scale. Why, these durable perennials can thrive for 20 years or more without needing to be divided! Since you

Jerry's TIMELY TIPS

"Peonies are pretty trouble-free, but there's one dastardly disease problem that might strike: botrytis. Affected shoots look rotted or scorched, and flower buds turn brown or don't open. To keep these funky fungi from pilfering any more of your peony pleasures, cut off any affected parts right away, and toss 'em in the trash. Also rake away the mulch and the top half-inch of soil around the plant, and replace it with fresh soil and mulch. Cutting off and destroying the remaining leaves at the end of the season'll help prevent disease problems next year."

won't be moving them often, it's worth taking the time to make them an extra-good bed to live in.

A couple weeks before planting, dig a big hole—1 foot deep and 2 feet wide is about right. Work a shovelful of compost into the bottom of the hole, and another into the soil you took out; toss a handful or two of bonemeal into the hole, too. Add the soil back in, then let the area settle a bit until planting time. When you set out your peony plants in this super-energized soil, they'll be off to a rip-roarin' start come spring!

Staking Secrets

The trick to successful peony staking? Do it *before* your plants really need it! When the emerging shoots are 6 to 12 inches tall, use stakes and string to surround the clump, or set out a store-bought "peony hoop." The stems'll grow up through the hoop, and by bloom time, you won't even see the supports!

Really hate staking? Then stick with single-flowered peonies! They're a whole lot less likely to flop over.

FLOWER POWER TONICS

Fungus Fighter

Get sweet on your peonies, and give 'em a dose of molasses to keep dastardly diseases away! At the first sign of trouble, try this tonic.

½ cup of molasses
½ cup of powdered milk
1 tsp. of baking soda
1 gal. of warm water

Mix the molasses, powdered milk, and baking soda into a paste. Place the mixture into the toe of an old nylon stocking, and let it steep in the warm water for several hours. Then strain, and use the remaining liquid as a fungus-fighting spray for peonies and other perennials every two weeks throughout the growing season. I guarantee you'll have no more fungus troubles! ✳

Perennials

Tired of planting the same old annuals year after year? Well, then, my friend—it's time to give perennials a try! Set 'em out once, then stand back to enjoy many seasons of beautiful blooms. Best of all, perennials are adaptable, too. Whether you have shade or sun, rich soil or poor, perennials are guaranteed to make your garden pretty as a picture!

Sea pink
Armeria maritima

Many Happy Returns

The greatest thing about growing perennials is that they come back every year—or at least, they're *supposed* to! You can increase the odds that yours will make a return appearance by choosing plants that are adapted to your climate. The easiest way to know this is to look at each plant's hardiness rating. Based on a map put out by the USDA, the hardiness rating tells you where a given plant is likely to survive the winter.

So before you choose perennials for your yard, make sure you know your hardiness zone—turn to the map on page 356 if you're not sure—then check the hardiness ratings of the plants you're considering. (You'll find hardiness ratings given in many gardening books, magazines, and catalogs, and sometimes on plant labels, too.) To be absolutely sure your perennials will survive the winter, do what I do, and pick ones that are hardy to one zone number

Landscape Lingo

All perennials aren't created equal! Check plant labels for these two terms, so you'll know how to treat the perennials you bring home.

Hardy perennial. A perennial that withstands cold and can be grown outdoors year-round. (The amount of cold a plant can survive varies, so check the USDA hardiness zone to be sure.)

Tender perennial. A plant that's perennial in southern zones, but killed by winter cold in the north. Some can't take any frost, while others can tolerate short periods of below-freezing temperatures. Read labels and check with garden center staff to find out how a plant labeled "tender perennial" will perform in your climate.

Rose campion
Lychnis coronaria

lower than that of your garden. If you live in Zone 5, for instance, choose perennials that are hardy through Zone 4.

Get Ready, Get Set...

What's better than spending a winter afternoon curled up in a cozy armchair with perennial catalogs and your favorite gardening books? Doing it when you have an empty flowerbed that's already dug and ready to fill! So, take advantage of cool fall days to dig new perennial beds, amend the soil with compost, and cover 'em with mulch. Come spring, simply rake off the mulch, and you're good to grow!

Spring or Fall? It's Your Call

In most areas, early spring and early fall are ideal planting times for perennials. The best fall-planting conditions are a warm, long fall followed by a hard, freezing winter. But if your area tends to see a lot of freezing and thawing in winter, spring planting's a *much* better bet for you—*and* your plants!

FLOWER POWER TONICS

Fragrant Pest Fighter

People love perfumed perennials, but pests sure don't! So the next time you're out in your flower garden, gather the ingredients for this aromatic pest-control spray.

½ **cup of fresh tansy (*Tanacetum vulgare*) or mugwort (*Artemisia vulgaris*) leaves**
½ **cup of fresh lavender flowers and/or leaves**
½ **cup of fresh sage (*Salvia officinalis*) leaves**
Boiling water
2 cups of room-temperature water
1 tsp. of Murphy's Oil Soap

Place the leaves and flowers in a 1-quart glass jar; fill with boiling water, cover, and let sit until cool. Add ⅛ cup of that liquid to the 2 cups of room-temperature water and the Murphy's Oil Soap. Pour into a hand-held mist sprayer, and apply to all your flowers to keep pests at bay! ✳

Perfect Perennials for Shady Sites

Think you can't have a flower-filled garden in the shade? Think again, my friend! Here's a bouquet of fantastic flowering perennials that are tailor-made for shade:

Astilbes (*Astilbe*)

Foamflowers (*Tiarella*)

Hostas (*Hosta*)

Lenten rose (*Helleborus* x *hybridus*)

Lungworts (*Pulmonaria*)

Meadow rues (*Thalictrum*)

Primroses (*Primula*)

Siberian bugloss (*Brunnera macrophylla*)

Spiderworts (*Tradescantia*)

Toad lily (*Tricyrtis hirta*)

Violets (*Viola*)

Yellow corydalis (*Corydalis lutea*)

GRANDMA PUTT'S Handy Hints

Every year, my Grandma Putt had the prettiest perennials in town, and the neighbors were always after her secret. "It's simple," she'd say, "just give the plants what they want." In other words, choose plants that grow well in the sun, soil, and other conditions available in your garden! Don't plant sun-lovin' plants in shade, or they'll get leggy and won't bloom. And don't plant shade-lovin' perennials in sun, or they'll get scorched leaves and look just awful. Be realistic about the conditions your garden has to offer, then plant perennials that'll be happy there. They'll look great, bloom better, and have far fewer problems than perennials that are planted in the wrong place!

Hello Down There!

It never fails: Every spring, a few perennials make you nervous. They're the ones that don't come up when everything else seems to be goin' great guns. Instead of poking around in the soil trying to see if they're still alive, just be patient. Some perennials just naturally come up later than others—balloon flower (*Platycodon grandiflorus*) and common rose mallow (*Hibiscus*

Missouri evening primrose

Oenothera missouriensis

Blue false indigo
Baptisia australis

moscheutos) are two examples. Wait at least a month after the last spring frost date—two is better—to see if they sprout. If they haven't come up by then, officially declare them "dead," and replace 'em with something else. If they do come up, put a label there so the late sleepers won't worry you again next spring.

Bottoms Up!

Feed your perennials daily with this fortified drink from the kitchen sink, then stand back and watch 'em soar! Take any combination of plant-based kitchen scraps—like table scraps (no meat or fats), eggshells, and potato peelings—and put 'em in an old blender. Fill it to the top with water, blend it all up, then pour it around the base of your perennials. They'll thank you for it!

Much Ado about Mulch

Psst! Wanna know my number-one secret for happy, healthy perennials? It's *mulch*—and lots of it! Besides making your garden look tidy, it smothers weeds, keeps the soil moist and cool, and protects against erosion. Compost is a marvelous mulch, and it's easy to make, or you can buy it bagged. Shredded bark is another great mulch; pine needles are nice, too. And don't overlook one of the best mulches for perennial gardens: chopped leaves. There's always a plentiful supply in fall, and you can run 'em through a leaf shredder, or chop and gather 'em in one easy step with a bagging lawn mower.

Jerry's TIMELY TIPS

"If I have to water my perennial garden, I make sure I do it in the morning. That way, the plants are juiced up and ready to handle the heat of the day. It also means that the leaves have plenty of time to dry off before bedtime. You don't send your kids to bed with a wet head, so don't do it to your perennials, either!"

Water Wizardry

Wondering whether it's time to water? If you wait until your plants are wilting, it's almost too late! You're better off checking the soil instead. Pull back the mulch in a small area, then dig down a few inches with a trowel. If the top 2 inches of soil are dry, get out the hose, and get busy waterin'!

Don't Overdo It!

Perennials need plenty of fuel for the long haul, but giving 'em one big dose of fertilizer in spring isn't the answer. They'll just pig out, grow floppy, and may actually bloom less! Instead, give them a couple of light snacks during the growing season.

If you worked lots of compost into your soil at planting time, put a narrow ring of 5-10-5 fertilizer around each of your perennials in midspring and again in midsummer. Keep the fertilizer out at the tips of the shoots, where the roots are feeding most—not right up against the base of the stems.

If your soil isn't rich in organic matter, feed with fish emulsion (apply every two weeks at half the recommended rate, mixed with a cup of beer and a tablespoon of liquid dish soap per gallon of liquid). Plan on spreading some compost, too, to beef up your soil's organic matter.

FLOWER POWER TONICS

Double Punch Garlic Tea

Are thrips and other pesky insects bugging your perennials? Send 'em packing with a dose of this excellent elixir.

5 unpeeled cloves of garlic, coarsely chopped
2 cups of boiling water
1/2 cup of tobacco tea*
1 tsp. of instant tea granules
1 tsp. of baby shampoo

Place the chopped garlic in a heatproof bowl, and pour the boiling water over it. Let it steep overnight. Strain through a coffee filter, and then mix it with the other ingredients in a hand-held mist sprayer, and thoroughly drench your plants.

*Place three fingers of chewing tobacco in an old nylon stocking and soak it in a gallon of hot water until the mixture is dark brown. ❁

Gas plant
Dictamnus albus

Jacob's ladder
Polemonium

Lobelia
Lobelia

Meadow rue
Thalictrum

Bear's breeches
Acanthus

First-Year Fillers

Here's a handy rule of thumb that you need to know about perennials: First year, they sleep; second year, they creep; and third year, they leap! That first year, they're busy putting down roots, so you won't see much in the way of growth. The second year, they're a bit further along, but it's not until the third year that your garden will start looking like the lush, flower-filled paradise you planned for.

So, what's a gardener to do? For those first few years, fill in the gaps with annuals! Some of my favorite fillers include marigolds, impatiens, coleus, verbenas, and zinnias—but you can choose others, too.

Self-sowing annuals are a smart choice for filling up spaces between newly planted perennials. Plant 'em the first spring your perennials are in the ground, then let 'em sow around. They'll gradually die out once the perennials have filled in. Good choices for freely seeding fillers include love-in-a-mist (*Nigella damascena*), Brazilian vervain (*Verbena bonariensis*), and larkspur (*Consolida ajacis*).

Perennials for Privacy

Need some instant privacy around a deck, pool, or patio? Don't spend a fortune on a fence or wait years for a hedge to fill in—plant a border of big perennials instead! Here are 10 head-high perennials that are just the ticket for showy summer screening:

Boltonia (*Boltonia asteroides*)

Common rose mallow
    (*Hibiscus moscheutos*)

Cup plant (*Silphium perfoliatum*)

Cut-leaved coneflower
    (*Rudbeckia laciniata*)

Joe Pye weed
    (*Eupatorium fistulosum*)

Maximilian sunflower
    (*Helianthus maximiliani*)

Queen-of-the-prairie
    (*Filipendula rubra*)

Sneezeweed
    (*Helenium autumnale*)

Swamp sunflower (*Helianthus angustifolius*)

Tartarian aster (*Aster tataricus*)

FL✽WER POWER TONICS

Mulch Moisturizer Tonic

When you give your perennial beds a fresh layer of organic mulch in spring, overspray it with this super tonic to give it a little extra kick.

1 can of regular cola (not diet)
1/2 cup of ammonia
1/2 cup of antiseptic mouthwash
1/2 cup of baby shampoo

Mix all of these ingredients in your 20 gallon hose-end sprayer, and give your mulch a long, cool drink. ✽

Perfect Perennial Plotting

If you can't stretch your budget far enough to plant the gigantic garden of your dreams, don't despair. Try any or all of these terrific tips:

Dig and plant sections. Tackle soil prep on a new section each year, then plant. In a couple of years, it'll all be done!

Buy the best stuff first. If you can afford only a few perennials a year, start with ones that you can divide, like daylilies and

Lenten rose
Helleborus x hybridus

Haage's campion
Lychnis haageana

hostas. Divide 'em after the first or second year to expand your garden.

Grow veggies among the perennials. I'm not kidding! Cherry tomatoes are pretty along the back of the border, and they'll fill up space while your perennials are growin'. Other pretty vegetables include peppers, 'Bright Lights' Swiss chard, lettuce, and eggplant.

Stagger Your Schedule

It's a fact of life: Happy, healthy perennials get bigger each year. At some point, you'll need to dig 'em up and divide 'em, to keep 'em from outgrowing their allotted space, to relieve overcrowding within the clump, or to make more plants to fill other parts of your yard.

To keep your perennials in peak condition, plan on dividing most of 'em every three to five years. But don't divide all the perennials in one bed at one time; if you do, you'll have to wait a few years for them all to fill in and bloom well again. Instead, do a few each spring and fall. Besides saving you lots of work at one time, this trick'll keep your perennial plantings looking great year after year!

Petunias • *Petunia*

Let's face it, folks—summer just wouldn't be the same without the bright, beautiful blooms of petunias! These old-fashioned favorites are still popular today, and no wonder—they flower from summer right up to frost, with showy, trumpet-shaped blooms in shades of pink, red, burgundy, purple, blue, and yellow. You can even find hybrids with stripes, edges, or veins in contrasting colors—wow!

 ## GROW IT!

Full sun or light shade
Average to rich, moist,
    well-drained soil
6 to 18 inches tall
Plants tolerate poor soil and
    are super for seaside gardens
Warm-weather annuals

 ## PLANT IT!

Petunias look great cascading
    from window boxes and
    hanging baskets
They're excellent edging
    plants for beds and borders
The blooms attract both
    hummingbirds and moths

Petunia
Petunia

 ## GETTING STARTED

Petunia plants are available everywhere in spring, but you can also grow them from seeds. The seeds are tiny—like dust—but they'll grow if you sow them indoors 10 to 12 weeks before your last frost date. Press the seeds into the soil surface—don't cover 'em up, because they need light to sprout—and keep the pots at 65° to 70°F. Set transplants outside after all danger of frost has passed.

Perennial Annuals?

Although petunias are normally grown as annuals, they're actually tender perennials. That may not seem like a big

I get asked quite often, "Hey—what happened to my petunias? They used to have a white edge on each bloom, and now they're all one color!" What's up? Well, the culprit is a change in the growing conditions, not any kind of disease. When the white edge gets smaller, it means the weather's been cool, and the water and soil nutrients are in ample supply. If the white increases, it means the weather's been hot, and the soil is dry and/or low in nutrients.

Landscape Lingo

Pick a peck of petunias—there are lots to choose from! Here's a run-down of what you'll find at your local garden center:

Grandiflora petunias. These have the biggest blooms (about 4 inches across). The large flowers are prone to damage from rain and wind, so grandifloras are best for sheltered spots. They spread to 3 feet.

Multiflora petunias. Bushy plants with loads of smaller (2-inch-wide) flowers that hold up well in less-than-ideal weather. The popular Wave Series petunias are extra-vigorous multifloras—they make great groundcovers! Multifloras spread to 3 feet.

Milliflora petunias. This class contains the Fantasy Series petunias. The densely branched plants spread to about 8 inches and produce masses of 1- to 1½-inch-wide flowers.

Supertunia and Surfinia Groups. These are compact, heavy-blooming hybrids (propagated by cuttings only) with 2- to 3-inch-wide flowers; their height and spread vary.

deal, but look at it this way: That means you can keep your favorite colors and flower forms from year to year if you bring 'em inside for the winter! Dig whole plants, or take cuttings in late summer. Indoors, keep 'em in a bright, cool (55° to 65°F) place, then set 'em outside again next year.

Dog Day Blues

When temperatures soar in summer, petunias aren't exactly happy campers: They stop blooming and start sprawling. Whatever you do, don't rip 'em out; just take your pruning shears and clip the stems back by half. That'll encourage the plants to produce bushy new growth and more blooms. Here's another handy hint: Cut 'em back again in late summer, and you'll get a good show of bountiful blooms right up until frost.

Seed Secret

When potting petunia seedlings, don't be too quick to toss out the smallest ones—they're often the ones that'll produce the best blooms! This is especially true if you're trying to grow double-flowered petunias from seed; the smallest seedlings are the most likely to have fully double flowers.

Do you have a sunny garden that could use some summer color? Then fill it with a flock of phlox! Stuck with a shady site instead? Don't despair—there are fabulous phlox for you, too! These flower garden favorites come in a wide range of colors, from show-stopping crimson-red and magenta-pink to softer shades of pink, white, lavender, and purple.

GROW IT!

Sun to shade, depending on the type
Average to rich, moist, well-drained soil
6 inches to 4 feet tall
Cool-weather annuals or hardy perennials (Zones 2 to 9)

PLANT IT!

Low-growing, sun-loving phlox make great groundcovers and edging plants
Shade-loving phlox are perfect partners for hostas, ferns, and foamflowers (*Tiarella*)
Grow tall types in beds and borders with other showy summer flowers, such as daylilies (*Hemerocallis*) and hollyhocks (*Alcea rosea*)

Prairie phlox
Phlox pilosa

GETTING STARTED

To grow **annual** phlox, buy transplants in spring, or sow seeds directly in your garden several weeks before your last frost date. For **perennial** phlox, buy plants to make sure you get exactly the colors you want.

Suitable for Shade

Most phlox are real sun-worshippers, but you shady-site gardeners can enjoy these beautiful bloomers, too—*if* you choose your plants wisely. Try wild blue phlox (*P. divaricata*), with clusters of fragrant, lavender flowers, and creeping phlox (*P. stolonifera*), in pink, lilac-blue, or white. Both perennials form broad clumps that'll really knock your socks off when they do their thing in spring!

FLOWER POWER TONICS

Powdery Mildew Control

Don't let mildew mess up your phlox! Try this terrific tonic instead.

4 tbsp. of baking soda
2 tbsp. of Murphy's Oil Soap
1 gal. of warm water

Mix all of the ingredients together. Pour into a hand-held mist sprayer, and apply liberally as soon as you see the telltale white spots on your phlox. ✳

Phabulous Phlox for Sun

Once you get hooked on phlox, you'll want to enjoy their beautiful blooms for as long as possible! Here's the scoop on some for spring and some for summer:

Ground-huggers for spring. The best-known, early bloomer is moss phlox or moss pink (*P. subulata*), with lavender, purple, pink, or white flowers on low-growing plants with evergreen, needle-like leaves. For something a little different, try sand phlox (*P. bifida*) and Douglas' phlox (*P. douglasii*). All three of these perennials tolerate poor, dry soil.

PROBLEM SOLVED!

If you grow garden phlox, there's a good chance you'll have to deal with a funky fungal disease called powdery mildew—*unless* you start with one of the newer mildew-resistant cultivars. Try the white-flowered 'David', as well as 'Katherine', 'Pax', and 'Sandra' in shades of pink, then say good-bye to spraying forever!

Taller phlox for summer. Stately garden phlox (*P. paniculata*) is a charmer, but it needs staking and is prone to powdery mildew. For easy-care substitutes, consider disease-resistant Carolina phlox (*P. carolina*) and wild sweet William (*P. maculata*). Divide all of these every two or three years in fall or spring to keep 'em vigorous.

Just Say No to Seeds

Did you ever plant a white (or pink, or red) cultivar of garden phlox, only to end up with a bunch of purplish pink blooms after a few years? It's not that the original plant changed color; what you're seeing is the seedlings that have come up and crowded out the pretty parent plant. To keep those pesky seedlings from getting started, try this trick: Always cut off the spent flower heads after your plants are done blooming.

Poppies • *Papaver*

If you're looking for an exciting way to kick off the summer gardening season, you just can't beat the snap and crackle of poppies! The bowl- or cup-shaped blooms have silky petals that are crinkled just like crepe paper, and they come in a wide range of bright and pastel colors. Once the flowers fade, they're replaced by distinctive, rounded seed capsules that are very pretty in flower arrangements.

 GROW IT!

Full sun
Average to rich,
   evenly moist,
   well-drained soil
1 to 3 feet tall
Cool-weather
   annuals or hardy
   perennials (Zones
   2 to 8)

 PLANT IT!

Scatter seeds of annual poppies to fill in around newly planted perennials
Plant poppies in beds and borders with other late-spring and early-summer bloomers, including irises and bellflowers (*Campanula*)
Pair Oriental poppies (*P. orientale*) with later-blooming perennials that'll fill in after the poppies go dormant

Oriental poppy
Papaver orientale

 GETTING STARTED

To make sure you get the colors you want, buy Oriental poppies as plants; for other poppies, seeds are the best route. Sow the seeds directly in your garden several weeks before your last spring frost date, or in late summer or fall for flowers the following spring. Barely cover the seeds with soil, then keep 'em evenly moist until sprouts appear.

Do Not Disturb

Oriental poppies are happiest if they're left undisturbed, but they do spread some, so you'll probably want to divide them every five years or so. Dig 'em up in late summer to early fall, just as the new leaves appear. (Be sure to dig deeply, to get as many roots as possible.) Replant the most vigorous parts of the clumps, and compost the rest.

To the Rescue!

Unless your Oriental poppies already have bright orange blooms, make sure you cut off the seedpods before they turn brown. Otherwise, you'll end up with an abundance of orange-flowered seedlings, and they'll crowd out the other colors in no time at all!

Summer Solutions

Oriental poppies call for a bit of special planning, because their big leaves die back to the ground by midsummer. That'll leave a big hole in your border if you're not prepared! Here are a couple of terrific tips to help you handle this challenge:

Add annuals. Buy a few pots of your favorite annuals when they go on sale in early summer, then plant 'em as the poppy leaves die back.

Plan a cover-up. Plant a pretty summer- or fall-flowering perennial in front of the poppy clump to hide the bare spot.

Pair poppies with shrubs. Plant your poppies in front of low-spreading evergreens. When they're in bloom, the poppies'll really show up against the dark background, but when they're dormant, they'll just disappear.

FLOWER FUN!

Poppies sure are pretty in bouquets, but it's tough to get them to last for more than a day or two—*unless* you know my sure-fire secret to poppy longevity! First, cut the flowers just as the buds begin to open. Next, recut the stems, and dip the cut ends into an inch or two of boiling water for a few seconds, or else sear the ends with a match. Stand the flowers in cold water for several hours, then add 'em to your arrangement. They'll last up to a week this way—*guaranteed*!

Let 'Em Sow!

One of my favorite things about annual poppies—like corn poppy (*P. rhoeas*)—is how easy they are to grow: You just plant 'em, and forget 'em! Don't bother with removing the spent flowers, either; just let the seeds drop, and you'll have poppies every year without buying and sowing new seeds season after season.

Iceland poppy
Papaver nudicaule

I can't think of a better way to celebrate spring than with the bright blooms of primroses! These easy, early bloomers have flat-faced or trumpet-shaped flowers in a real rainbow of colors, and some are pleasingly perfumed, too. Let me tell you—that's a whole lot of flower power from one little perennial!

 ## GROW IT!

Partial shade
Rich, evenly moist soil
8 inches to 2 feet tall
In areas with warm summers, give 'em a spot that's shaded during the hottest part of the day
Hardy perennial (Zones 3 or 4 to 9)

 ## PLANT IT!

Primroses are superb for spring color in shade gardens
Plant 'em along mulched walkways to create a pretty primrose path
Perfect partners for early-spring bulbs, and for moisture-loving perennials, like hostas and ferns

English primrose
Primula vulgaris

 ## GETTING STARTED

Buy primrose plants in spring, or grow 'em yourself from seeds. Simply sow seeds in pots in fall or early spring, then set the pots in a cold frame or a protected location outdoors.

Everything's Coming Up Primroses

I'll let you in on a little secret, folks: The hardest part of growing primroses is deciding which ones you like best! Here are a few of my favorites for early to midspring bloom:

❀ **Cowslip primrose** (*P. veris*): Sweet-scented, yellow flowers. Zones 4 to 8.

❀ **English primrose** (*P. vulgaris*): Many colors. Zones 4 to 8.

❀ **Polyanthus primrose** (*P.* Polyanthus Group): Many colors. Most are hardy in Zones 3 to 8.

GARDEN SMARTS

Are your primroses looking a little peaked? If so, they probably need to be divided. Dig 'em up just after the flowers fade, replant the divisions, and water 'em regularly for several weeks until they're settled in again.

Red-Hot Pokers • *Kniphofia*

Once you see these no-fuss perennials in full flower, you'll know right away how they got their name! As soon as the weather heats up, red-hot pokers produce tall, spiky, tropical-looking blooms in a range of summer-bright colors.

Red-hot poker
Kniphofia

GROW IT!

Full sun
Average to rich, moist,
    well-drained soil
1 to 4 feet tall
Hardy perennials
    (Zones 5 to 9)

PLANT IT!

Enjoy red-hot pokers as eye-catching
    accents in summer beds and borders
Perfect partners for perennials with
    flat or trumpet-shaped flowers, like
    yarrows (*Achillea*) and daylilies
    (*Hemerocallis*)

GETTING STARTED

Add red-hot pokers to your garden by buying plants in spring. Make sure you give 'em a site that's well drained, especially in winter. Nothing'll kill a red-hot poker faster than soggy soil!

Color Choices

Red-hot pokers are some of the longest-lived, easiest-care perennials you'll ever find. Since you'll be enjoying 'em for many years, it makes sense to start with the very best cultivars available. Choosing a few that flower at different times helps spread out the bloom season, too! Here's the best of the bunch:

'Earliest of All': Coral-rose blooms in early summer.

'Little Maid': Pale yellow blooms on compact plants from late summer to fall.

'Primrose Beauty': Yellow blooms from early summer to fall.

'Royal Standard': Scarlet buds opening into yellow flowers from mid- to late summer.

Jerry's TIMELY TIPS

"If you just want to share a piece of red-hot poker with a friend, don't bother digging up the whole clump. Simply push back the grassy leaves, and look for a small, rooted plant that you can cut off the outside of the clump."

Rhododendrons and Azaleas • *Rhododendron*

I can sum up the big, beautiful blooms of rhododendrons and azaleas for you in two words: *simply spectacular!* They come in an amazing array of colors, including white, pink, lavender, violet-blue, yellow, orange, and red. With so much to offer, these super flowering shrubs earn a place of honor in any flower garden!

 GROW IT!

Partial shade
Rich, moist,
    well-drained acid soil
1 to 12 or more feet tall
Hardy shrubs
    (Zones 5 or 6 to 8)

 PLANT IT!

Grow 'em in groups for a show-
    stopping display of color in spring
Plant under trees for color and year-
    round screening in shady sites
Grow shade-loving perennials under
    rhododendrons and azaleas for
    all-season interest

 GETTING STARTED

Shop for rhododendrons and azaleas at your favorite local nursery, so you can see them for yourself and choose the colors you like best. Spring and early fall are the ideal times to buy and plant potted clumps, but actually, you can set 'em out any time during the growing season; just be prepared to water during dry spells. If you buy balled-and-burlapped plants instead, late summer is the best time to get 'em in the ground.

Flame azalea
*Rhododendron
calendulaceum*

Get the Site Right

Give your rhododendrons and azaleas the right site, and you're in for a treat; give 'em a site that's hot, dry, soggy, or alkaline, and you'll be mighty disappointed. A lightly shaded site with loose, humus-rich soil that's neither bone-dry nor sopping wet is just perfect. Acid soil is a must—pH 4.5 to

As far as gardeners are concerned, rhododendrons and azaleas are different plants. But botanists see things otherwise, and they've lumped all of these great garden plants into one genus: *Rhododendron*. Don't worry about the distinctions between the two—just plant the ones you like. The differences are subtle anyway: **Rhododendrons** have 10 or more stamens, bell-shaped flowers, and leaves that are usually evergreen, while **azaleas** typically have five stamens, funnel-shaped flowers, and deciduous leaves.

Jerry's TIMELY TIPS

"Psst! Wanna know the secret to getting an eye-popping show from your rhododendrons and azaleas year after year? Grow as many different kinds as you can! Sure, masses of just one or two different cultivars may flower in a blaze of glory in good years, but if the weather is bad or a late freeze occurs, you can lose all of that year's blooms in a single night. A mix of different cultivars guarantees you'll have plenty of blooms from early spring right into summer—plus, you won't miss a whole bloomin' show due to bad weather!"

6.5—so start with a soil test.

What if you're not lucky enough to *start* with ideal conditions? Well, then, *make* them! In wet-soil sites, build raised beds to elevate the roots above the muck. And in dry sites, work plenty of compost into the soil before planting, and keep plants well mulched with pine needles or chopped leaves after planting.

Walnut Woes

If you have black walnut trees (*Juglans nigra*) in your yard, growing rhododendrons and azaleas is definitely a problem. That's because walnuts produce a substance called juglone in their roots, and it kills some kinds of plants, including—you guessed it—rhododendrons and azaleas! So whatever you do, keep these plants well away from walnuts—at least 50 feet, and farther if possible.

The Foundation of Success

Planting rhododendrons and azaleas right against the foundation of your house is one of the worst things you can do to them. The soil tends to be dust-dry there, and it's often alkaline, too. The plants may survive in these tough conditions, but they'll look spindly and yellowish, and they'll be a magnet for pest and disease problems. So what's a body to do if you've got rhodies and azaleas that're

Rosebay rhododendron
Rhododendron maximum

suffering in this kind of site? Here are three handy hints to help you set things right:

❁ If possible, move the plants to shade. Or, bring the shade to the plants by planting a small tree near the house.

❁ Install soaker hoses, so it's easy to give the shrubs a thorough watering about once a week through the summer.

❁ Keep the soil (and soaker hoses) covered with a 3-inch layer of mulch—ideally, a mix of compost and shredded bark or chopped leaves.

Catawba rhododendron
Rhododendron catawbiense

Cold Hardy Choices

Don't despair if you live in Zones 3 and 4, where winters are too cold to grow most azaleas. Get your hands on some of the Northern Lights cultivars, which were developed by the University of Minnesota! These rugged rhodie relatives are generally hardy to -40°F, and they bear fragrant flowers on 6- to 7-foot-tall plants. Cultivars include 'Apricot Surprise', 'Golden Lights', 'Northern Hilights', 'Rosy Lights', and 'Spicy Lights'.

PROBLEM SOLVED!

Wondering what's bugging your rhododendrons and azaleas? Here's the scoop on the two most likely culprits:

• **Lace bugs** cause mottled leaves with black flecks—turn a leaf over to look for the tiny bugs. Azaleas that are stressed out from too much sun are like magnets to these pesky pests. For a quick fix, spray with insecticidal soap; to prevent future problems, move the plants to a shady site.

• **Black vine weevils** chew notches along the edges of rhododendron leaves. While the adults are chewing up the leaf edges, the larvae are feeding on the roots. Spray weekly with pyrethrin several times to send these pests packing. To get rid of the larvae, drench the soil with a solution of parasitic nematodes (available at your local garden center).

FLOWER FUN!

For fabulous cut flowers, pick your rhododendrons when no more than half of the flowers in a cluster are open. Submerge the entire cluster in water for an hour or two, then split the stems at the base with a knife. Keep the blooms in cold water overnight, or until you're ready to arrange 'em.

Everything Old Is New Again

If you've got huge, overgrown rhododendrons you hate, don't just live with them that way; give 'em some tough love! In early spring, cut all the stems back to about 1 foot, then keep the plants well watered during the summer. Don't want to gamble with your plant? Before you prune, look for small shoots near the base of the shrub. Plants that have new growth there—on old wood—usually survive severe pruning just fine. If you don't see any, try cutting back a branch or two without chopping down the entire plant. Then, if new shoots form, you can whack back the rest of the stems the following spring!

Java Jolt

Want to give your rhodies and azaleas a real treat? Then do what I do: Each time you brew a pot of coffee, dump the grounds around your shrubs, and scratch 'em into the soil. Besides adding a small but steady supply of nutrients, coffee grounds help make the soil more acidic—and that's just what azaleas and rhododendrons love!

Swamp azalea
Rhododendron viscosum

Roses • *Rosa*

Roses aren't just for rose gardens anymore! And there's no law that says you need to keep these beauties stuck off in a corner bed by themselves. So get 'em out front and center in your garden, and let 'em mingle with your other flowers. When roses are in their glory, your beds and borders will look as pretty as a postcard, and once they're done, the annuals and perennials will still be there to carry the show!

Sweetbrier rose
Rosa eglanteria

GROW IT!

Full sun
Rich, loose,
 well-drained soil
1 to 12 or more
 feet tall
Perennial shrubs
 (Zones 2 to 9)

PLANT IT!

Pair 'em with low-growing perennials,
 such as lavender, catmints (*Nepeta*),
 and feverfew (*Tanacetum parthenium*)
Low-growing roses make great groundcovers
Enjoy shrub-type roses at the back of a
 border, or as a fabulous flowering hedge
Of course, roses are top-notch cut
 flowers, too!

GETTING STARTED

You've got plenty of options when it comes to buying roses! Bare-root roses—dormant plants with no visible leafy growth—are sold in stores in bags or boxes, or shipped from mail-order nurseries with moist packing material around their roots. They're normally sold or shipped at the perfect planting time in your area—mid- to late fall, or very early spring. When you get these babies home, immediately take 'em out of their packaging, then plunk the roots in a bucket of warm water or my Rose Rousin' Elixir overnight to get them juiced up again. Get 'em in the ground as soon as you can—ideally, within a day or two after you get 'em. Timing is less critical when you're dealing with potted roses; you can plant these any time the ground's not frozen.

FLOWER POWER TONICS

Rose Rousin' Elixir

To get bare-root roses off to a rip-roarin' start, give 'em a taste of this magical mixer before you plant.

**1 tbsp. of 5-8-5 or 5-10-5
 garden fertilizer
1 tbsp. of baby shampoo
1 tbsp. of corn syrup
1 gal. of warm water**

Mix these ingredients together in a bucket, and soak the roots in the solution overnight. When you're done, sprinkle this mixture around all your other rosebushes, too—they'll love you for it! ✿

Soggy sites and hard, heavy clay can be real drags when you want to grow roses. Don't waste your weekends digging and tilling to get poor soil in better shape; instead, build a few raised beds! Fill 'em with a mix of good-quality topsoil and compost, and in return for just a few hours work, you'll enjoy a lifetime of happy, healthy roses.

The Bare Facts

Whenever I have a choice between bare-root and container-grown roses, I always go for the bare-root ones, and I'll tell you why. In my experience, they just seem to settle in quicker than their potted counterparts. And, I'd rather buy them from a mail-order nursery than a local source, because then I know the roots haven't been chopped to fit into a tiny bag or box to fit on a display shelf.

In fact, the only downside to bare-root roses is having to plant them when the weather's pretty chilly—usually late fall or very early spring. But I've found an easy way to get around that: by getting the beds ready well in advance! Pick a nice day in early fall, and decide where you're going to plant, then dig the holes and get the soil all ready for your roses. When they finally arrive, it'll take just a few minutes to get 'em snug in their beds, and they'll be rarin' to grow when the warm weather returns!

Hybrid tea rose
Rosa hybrid

Windy Warning

What do roses and real estate have in common? It's all about *location, location, location!* Planting roses in an open, airy site will go a long way toward keeping dastardly diseases from getting a foothold. But you don't want 'em exposed to strong *northwest* winds, 'cause these chilly breezes can dry out the canes in a flash during rough winter weather. So what's the answer? A south- or east-facing site, with some sort of shelter or windbreak to the northwest side, is the perfect spot for growing great roses!

Rosy Thoughts

There's no getting around it, folks—if you want great-looking roses, it'll take a bit of effort on your part, in the form of fertilizing, watering, pruning, and pest control. Fortunately, not all roses are garden prima donnas; in fact, a fair number of them'll do just fine with the same good care you give other garden shrubs! So if you don't want to be a slave to your garden, look for these easy-care roses when you're adding new bushes to your borders:

English roses: Full, fragrant flowers that look like old roses, but rebloom like modern ones.

Canadian roses: Super-hardy cultivars (most to Zone 3; some even to Zone 2) with good to excellent disease resistance.

Modern shrub roses: A catchall category of sturdy plants with abundant flowers and attractive shapes; they do fine with minimal pruning.

Polyantha roses: Tough, disease-resistant, easy-to-grow roses with large clusters of small flowers borne in flushes from spring through fall. Pink-flowered 'The Fairy' is one of the best.

Rugosa roses: Rugged, disease-resistant roses with showy, fragrant flowers through the summer—and showy red fruits, too!

Jerry's TIMELY TIPS

"Most times, the roses you buy will be grafted plants— the top growth of a desirable rose growing on the roots of another rose. You can tell when you look at the base of the plant, 'cause grafted roses have a knobby-looking area just above the roots. It's important to know where the graft union is, since it'll tell you how deep to set the plant in the ground. In the North (Zone 6 and colder), set the graft union 3 inches below the soil surface. In the South, set it 1½ inches above the soil line."

Roses, continued

FLOWER POWER TONICS

Rosy Feeding Regime

Believe you me, roses are the hardest-working flowering plants in your garden. These beauties bloom only for the sake of showing off, as much as they can, for as long as they can. All this hard work takes lots of energy—and that's where you come in! Follow this simple feeding routine, and your roses will have all the food they need to keep those blooms comin' along! Start with a dose of this elixir in mid- to late spring.

4 cups of bonemeal
1 cup of 5-10-5 garden fertilizer
1 cup of Epsom salts

Mix these ingredients together in a bucket, then give each bush 1 heaping tablespoon, or work in 4 pounds per 100 square feet of rose bed. Then every three weeks after that, give 'em a drink of this terrific tonic.

1 cup of beer
2 tsp. of instant tea granules
1 tsp. of 5-10-5 fertilizer
1 tsp. of fish emulsion
1 tsp. of hydrogen peroxide
1 tsp. of liquid dish soap
2 gal. of warm water

Mix the ingredients together, then water each plant with 1 pint of the solution in the morning. Stop feeding by July 15 in the North, and August 15 in the South. ❋

Out on Their Own

Hey, cold-climate rose lovers—have I got a tip for you! Whenever you can, buy roses that are grown from cuttings (called *own-root* roses), instead of grafted ones. It may take a bit of searching, but I promise it'll be worth it! You see, if cold winter weather kills the top of a grafted rose, any new shoots you get will be from the roots, not the desirable top growth you chose the rose for. But if an own-root rose dies back, the new shoots will be the same rose you started with! And here's a bonus tip: Set the crown of own-root roses (the point where the roots and stems join) 1 inch below the soil surface to give it extra protection from severe winter weather.

Rose Pruning 101

When it comes to pruning roses, knowing what to cut and what to leave can be a really thorny problem! To de-stress the pruning process, I've simplified it into four easy steps for you. So read on, and find out how easy rose pruning can be:

Step 1: First, cut out any dead and damaged wood. You can tell the health of canes by their color: green, light brown, or gray canes are alive, while black or dark brown canes are dead. Cut dead and dying canes back to healthy wood (where the center of the cane is white) if you can; if not, cut them off right at ground level.

Step 2: Remove crossing or rubbing canes. Repeated rubbing can cause disease-drawing wounds on both stems, so prevent the problem by cutting out and removing the smaller of the two canes.

Step 3: Prune spindly or weak branches. Scrawny stems won't bloom well, so there's no point in keeping them. For large roses, such as Hybrid Teas, this means shoots thinner than a pencil.

Step 4: On established roses, remove a few older canes. Cutting out up to a third of the oldest stems each year will encourage vigorous—and free-flowering—new growth to form.

PENNY WISE

Are your roses looking a little run-down? Don't worry; there's a quick-and-easy cure, and it's as close as your local drug-store! Epsom salts are prefect for perking up tired, spindly rosebushes, and all for just pennies per plant. Simply rake the mulch away from around your roses in early spring, then sprinkle two or three tablespoons around each bush, out toward the tips of the branches. Scratch the Epsom salts lightly into the soil, then put the mulch back. You'll notice a big difference in just a few weeks!

The Kindest Cut

On roses, knowing *how* to make a good pruning cut is just as important as knowing *where* to make it! So do what the pros do: Always cut just above a bud, and slope the cut at a 45° angle *away* from the bud. (This directs water away from the bud and prevents rotting.) Cutting above a bud that faces toward the outside of the bush is

Cut blooms with short stems to leave plenty of leaves on the bush!

usually the best idea, but if the center of your bush has a big gap, cut above a bud that faces that way, in the direction you'd like to have a new stem form. And don't forget this bonus tip: A touch of fingernail polish or white craft glue on new cuts prevents bothersome borers from chewing into the cut cane ends.

Prudent Pruning

To keep your Hybrid Tea and Grandiflora roses healthy and full of flowers, heavy pruning is the key. Each spring, cut off all but three to six of the youngest, healthiest canes. In the North, cut the remaining canes back to 12 to 14 inches; in the South, leave them 18 to 24 inches tall. Floribunda and Polyantha roses do better if you leave a few more stems, so I suggest keeping six to eight of the youngest canes; then prune as you would for Hybrid Teas.

GRANDMA PUTT'S
Handy Hints

Want to get twice the flower power from your rose? Then try this trick I learned from Grandma Putt: Plant a clematis next to it! The clematis will climb up and over the rose, so it'll look like the rose has two different kinds of flowers. You can pair a clematis and a rose that bloom at the same time for one spectacular show, or choose ones that flower at different times to extend the show. Sturdy shrub roses make the best supports, while smaller clematis (those that mature at 8 to 10 feet tall) are the best choice for climbers.

Bloom Once? Prune Once!

Deciding when to prune once-blooming roses is a no-brainer—simply trim them as soon as their flowers fade. In early to midsummer, prune out one or two of the oldest canes to make room for vigorous new growth. Then cut off the top third of each remaining cane, and snip side shoots by up to two-thirds. (If the roses you're growing produce pretty "hips," hold off on pruning the side shoots until late winter or early spring, so you can admire the fruits through the off-season.)

American beauty
Rosa 'American Beauty'

Tiny, But Tough

When it comes to roses, bigger isn't always better! Sure, I love the large flowers of Hybrid Teas, but when I want *lots* of color for beds and borders, miniature roses are at the top of my list. You might think I'm talking about tiny rosebushes, but actually, "miniature" refers to the size of the flowers, not the plants. Mini rosebushes can be anywhere from 6 inches to 6 feet tall, but most fall into the 1- to 2-foot-tall category—just right for planting near the front of a flower garden among annuals, perennials, and bulbs. Monthly feedings, plus a heavy pruning in spring and a light shearing in midsummer, are the secret to keeping your minis making more blooms all season long. Spraying for powdery mildew and blackspot is a good idea, too.

No Moo Mildew

Tired of powdery mildew on your roses— you know, those dirty white spots that start on the leaves and spread to the whole plant? I've got an amazing secret weapon for you, and it's as close as your refrigerator! Simply stir up a 50-50 mix of milk and water, then spray away; once a week is about right. Sounds too good to be true, I know, but it really works!

Jerry's TIMELY TIPS

"The best time to prune most roses? Late winter or early spring—just as some of the buds on the largest canes are beginning to swell, but before the plants are sending out shoots and leaves. One exception is roses that bloom once in late spring to summer—this includes many old roses, and some shrub roses. If you prune these roses in spring, you'll cut off all of this year's blossoms! So wait until after flowering to prune these one-time-only bloomers."

Little gem
Rosa 'Little Gem'

Rose Disease Wrap-Up

Roses are notorious for being disease magnets, but you don't have to be a slave to your sprayer if you know how to keep diseases at bay right from the start. Here's my four-step solution to keeping rose woes to a minimum:

Step 1: Start with disease-resistant plants, and give 'em the best possible site: well-drained soil, full sun, and plenty of good air circulation.

Step 2: Keep leaves dry when you water. Soaker hoses wet the soil, not the plants, so they're a much smarter irrigation option than sprinklers.

Step 3: If you see only one or two diseased leaves, pick them off and destroy them; that way, you might stop the problem before it starts. But if the fungi have gotten a head start on you, don't wait to spray; get out there as soon as possible to stop the spores from spreading to still-healthy shoots.

Step 4: At the end of the growing season, give your rose beds a thorough clean-up: Rake up all the dropped leaves, so the fungi don't have a place to hang out over the winter.

To the Rescue!

When extra-vigorous canes shoot up from grafted roses, take a close look at 'em. Root suckers usually have leaves and thorns that look different from the grafted part of a plant, along with slender, more arching canes. They'll also have different flowers. To keep these suckers from taking over, you need to get rid of 'em, *pronto!* Dig next to the plant to see where they're attached, then pull or snap them off by hand. If you can't find where the sucker is attached, cut it off as deeply as possible. And never cut off root suckers right at the soil line—this simply encourages 'em to grow right back!

Put Your Roses to Bed...

For the winter, that is! To get 'em in the mood for a long winter's nap, stop removing spent flowers in late summer or early fall, three to five weeks before the first frost in your area. Also, stop fertilizing after midsummer, but keep on watering, so your plants don't go to bed thirsty.

If you live where winter temperatures dip below 0°F (Zone 6 and north), it's a good idea to protect Hybrid Teas, Grandifloras, Floribundas, and most English roses. Once the ground has frozen, pile shredded bark, soil, or compost over the base of the stems, in an 8- to 12-inch-tall mound. Remove the mound in early spring, so new shoots can emerge.

Gone, But Not Forgotten

If you've had a rosebush die, you know how tempting it is to rush right out and buy another one to fill that very same spot. But planting a new rose in a dead rose's grave isn't a good idea. Why? Diseases, insects, or other problems in that spot probably will attack the new plant just like they did the old one. So sure, go out and buy a new plant to replace the one you lost, but look for a brand-new spot to plant it in!

Tea Suits 'Em to a "T"!

When Grandma Putt wanted to give her roses a post-pruning pick-me-up, she'd tuck used tea bags into the mulch around

---

FLOWER POWER TONICS

Mildew Relief Elixir

If you've had problems with powdery mildew on your roses, try this tonic to keep it from spoiling your fun again this year.

1 tbsp. of baby shampoo
1 tbsp. of hydrogen peroxide
1 tsp. of instant tea granules
2 cups of water

Mix all of these ingredients in a hand-held mist sprayer and apply to rose leaves, stems, and buds. Midafternoon on a cloudy day is the best time to apply it. ✻

Roses, continued

Roses and other pretty petals are perfect for making garden gifts.

the base of her bushes. The tannic acid in the tea made the soil slightly acidic, which made her roses pleased as punch!

Roses with A-Peel

If you want the best-looking and most trouble-free roses in your neighborhood, do what Grandma Putt did: Work banana skins, or whole, rotten bananas, into the soil near the base of your bushes. The potassium in their skins gives 'em a power-packed snack that'll help the plants fend off pests and diseases, plus deliver boatloads of beautiful blossoms!

How Dry I Am!

What's the trick to drying rose petals so they keep their color and scent? Start with the best petals, and then get 'em dry lickety-split. Pick blooms when they are just fully open; avoid ones that have been open for several days, or that have started to brown around the edges. Gather 'em in late morning, after the dew has dried, then separate the petals and spread them out on old window screens in a warm, dry, dark spot.

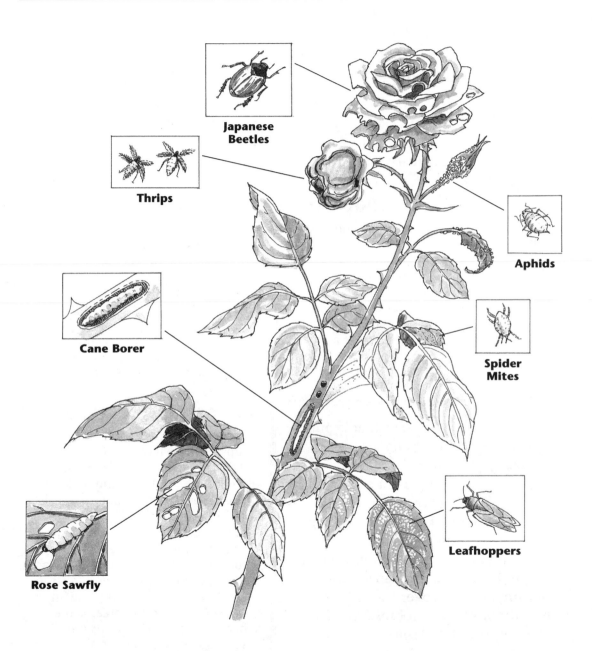

Japanese Beetles

Thrips

Cane Borer

Rose Sawfly

Aphids

Spider Mites

Leafhoppers

Rose growers: Know your enemies, so you're ready to take action, if needed!

Rudbeckias • *Rudbeckia*

Three-lobed coneflower

Rudbeckia triloba

Call 'em what you will—orange coneflowers, black-eyed Susans, or rudbeckias—you're guaranteed to get your money's worth out of these tough-as-nails beauties! The bright, daisy-like blooms of these native American wildflowers have black or brown centers, and petals in shades of yellow to yellow-orange. Gloriosa daisies, which are rudbeckias, too, come in shades from yellow to red-brown and rusty orange.

 GROW IT!

Full sun to light shade
Average to rich, well-drained soil
1 to 9 feet tall
Evenly moist soil is ideal, but plants tolerate drought once established
Cool-weather annuals, biennials, or perennials (Zones 3 to 9)

 PLANT IT!

Super for summer color in sunny beds and borders
Combine rudbeckias with ornamental grasses for a casual, country look
Perfect partners for other bright bloomers, including purple coneflowers (*Echinacea purpurea*), daylilies (*Hemerocallis*), and yarrows (*Achillea*)

 Who says that groundcovers have to be green and boring? If you've got a sunny space to fill, you can't do better than a big batch of orange coneflower (*R. fulgida*), including its popular cultivar, 'Goldsturm'. Set the plants 12 to 18 inches apart, and in no time, they'll cover the area in a bounty of golden blooms from midsummer into fall. *Wow!*

 GETTING STARTED

Pick up a few plants in spring, or grow your own from seed; either way, it's super-easy! Sow gloriosa daisies (*R. hirta*) in spring, either indoors, several weeks before the last spring frost date, or directly in your garden, two weeks before the last spring frost date. Sow the other rudbeckias in your garden in spring or fall, or plant the seeds in pots in early spring or fall, and set them outdoors in a protected area. Remember: Press rudbeckia seeds into the soil surface, but *don't* cover 'em up, 'cause they need light to sprout!

Reach for the Sky

Most rudbeckias grow anywhere from knee- to waist-high, but there's one kind that you sure won't look down on: giant coneflower (*R. maxima*). This towering perennial produces handsome clumps of smooth, gray-green leaves, then rockets upward in summer, with 6- to 9-foot-tall flower stems topped in brown-centered, orange-yellow blooms. It's sure to grab your attention, no matter where you plant it!

Glorious Gloriosas

Rudbeckias, as a group, are some of the best bloomers around, but for pure flower power, gloriosa daisies have to be the winners, hands down! These biennials or short-lived perennials positively bloom their heads off from midsummer to fall, with 3- to 6-inch-wide flowers in rich combinations of yellow, gold, maroon-brown, and bronze. In fact, they bloom so much that they can even wear themselves out after only a season or two. If you want the biggest flowers on the block, start new plants from seeds each spring. Or just let the flowers go to seed, then look out for self-sown seedlings the following spring.

Jerry's TIMELY TIPS

"It's tough to imagine plants that need less coddling than rudbeckias! These sturdy garden stars stand tall without staking, and they also don't need dividing regularly. But if your plants do get overgrown, simply dig 'em up and divide 'em in spring or fall."

They're for the Birds!

Sure, rudbeckias are beautiful, but they're more than just pretty faces: They're a must-have if you want to attract birds to your backyard! Their seeds are a favorite food of goldfinches and purple finches, as well as chickadees, cardinals, sparrows, and nuthatches. Just remember to spare the clippers when you're cleaning up around your rudbeckias in the fall; if you get too tidy and cut off the brown cones, you're taking away all those seeds, too!

Pretty flowers, fragrant leaves, and tasty shoots, too—sages have it all! These versatile plants bloom in every color of the rainbow, so there's sure to be at least one you'll love. What are you waiting for? It's time to get growing with sages!

Scarlet sage
Salvia splendens

 GROW IT!

Full sun or very light shade
Average, well-drained,
    evenly moist soil
1½ to 4 feet tall
Most sages are tough
    and drought tolerant
    once established
Warm-weather annuals, tender
    perennials, or hardy perennials (Zones 3 to 10)

 PLANT IT!

Grow sages in herb gardens
    or sunny beds and borders
    with annuals and perennials
Mix 'em with rudbeckias,
    daylilies (*Hemerocallis*),
    yarrows (*Achillea*), and other
    showy summer flowers
Sages make super container
    plants, too!

 GETTING STARTED

It's a snap to start many sages right at home; simply sow the seeds indoors six to eight weeks before your last spring frost date. Press the seeds onto the soil surface, but don't cover them up; light is a must for quick sprouting! If you only need a few plants, or if you want particular colors of perennial sages, then pick up cell-pack or potted plants at your local garden center in spring.

GRANDMA PUTT'S
Handy Hints

Every summer, Grandma Putt made sure she planted plenty of sages in her garden. But it wasn't just because she liked to look at the flowers; she knew that they were like candy to any hummingbirds and butterflies in the area!

Cut and Come Again

Sure, you can buy new annual and tender perennial sages every year, but why spend the dough? You won't believe how easy it is to keep your favorites from year to year! Simply take cuttings in late summer to early fall, or dig entire plants and pot 'em up. Keep your sages in a sunny, cool spot over the winter, then plant 'em out in the garden in spring once there's no chance of frost. Wait 'til you see how well these older plants bloom—they'll outflower first-year sages by a mile!

Picture-Perfect Perennials

When it comes to keeping perennial sages at their peak, you have two choices: You can pinch, or you can chop! Pinching off the spent bloom clusters just above a new bud will keep your plants producing new spikes. Do this every few days, and your sages will keep flowering for weeks longer than they normally would. If you'd rather get the job done in one fell swoop, simply chop all the stems down to ground level right after the first flush of bloom is done. Within a few weeks, you'll have a tidy new clump of foliage to enjoy for the rest of the season—and *maybe* another round of flowers, too!

PROBLEM SOLVED!

If your sage plants sprawl, there's a good chance you're being too nice to them. Overly rich soil leads to lush growth that tends to flop; plus, you're likely to get more leaves than flowers. So save your compost to make a nice bed for your other annuals, and hold off on the fertilizer, too. Your sages'll thank you!

Sage Advice

Some snooty gardeners may look down on scarlet sage (*S. splendens*) as too common, but not me! When it comes to flowers, I say, the brighter, the better! But even if shocking scarlet just doesn't work for your color scheme, you can still enjoy the spiky blooms of this dependable annual. Thanks to busy plant breeders, scarlet sage now comes in a whole host of colors, including purple, pink, salmon, burgundy, lavender, and creamy white. The red-flowered ones'll take as much sun as you can give 'em; the other colors seem to do better with a little bit of shade.

Scabiosas • *Scabiosa*

Scabiosas—also known as pincushion flowers—were mighty popular back in Grandma Putt's day, and nowadays, they're better than ever! So, if you're looking for something a little different than the standard flower garden fare of marigolds and geraniums, give scabiosas a try—you'll be glad you did.

Pincushion flower

Scabiosa

GROW IT!

Full sun
Average, well-drained soil
1½ to 3 feet tall
Neutral to slightly alkaline pH is best
Warm-weather annuals or hardy perennials (Zones 3 to 9)

PLANT IT!

Scabiosas are beautiful in mixed beds and borders—and casual cottage gardens, too!
The flowers are favorites with both hummingbirds and butterflies
The seedheads of star flower (*S. stellata*) are eye-catching in dried arrangements

GETTING STARTED

It can be tough to find transplants of annual scabiosas for sale, so you're best off growing your own. Sow the seeds indoors a few weeks before your last frost date, or sow directly in your garden after all danger of frost has passed. Most garden centers carry the perennial kinds as plants, so you don't need to bother with seed for these; buy the kinds and colors you want in spring.

What's the trick to keeping scabiosas bloomin' their hearts out? Keep the spent flowers pinched off, and the plants'll keep makin' new blooms all summer long!

SOS—Save Our Scabiosas!

Are you having trouble with your perennial scabiosas disappearing after only a year or two? The solution is simple: Improve the drainage before you replant! Scabiosas are generally tough and trouble-free, but the one thing they can't stand is soggy soil, especially in winter. So if your soil tends to be on the heavy (clay) side, dig deep to loosen the soil before planting, and work a shovelful of compost into the hole, too. Or grow 'em in raised beds, instead.

Sedums • *Sedum*

To sedum is to love 'em! Okay, maybe that's a little corny, but seriously, folks—what's *not* to love about sedums? These tough-as-nails perennials shrug off heat and drought, and they're about as low-maintenance as you can get. Best of all, they come in a wide range of heights and habits, from mat-forming evergreen groundcovers to mounding perennials. If you've got a sunny site, there's sure to be a super sedum that's just perfect for it!

 GROW IT!

Full sun
Average to rich,
    well-drained soil
2 to 30 inches tall
Sedums also grow
    in poor, dry soil
Hardy perennials
    (Zones 3 to 9)

 PLANT IT!

Low-growing sedums make great
    groundcovers and edgings
Grow clump-forming sedums in beds
    and borders for summer and fall color
Pair 'em with other drought-tolerant
    perennials, like rudbeckias and
    ornamental grasses
They're perfect perennials for
    beginning gardeners!

Showy sedum
Sedum spectabile

 GETTING STARTED

Shop for sedum plants at your local garden center; you'll be amazed at the wide variety you have to choose from! Spring and fall are the best planting times, but you can plant in summer, too; just plan to water them every few days during dry spells that first year.

Creepy Carpeters

Need to get some ground covered in a jiffy? Two low-growing sedums spread too much for the polite society of flowerbeds, but are perfect for filling up tough, dry sites:

Gold moss sedum (*S. acre*). This speed-demon of a creeper has long, trailing stems clad in tiny, evergreen leaves. It forms ground-hugging carpets that are spangled with starry, yellow-green flowers in summer.

Two-row sedum (*S. spurium*). Clusters of starry, pinkish-purple or white flowers show up in late summer, but mostly, you'll grow this sedum for its good-looking, evergreen leaves. 'Dragon's Blood', with purple-tinted leaves and dark pink flowers, is especially popular. Also look for 'Tricolor', with pink-, white-, and green-striped leaves.

Joy for All Seasons

I'll be honest, folks: I've never met a sedum I didn't like. But if you asked me to tell you the best of the bunch, it'd be easy: The cultivar called 'Autumn Joy' is my favorite by far! This trouble-free trouper looks great for just about 11 months of the year. The fun starts with the fresh new foliage in spring and broccoli-like flower buds in summer; by fall, those buds open into dark pink blooms in clusters up to an amazing 8 inches across! As the season draws to a close, the flower heads age to bronze, then hold their shape all through the winter. What's your role in helping this spectacular show along? Just cut the stems down in late winter or early spring. You can't get much easier than that!

Jerry's TIMELY TIPS

"If there's one thing all sedums hate, it's wet feet. Soil that's too wet causes the crowns and roots to rot, and eventually kills the plants. So if you want to have success with sedums, be sure to give 'em a site where they'll stay high and dry!"

Divide and Conquer

Growing sedums is kind of like eating potato chips: You can't have just one! But you don't have to go broke in the process—buy only one or two plants of each kind you can find, then plan on propagating them. Sedums are a snap to divide in spring or fall, and you can't fail with cuttings taken any time the plants aren't flowering. (Just make sure you give the cuttings a well-drained rooting medium, like a 50-50 mix of perlite and vermiculite.) And creeping sedums are the easiest—simply pull up pieces with your fingers and pat 'em down in a new spot of loosened soil—no tools needed!

Shrubs

I know what you're thinking, folks—why am I talking about shrubs in a book about flower gardening? Well, when you think about it, some of our best-loved flowers—including roses, lilacs, hydrangeas, and forsythias—actually are shrubs! These versatile plants can look great in all parts of your yard: along the foundation of your house, as hedges and screens, as accent plants, and as partners for annuals and perennials. Shrubs can make flowers like crazy, create private places to sit, shield you from wind, and attract birds to your garden. So, what are you waiting for? Let's get growing with shrubs!

Weigela
Weigela rosea

Shrub Planting—The Next Generation

Here's a news flash, friends: *Forget everything you know about planting shrubs.* There's a new way to do it, and you'll be *amazed* at how much easier it is! No more lugging bales of peat moss or hauling compost to the planting hole; keep these goodies for fixing up your flowerbeds, and keep 'em *away* from your shrubs!

You see, experts have found it's not a good idea to dig a deep hole, then set the plant in soil that's been mixed with organic matter and fertilizer. Why? When you make a nice, loose, rich bed for your shrubs, they don't want to send their roots out into the harder, less-fertile soil outside the hole. Instead, the roots'll keep windin' around and around to stay in the hole, just as if they

PROBLEM SOLVED!

Whoa, partner! Before you set that new shrub in its hole, take a good, hard look at the roots. If you see any that are circling around the outside of the root ball, slice 'em with a sharp knife. Or, if all you see is a solid mass of roots, use that knife to make three or four cuts from top to bottom around the root ball, about a half-inch deep. Then use your fingers to work loose some of the root tips, too, just before you set the root ball in the planting hole. It sounds pretty rough and tumble, but trust me—your shrubs'll thank you!

were growin' in a pot.

So what's the solution? Go ahead and dig a big hole, but don't make it *deep;* make it *wide!* It should be only as deep as the root ball of the shrub you're planting, but three times the width. Loosen the soil on the sides of the hole, too. Set the root ball in the middle of the hole, then refill the hole with the soil you took out—and don't add any compost, peat moss, or fertilizer!

Three Steps to Shrub Success

While it doesn't pay to pamper shrubs when you're makin' their bed, it's good green-thumb sense to give 'em some TLC *after* you get 'em in the ground. Just follow these three easy steps:

Step 1: First, use the leftover soil to form a raised ring around the edge of the planting hole. That'll make a basin that directs water down to the roots, instead of lettin' it run off.

Step 2: Using a gentle flow from a hose or watering can, fill the basin two or three times with water to give the roots a real thorough soaking.

Step 3: Finally, finish up by covering the soil with a 2-inch layer of mulch, such as shredded bark or chopped leaves, to keep the soil moist and those wicked weeds at bay.

Do Your Level Best

When you set out a shrub (or *any* plant, for that matter), always make sure you're planting it at the same depth it was growing in the pot. Sure, it

FLOWER POWER TONICS

Super Shrub Stimulator

Want to get your shrubs off to a rip-roarin' start in spring? Give 'em a taste of this excellent elixir!

4 tbsp. of instant tea granules
4 tbsp. of bourbon, or ½ can of beer
2 tbsp. of liquid dish soap
2 gal. of warm water

Mix all of these ingredients together, and sprinkle the mixture over all your shrubs as soon as their leaves are out.

takes an extra few seconds, but it'll make a *big* difference in the long run! And it's easy to do: Simply dig the hole, set the plant in place, and then lay the handle of your shovel across the hole. Look at the plant carefully from the side. The handle should rest on the soil line on both sides of the hole and touch the crown of the plant in the center.

If you need to, adjust the depth of the plant by digging deeper, or by adding soil under the root ball. If you do end up putting some soil under the roots, add enough to raise the root ball about a quarter-inch above the soil line, because it'll settle a bit after you water.

Check the Ratings

It's one thing to gamble with perennials—they're pretty inexpensive to replace, after all—but for the main shrubs in your landscape, stick to plants that are dependably winter-hardy. To be extra safe, it's a good idea to pick shrubs that are rated a whole zone colder than where you live—if you live in Zone 5, for example, choose shrubs that are hardy to Zone 4. That way, your shrubs should sail right through the winter, even if it's extra-cold one year!

Showy Shrubs All Year

If space for shrubs is at a premium in your yard, it just makes sense to choose the ones that'll work the hardest! Pretty flowers

FL*WER POWER TONICS

Super Shrub Elixir

Don't waste your hard-earned dough on fancy, pre-packaged shrub fertilizers from your local garden center! Instead, just whip up a batch of this terrific tonic, and you'll have the best-looking flowering shrubs on the block.

½ **can of beer**
½ **cup of fish emulsion**
½ **cup of ammonia**
¼ **cup of baby shampoo**
2 **tbsp. of hydrogen peroxide**

Mix all of the ingredients together, and pour into your 20 gallon hose-end sprayer. Every three weeks during the spring and summer, spray your shrubs until the tonic starts dripping off their leaves. That'll really get 'em growin' like gangbusters! ✳

are a great start, but shrubs can have a whole lot more, too—good-looking leaves, showy berries, bright fall foliage color, or interesting bark. Here's my top-10 list of super-showy shrubs that I *guarantee* you'll love:

GRANDMA PUTT'S
Handy Hints

When it came to pruning her shrubs, Grandma Putt had a handy-dandy rule of thumb: Prune spring-flowering shrubs right after they bloom, and prune later-flowering shrubs in spring. If she really needed to cut back any shrub, she'd do it in late winter or early spring, regardless of when it bloomed. She might miss out on the flowers that year, but at least the job would be done, and the shrub would have a whole growing season to recover!

Blueberry (*Vaccinium corymbosum*)

Cornelian cherry dogwood
(*Cornus mas*)

Fringe tree (*Chionanthus virginicus*)

Hollies (*Ilex*)

Oak-leaved hydrangea
(*Hydrangea quercifolia*)

Oregon grape-holly
(*Mahonia aquifolium*)

Red-twig dogwood (*Cornus alba*)

Rockspray cotoneaster
(*Cotoneaster horizontalis*)

Rugosa rose (*Rosa rugosa*)

Viburnums (*Viburnum*)

Go Natural

If there's one drawback to flowering shrubs, it's that they don't die back to the ground each year like perennials do—and that means they can get pretty big over the years! But if you think pruning is a pain in the neck, you can still enjoy growing these bulky beauties—just follow my three simple secrets to successful shrub management:

❀ **No more squares and gumdrops.** Instead of carving your shrubs into shapes, let them have a looser, more natural shape. That'll mean a *lot* less work for you!

❀ **Shearing doesn't keep 'em small**. Cutting back the tips of branches actually makes 'em grow faster, so it's the wrong thing to do if size control is your goal! Instead, cut out a few whole branches each year—back to a main stem, or all the way back to the ground.

❀ **Replace or transplant.** Rather than fight with a shrub that's too big, either dig it up and throw it away, or move it to a spot where its size won't matter.

Double the Color

Here's a great trick for getting your spring-blooming shrubs to do double duty: Train vines to grow over them! Create an amazing display with summer-blooming annual vines, like morning glories (*Ipomoea*), scarlet runner beans (*Phaseolus coccineus*), or hyacinth beans (*Lablab purpureus*). Or, for plant-it-once color, try hardy vines instead; clematis and honeysuckle (*Lonicera*) are two top-notch choices.

Don't be tempted to plant any kind of climber too close to the trunk of the shrub, or the vine'll get shaded out before it can get growing. Instead, set it just outside of the farthest reach of the shrub's stems, so it'll get all the sun and rain it needs to thrive. Once the vine starts to climb, simply stand back and enjoy the two-for-one show!

Do Your Homework

Every time you choose a new shrub for your yard, you have a chance to save yourself hours and hours of headaches down the road. How? *Before* you buy, find out how tall it will get—and how wide—once it's full grown. If this information isn't on the shrub's label, check with the nursery personnel, or look it up in a shrub book. Whatever you do, don't assume that the cute little potted shrub is going to stay the same size for the rest of its life!

Shrub Buddies

To my mind, nothing looks lonelier than a few shrubs stuck out in the middle of a lawn. So, instead of spending every weekend mowing, trimming, and weeding around a bunch of boring shrubs, why not pair 'em up with some pretty flowers? Besides sprucing up your yard, you'll save yourself a whole lot of maintenance time, too!

PROBLEM SOLVED!

Have a shrub that's just stopped blooming? Maybe it needs to be trimmed up a bit! To rejuvenate a tired shrub gradually, cut out one or two of the oldest stems each year to make room for new ones. Want to try a radical renewal? Before you do, look for suckers or new shoots at the base of the plant; if you see them, there's a good chance that shrub can stand severe pruning. Wait until late winter or early spring, then cut the entire shrub down to within 6 to 12 inches above the ground. It'll grow back even better than ever!

❀ **Bulbs.** For pop-up color, fill the space under deciduous shrubs with a bounty of spring bulbs, like crocuses, daffodils, and snowdrops (*Galanthus*).

❀ **Groundcovers.** Plant bugleweeds (*Ajuga*), deadnettles (*Lamium*), or plumbago (*Ceratostigma plumbaginoides*) around the base of each shrub. They'll outcompete weeds, and add color in the process!

❀ **Perennials.** Spice up the space around your shrubs with vigorous perennials like hostas, daylilies (*Hemerocallis*), and Lenten rose (*Helleborus* x *hybridus*). Keep the space mulched until the perennials have filled in, or plant some annuals for instant color, and you've got yourself a new garden that'll look great all year round!

Snapdragon • *Antirrhinum majus*

There's just something about snapdragons that brings out the kid in all of us! I remember spending many happy hours as a boy in Grandma Putt's garden, showing all my friends how to pinch the blooms to get the "dragon's mouth" to pop open. Many years later, I still enjoy growing these elegant annuals for their tall, spiky flowers.

 GROW IT!

Full sun
Rich, well-drained soil
Dwarf types grow 8 to 12 inches tall; others range from 1 to 3 feet tall
Cool-weather annual or tender perennial (Zones 6 to 9)

 PLANT IT!

Snaps are equally at home with annuals and perennials in beds and borders
Grow some in a cutting garden so you'll have plenty for bouquets
Dwarf and trailing snapdragons are eye-catching in containers

Snapdragon
Antirrhinum majus

 GETTING STARTED

Buy snapdragon plants in spring, or start your own from seeds—either way, it's a snap! Simply sow the seeds indoors 8 to 10 weeks before your last spring frost. Press the tiny seeds onto the surface of the medium, but don't cover 'em, because they need light to sprout. Once they sprout, keep 'em cool—around 55°F—and they'll stay nice and stocky.

Cool Cuts

If your snaps aren't lookin' too snappy when the sultry summer weather arrives, don't despair! You can help them beat the heat with this simple trick: Give 'em a good trim (by about half their height), then douse 'em with a shot of my Flower Feeder tonic (see page 110), followed by a good drink of water.

If you think you're seeing orange spots on your snaps, it's not your imagination—it's a fungal disease called rust. If you catch it early, dusting the plants with powdered sulfur can help stop the spread of these funky fungi. Otherwise, pull out infected snaps and toss 'em in the trash. Next year, try a rust-resistant cultivar. Dwarf strains, such as 'Floral Carpet', are much less susceptible to this disease than old-fashioned tall types.

Speedwells • *Veronica*

With a name like "speedwell," it's easy to see why these vigorous perennials have a reputation for being garden thugs! But don't throw the baby out with the bathwater—most speedwells are quite well-behaved enough for any flower garden. I wouldn't be without their summer spikes of blue, pink, or white flowers in my own yard, and I know that if you try 'em, you'll love 'em, too!

Spike speedwell
Veronica spicata

 GROW IT!

Full sun or partial shade
Average to rich, moist,
   well-drained soil
3 inches to 3 feet tall
Hardy perennials
   (Zones 3 or 4 to 9)

 PLANT IT!

Taller speedwells are terrific
   in beds and borders
Shorter species are great in rock
   gardens or as groundcovers
Most speedwells make excellent
   edging plants

 GETTING STARTED

It's easy to find speedwells for sale at garden centers in spring, and that's the ideal time to plant 'em, too. Would you rather wait to see what color the blooms are before you buy? Speedwells are tough enough to tolerate transplanting even in full flower without missing a beat!

Jerry's TIMELY TIPS

"If your speedwells aren't blooming too well, it's time to divide them. Every three or four years, dig up the clumps in spring or fall. Replant the vigorous new growth from the outside of the clump, and toss the old, woody pieces in the trash."

Sorting Out Speedwells

I'm as fond of swapping plants as the next person, but usually, if someone has lots of speedwell to share, they've got a fast-spreading kind—and you *don't* want it!

You're much better off buying a good, named cultivar, then propagating it by division or summer cuttings if you want to make more. Two top-quality speedwells that I highly recommend are the violet-blue-flowered 'Goodness Grows' spike speedwell (*V. spicata*), and the hybrid speedwell 'Sunny Border Blue', which blooms from midsummer to fall if you pinch off the spent bloom spikes.

Spurges • *Euphorbia*

At first glance, you'd never guess that these hardy, tough-as-nails perennials are close relatives of that tender Christmas classic, the poinsettia. A close look at the blooms reveals the relationship: The true flowers are tiny, surrounded by colorful parts that are actually modified leaves, called bracts—red in poinsettias, and yellow or orange in garden spurges!

 GROW IT!

Light shade to full sun
Loose, well-drained soil
1 to 4 feet tall
Established plants are usually very drought-tolerant
Hardy perennials (Zones 4 to 9)

 PLANT IT!

Pair spurges with other early bloomers, such as columbines (*Aquilegia*) and spring bulbs
They're great in rock gardens, or in raised beds
Enjoy 'em as groundcovers on dry or rocky slopes

Cushion spurge
Euphorbia polychroma

 GETTING STARTED

To start with spurges, pick up a plant or two at your local garden center in spring. When you plant, dig the soil deeply, and work in some compost to ensure good drainage around the roots.

Spurge Scourge

The only problem with growing spurges is that some of them can get a bit too generous when it comes to making babies! A few seedlings are welcome—you can move them to new parts of your garden, or share 'em with friends. But if you find they're getting out of hand, there's a simple solution—just whack 'em back by one-third to one-half their height, right after they're done blooming. Hedge shears make quick work of the cutting. Besides eliminating self-sown seedlings, this trim'll also get plants to bush out and make fresh new growth, so they'll look all the better for the rest of the growing season!

PROBLEM SOLVED!

Like poinsettias, spurges have sticky, milky sap in their stems and leaves. Some people are allergic to the sap, so it's a good idea to wear gloves while working around your spurges!

Sunflowers • *Helianthus*

Sum-, sum-, summertime means sun-, sun-, sunflowers! The ones that first come to mind are the shaggy-headed, bright yellow, annual kinds, but did you know there are perennial sunflowers, too? Whichever you choose, you'll get months of knock-your-socks-off blooms for practically no work on your part!

Annual sunflower
Helianthus annuus

 GROW IT!

Full sun
Average to rich, moist,
    well-drained soil
2 to 10 feet tall
Drought-tolerant, once established
Warm-weather annuals and hardy
    perennials (Zones 3 or 4 to 9)

 GETTING STARTED

To get growing with **perennial** sunflowers, it's easiest to start with spring-purchased plants. **Annual** kinds are a snap to start at home: Simply sow the seeds outdoors after all danger of frost has passed, or start 'em indoors, in individual pots, four to six weeks before your last spring frost date.

 PLANT IT!

Grow annual sunflowers
    in beds and borders for
    summer color
They're favorites with a
    wide variety of birds
All sunflowers are beautiful
    in bouquets!

The end of summer doesn't have to mean the end of your sunflowers! Swamp sunflower (*H. angustifolius*), willow-leaved sunflower (*H. salicifolius*), and other perennial sunflowers come into their own closer to the end of the growing season. Most of these get pretty tall, but you can keep 'em shorter and bushier if you whack 'em back by half in early summer.

Fun in the Sun

When it comes to easy-care garden bloomers, sunflowers are tough to beat! They have no special problems, except maybe that the tall annual kinds can blow over in strong winds. If that's a problem in your yard, check out some of the newer, more compact cultivars, such as 3-foot-tall 'Teddy Bear' and 15-inch 'Big Smile'.

When it comes to tulips, I'm not one to tiptoe around! I've fallen head over heels for these big-bloomed spring beauties, and once you learn my secrets to growing top-notch tulips, you'll be crazy about 'em, too.

 ## GROW IT!   ## PLANT IT!

Full sun
Rich, well-
   drained soil
4 to 30 inches tall
Hardy bulbs
   (Zones 3 to 8)

Tuck 'em into beds and borders for a
   spectacular spring show
Tulips pair perfectly with pansies, other
   early bulbs, and early-blooming
   perennials, like lungworts (*Pulmonaria*)
Plant extras to have plenty for bouquets

Single early tulip
Tulipa hybrid

GETTING STARTED

To enjoy a yard full of tulips in spring, you need to plan ahead, and plant 'em in fall. If you only want a dozen or so, it's fine to buy 'em at your local garden center. But if you have enough room to plant lots of tulips, do what I do, and buy from a mail-order source. You'll have a much wider selection, the prices are a lot cheaper—especially if you order early—and the bulbs will arrive on your doorstep at the perfect planting time for your area!

New Bulbs Don't Bloom?

All leaves and no flowers make tulips mighty dull, indeed! So what happened? It's likely that the bulbs you bought weren't stored or handled properly. Tulips exposed to temperatures above 70°F in storage don't bloom well—if they bloom at all. There's not much you can do except be patient; you should have flowers the following year.

   If you don't even see leaves where your tulips are supposed to be, suspect voles, mice, chipmunks, or squirrels, all of which consider tulips a tasty treat. The next time

When you're picking out tulips, look for fleshy, solid bulbs with no signs of mold or black, rotted blotches. It's best if a bulb's brown jacket (called a tunic) is intact, too.

Tulips, continued

you plant, surround your tulip bulbs with sharp, crushed gravel, or work bloodmeal into the soil you use to refill the planting holes. For a more permanent solution, line planting beds with ½-inch hardware cloth before you set out your tulips, or plant groups of bulbs in wire mesh baskets. Sure, it's extra work—but believe me, it'll all be worthwhile when you see those beauties strut their stuff in spring!

Many Happy Returns

Are you tired of having to buy new tulip bulbs each year, because the old ones never seem to bloom well after the first year? It's easy to have the same tulips come back spring after spring—*if* you choose the right ones! Your best bets are Kaufmanniana, Fosteriana, and Greigii tulips, along with Darwin Hybrid or Triumph tulips. Species tulips are good choices, too—especially *T. saxatilis*, *T. batalinii*, and *T. tarda*.

Don't Kill 'Em with Kindness

Tulips thrive where the soil is dry after their leaves die back. If you usually water your flower garden regularly in summer, consider digging a separate bed just for tulips, and don't water it. Your tulips'll be much happier there!

Verbenas • *Verbena*

If you've never been a fan of verbenas, then you haven't tried 'em for a while! These bright-blooming beauties used to have a reputation for being a little fussy, but nowadays, they're a whole lot easier to grow—and they come in a wider range of colors, too. So go ahead and give verbenas a try—I *guarantee* you'll thank me!

 GROW IT!

Full sun or light shade
Average, well-drained, evenly
    moist soil
12 to 18 inches tall
Warm-weather annuals, tender
    perennials, or hardy perennials

 PLANT IT!

Enjoy verbenas as eye-
    catching fillers in first-year
    perennial gardens
Plant 'em in containers for
    months of color
The flowers attract humming-
    birds and butterflies, too!

Verbena
Verbena

GETTING STARTED

Buying plants is by far the easiest way to get growing with most verbenas. To start your own common garden verbena (*V. x hybrida*) plants, sow the seeds indoors 8 to 10 weeks before your last spring frost date. Move plants to the garden a few weeks after the frost date, once the soil has warmed up and the weather has settled.

Be a Cutup!

The verbenas you see sold as annuals are actually tender perennials—they'd live through the winter if temperatures didn't dip below freezing. That means you can keep your favorite plants from year to year—simply by taking cuttings in late summer, then keeping 'em on a sunny windowsill until the warm weather returns!

FLOWER POWER TONICS

Chamomile Mildew Chaser

If your verbenas are looking gray and dusty, there's a good chance they've got powdery mildew. Apply this elixir at the first sign of trouble.

4 chamomile tea bags
2 tbsp. of Murphy's Oil Soap
1 qt. of boiling water

Make a strong batch of tea by letting the tea bags steep in the boiling water for an hour or so. Once the tea cools, mix with the Murphy's Oil Soap. Apply once a week with a 6 gallon hose-end sprayer. ✻

If you're as crazy about flowers as I am, you're always looking for new ways to fit more blooms in the same amount of space. Well, here's a suggestion: Grow up! No, I'm not being rude; I'm suggesting you fill your yard with flowering vines! Try 'em on a trellis, festoon a fence, or turn a boring wall into a flower-filled spectacle; vines'll grow in all those awkward spaces where other plants just can't fit. So now that I've got you excited about your upward options, let's look at some great ways to put vines to work for you!

Wisteria
Wisteria

Put Up, Then Plant Up

My number one rule for great vine gardening? Always, always, always put the support in place *before* you plant! If you're planting against an existing wall or fence, you're already good to go. But don't even *think* about putting up a trellis after your vine's in the ground. Inevitably, you'll end up stepping on and compacting the soil—or worse yet, cutting the roots when you set in the trellis. You might even trample the vine itself! So remember: Get a support system in place first, then stand back and let your vine do its thing.

Rosy Thoughts

Climbing roses aren't true vines, since they don't climb on their own; you need to tie them to a trellis, fence, or other supports. But who cares? You can use them the same way—on walls, fences, and even older trees (just make sure they still get at least six hours of sun a day). For pure flower power, you can't beat large-flowered climbers like 'Dublin Bay' and 'New Dawn'; both have excellent disease resistance. Other outstanding climbers include 'Dortmund', 'William Baffin', 'American Pillar', and 'Dorothy Perkins'. For thorn-free beauties, try 'Zéphirine Drouhin'—its stems are as smooth as a baby's bottom!

Think Twice

There's a lot to love about flowering vines, but my favorite thing about them is their vigorous nature. You start with one seed or a single stem, and by the end of one season, you've got yourself a flower-filled plant that's at least up to eye level! But there are a few bad apples in the bunch, so don't go planting just any vine before you do your homework. Here are three real invasive thugs that will take over your garden in no time!

Japanese honeysuckle (*Lonicera japonica*)

Oriental bittersweet (*Celastrus orbiculatus*)

Silver-lace vine (*Polygonum aubertii*)

Landscape Lingo

The secret to picking the perfect support for your vine is knowing how it climbs. Here's an overview:

Clinging vines. Vines that have rootlets or "hold-fasts" along their stems attach themselves directly to surfaces and climb with ease; think of English ivy (*Hedera helix*) and Virginia creeper (*Parthenocissus quinquefolia*). Train these climbers up trees, stone walls, or other maintenance-free surfaces; keep 'em away from aluminum or vinyl siding, or wood walls that need painting periodically.

Tendril vines. These climbers hold themselves to supports using little shoots that grow out from the main stems; sweet pea (*Lathyrus odoratus*) is one example. Clematis don't have true tendrils—they wrap their leaf stems around a support—but they like the same kinds of supports: strings, netting, branches, and small trellis slats.

Twining vines. These vines climb by winding their stems around a support. Annual twiners, like morning glories (*Ipomoea*), can climb strings or lightweight trellises; woody twiners, like wisteria, need sturdy structures.

Bleeding heart vine
Adlumia

When Grandma Putt planted a new vine, she'd make it a point to check back every few days, to see if it needed any help. Sometimes, she'd just have to twirl the stem tips around the support to get them growing onward and upward. If a little extra assistance was in order, she'd tie the stems to the trellis with soft yarn, or strips of old panty hose. Once they grabbed hold, an occasional pinch or snip was enough to keep wayward stems going in the right direction!

For Something Completely Different

Vines show off best when they can rise up high, but many can do double duty as groundcovers if you let 'em sprawl. They're especially nice cascading down slopes, and they'll smother weeds like a pro! Here's a rundown of my five favorite vines for growin' at ground level:

Climbing hydrangea
(*Hydrangea petiolaris*)

Five-leaved akebia (*Akebia quinata*)

Honeysuckles (*Lonicera*)

Mountain clematis
(*Clematis montana*)

Sweet autumn clematis
(*C. terniflora*)

Room to Roam

To save yourself loads of work down the road, read the fine print on the label *before* you buy any climber. A vine that's too big for your garden can be a headache—once it's grown for a few years, you'll have to hack it back into submission every spring just to keep it in bounds! Instead, look for a smaller vine that just fits the space you can give it.

String 'Em Up!

Are you planning to support your annual vines with string? Whatever you do, my friend, *don't* use the plastic kind! Sure, it'll last for more than one year, but then you'll be stuck unwinding the dead vines when you put the garden to bed for winter. Instead, use biodegradable cotton string, or uncoated jute. At the end of the season, simply cut down the whole mass of withered stems and string, and chuck it onto your compost pile.

Watch Out for Wood

Flowering vines look fantastic growing against a home, but it's smart to take a few precautions to make sure they don't do more harm than good. Always keep vines pruned away from the woodwork on your house, because they hold in moisture that can cause wood to rot. I like to keep my vines on a lattice trellis that's stationed about 6 inches away from the exterior wall of my house. Besides keeping the wall clean and dry, this allows air to circulate behind the vine—and that'll go a long way toward stopping dastardly diseases in their tracks!

FL✿WER POWER TONICS

Clematis Chow

These regal beauties can take a lot of neglect, but if you want a really fine clematis vine, I've got just the ticket—this secret family recipe.

5 gal. of well-cured horse or cow manure
½ cup of lime
½ cup of bonemeal

Mix the ingredients together in a wheelbarrow and spread over the root zone of your clematis, first thing in the spring. Top that with a rich mulch of half-rotted compost to make sure the soil stays cool and moist, and your clematis will be as happy as a clam! ✳

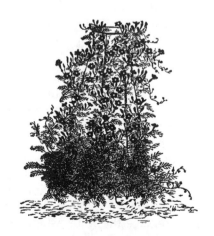

Cypress vine
Ipomoea quamoclit

Yarrows • *Achillea*

Yarrows may look delicate, but don't be fooled—these pretty perennials are really tough customers! Heat? Drought? Poor soil? No problem! Yarrows can take it all, and they'll fill your summer garden with a bounty of yellow, pink, or white blooms while they do it.

Yarrow
Achillea

 GROW IT!

Full sun
Average to poor,
    well-drained soil
1 to 3 feet tall
Hardy perennials
    (Zones 3 to 9)

 PLANT IT!

Grow yarrows in clumps or drifts
    on hot, dry sites, like slopes
Pair 'em with other drought-tolerant
    perennials, including coreopsis
    and catmints (*Nepeta*)
Yarrows make fantastic cut flowers!

 GETTING STARTED

Start off with purchased plants when you're looking for yarrows in a particular bloom color or height. If you enjoy variety, seeds can be a fun way to go: Sow 'em indoors in early winter, and the plants may flower the first year!

FLOWER FUN!

For the longest-lasting cut flowers, pick yarrows when about half the buds in the cluster have opened. It's easy to dry 'em, too: Simply hang them upside down in bunches in a warm, airy place. Or better yet, let 'em do double duty: Enjoy them as fresh flowers with 2 to 3 inches of water in the vase, but *don't* replace the water when it's used up—the flowers will dry in perfect shape, right in the vase!

No Fuss, No Muss

When I'm looking for a dependable, easy-care perennial to fill a sunny spot, yarrows are always at the top of my list! They'll bloom for two months or more with minimal maintenance—mostly just occasional deadheading to keep new blooms coming along. Over time, the clumps can get pretty crowded, so plan on dividing them every three to five years, either in spring or in early fall. That's all it takes to keep yarrows rollin' right along!

Grandma Putt never let a summer go by without zinnias in her garden—and neither do I! With such an amazing range of bloom colors, flower forms, and plant heights to choose from, it's easy to see why these annuals are so popular.

 GROW IT!

Full sun
Average to rich,
   well-drained soil
6 inches to 4 feet tall
Warm-weather annuals

 PLANT IT!

Grow tall zinnias at the back of a bed
   or border for quick height and color
Enjoy shorter zinnias as fillers
   among other flowers
They're terrific cut flowers, too!

Common zinnia
Zinnia elegans

 GETTING STARTED

Simply sow the seeds outdoors—after the last frost date—right where you want the plants to bloom, or start 'em indoors a few weeks before the last frost date. Transplant carefully—zinnias are happiest if their roots aren't disturbed!

Zany for Zinnias

Let me tell you, folks—if you haven't grown zinnias in a while, you don't know what you're missing! Here's a rundown of some of my favorites:

❀ For lots of flowers, look to "cut and come again" zinnias, like the Oklahoma Series. The more you pick, the more they bloom!

❀ Dwarf cultivars, like the Dreamland and Dasher Series, grow only 1 foot tall, so they're excellent for edging beds—and perfect for pots, too!

❀ If diseases like powdery mildew have kept you away from zinnias, try narrow-leaved zinnia (*Z. angustifolia*), which shrugs off heat and drought as well as disease.

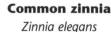

FLOWER POWER TONICS

Baking Soda Spray

If you're seeing gray spots on your zinnia leaves, whip up a batch of this simple solution.

2 tbsp. of baby shampoo
1 tbsp. of baking soda
1 gal. of warm water

Mix these ingredients together, and mist-spray your plants lightly once a week to keep diseases from zapping your zinnias! ❀

PART 4

PEST
and
PROBLEM
PATROL

othing can spoil your flower gardening fun quicker than bad bugs, cunning critters, and dastardly diseases. When you have a sick plant, finding the guilty party can be tough, but that's exactly what you have to do. Grandma Putt taught me that every pest and disease leaves telltale signs to say they've been there—you just need to know what to look for. After all, you've planned and planted, primped and pinched—now you should be able to enjoy those beautiful blooms. Don't let a bunch of bothersome bugs or funky fungi get you down—just send 'em on their way with my all-time favorite rescue remedies!

In this section, you'll learn all of Grandma Putt's secrets—and mine, too—for ratting out the culprits and getting 'em out of your garden *pronto!* You'll find plenty of terrific tips and timely tonics for getting these bad boys under control in a jiffy! Need to bring out the real big guns? Then turn to page 331, where you'll find an alphabetical roundup of my best magical mixers and excellent elixirs for gettin' your flowers as healthy as a horse—and keeping 'em that way, too!

A Rogues Gallery

🌸 For Grandma Putt, fending off pests and diseases wasn't simply a matter of waiting for the worst to happen, then deciding what to do about it. She knew that the key to having a fabulous flower garden was keeping an eagle eye out for potential problems, then nippin' them in the bud. And Grandma sure was right, folks: It's a whole lot easier to *prevent* pesky pests, crazy critters, and dastardly diseases, or to stop 'em early, than to fight a full-scale battle—with your flowers caught in the middle at ground zero!

In the following pages, I've turned a spotlight on the top 20 problems you're most likely to run into in your flower garden. You'll find checklists to help you confirm the culprit, plus plenty of my best tips and tricks for outsmarting even the wiliest flower pests!

Mix 'Em Up

One of the best ways I know of to keep bugs from buggin' your bloomers is to grow many different kinds of flowers. That way, most pesky pests will take one look and decide there's not enough of their favorite chow to hang around for!

Weeds to Welcome

Believe it or not, some weeds can actually be good for your garden! These five flowering weeds are wonderful for attracting beneficial insects, which help keep pernicious pests from getting the upper hand. Plus, they're pretty enough to do double duty as beautiful bloomers for your beds and borders!

Common yarrow (*Achillea millefolium*)

Goldenrods (*Solidago*)

Orange coneflowers (*Rudbeckia*)

Oxeye daisy (*Leucanthemum vulgare*)

Queen Anne's lace (*Daucus carota*)

Don't Let Diseases Get You Down

Well, plant diseases are a pain in the butt, and that's the truth. The good news is, your plants are more than happy to help you fight off even the worst of 'em! How's that work? Well, healthy, vigorous plants can shrug off most diseases without batting a leaf, so anything you do to keep 'em growin' strong is a big help. Pick the perfect site for your flowers, feed 'em regularly with compost, dose 'em with my tonics, keep 'em mulched and watered, and do anything else you can to keep 'em happy. If you take care of your plants, they'll take care of you!

We all know that hummingbirds sip nectar from flowers—but did you know that they're our buddies in the fight against garden pests, too? It's true! Hummingbirds dine on aphids, mosquitoes, flying ants, leafhoppers, flies, and many other pesky pests—and that's a great reason to welcome them to your garden! Some of their favorite flowers include coral bells (*Heuchera sanguinea*), snapdragons (*Antirrhinum majus*), and trumpet vines (*Campsis*).

A Soapy Solution

Wondering what to do about pest sprays that just don't seem to stick? Try adding a shot of liquid dish soap to the mixture. It'll help any spray stick to the leaves, so the tonic'll have a better chance to do its job.

Name any flower, and you can almost bet that there's an aphid that likes to dine on it. These plump, pear-shaped, winged or wingless pests are about as tiny as pinheads, but they spell big trouble if they get goin' in your garden! Aphids suck plant juices, ooze sticky stuff (called honeydew), and spread viruses among plants—all good reasons to get rid of 'em in a jiffy.

Aphid

🔍 FLOWER GARDEN DETECTIVE

Think aphids might be attacking your flowers?
Here's what to watch for:

☑ Green, pink, black, gray, or white insects clustered on stem tips and under leaves.

☑ Flower buds, flowers, and leaves are distorted.

☑ Badly infested plants become stunted.

☑ Black sooty mold growing on the honeydew that the aphids produce.

FLOWER POWER TONICS

Aphid Antidote

To keep aphids and other pests off your favorite flowers, mix up a batch of this amazing antidote.

1 small onion, chopped finely
2 medium cloves of garlic, chopped finely
1 tbsp. of liquid dish soap
2 cups of water

Put all of the ingredients in a blender, blend on high, and then strain out the pulp through cheesecloth or panty hose. Pour the liquid into a hand-held mist sprayer, and douse your flowers at the first sign of aphid trouble. ✺

Blast Away!

Need an easy *and* effective aphid control? The answer's as close as your garden hose! Simply blast the bugs off your plants with a strong stream of water. If you're worried about breaking the stems when you spray, support them with one hand and hold the hose with the other as you wash away the pests. Repeat every few days, until the aphids go away for good!

Beetles

Bad-guy beetles are chewers, and that's the truth. They come in all shapes and sizes, from tiny, black flea beetles to dime-sized, copper-colored Japanese beetles. The adults chomp holes in leaves and flowers, while the grubs chow down on the roots. That makes them double trouble!

 FLOWER GARDEN DETECTIVE

Think you have beetles? First, look for the little buggers themselves. Some feed at night, but others, like Japanese beetles, are brazen enough to chew up your flowers in broad daylight!

Japanese beetle

☑ Adult beetles have two hard wing covers. They're often brown or black, but may be metallic, striped, or brightly colored.

☑ Larvae are usually dirty white, dark-headed, C-shaped grubs that live in the soil.

☑ If leaves have many tiny, round holes, flea beetles are to blame.

☑ Many different beetles chew large, irregular holes in leaves, buds, and/or petals.

☑ When leaves are eaten right down to the main veins, the usual suspects are Japanese beetles.

Beetle Doom

Flea beetles are too tiny to catch, so blast 'em with my Beetle Juice Tonic. Handpick bigger beetles, and drop 'em in a can of soapy water to drown. For a long-term fix, spread Milky Spore disease and/or parasitic nematodes on your lawn and garden. These treatments will get the grubs under control—and that means fewer adults in the long run!

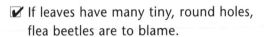

FLOWER POWER TONICS

Beetle Juice Tonic

This stuff will stop any kind of pesky beetle right in its tracks!

½ cup of beetles (alive or dead)
2 cups of water

Collect the beetles and whirl 'em up in an old blender (one you'll *never* again use for food preparation) with 2 cups of water. Strain the liquid through cheesecloth. Pour about ¼ cup into a 1 gallon hand-held sprayer, and fill the rest of the jar with water. Spray your plants from top to bottom, and make sure you coat both sides of the leaves. ❋

Bugs

We tend to call any creatures with six legs a bug, but true bugs are a special group of insects that grow a certain way. The babies look just like miniature adults, and they get bigger as they feed. True bugs have beak-like mouthparts that they use to chew into leaves and suck out plant juices. Bugs feed on lots of different flowers, so it's smart to be ready for 'em!

Squash bug

Tarnished plant bug

 FLOWER GARDEN DETECTIVE

Not sure if bugs are to blame for your flower damage? Here's what to look for:

☑ True bugs have wings that cross on the back to make a V-shaped pattern. Some are shield-shaped, others are round.

☑ The sharp mouthparts inject a toxin as they feed, causing yellow or white leaf spots.

☑ Leaves and/or flowers are puckered or distorted.

Stink bug

A Watery Grave

Bugs are slowest and easiest to find early in the morning, so head out to your garden while it's still cool. Hold a can of soapy water under a damaged leaf, and flick the bugs into the water with your finger. Whatever you do, don't smash 'em; many bugs are really stinky! For a bad infestation, spray with insecticidal soap or Plant Shampoo, or give 'em a blast of my super Bug-Be-Gone Spray (see page 116).

To the Rescue!

Lace bugs may sound pretty, but the damage they do sure isn't! These tiny, lacy-winged pests hide under leaves to feed, causing leaf surfaces to turn yellow or even white. Azaleas are particular favorites, but these bugs can trouble many other flowers, too. Send these pests packin' by mixing up 2 tablespoons of Murphy's Oil Soap and 2 tablespoons of canola oil in a gallon of water. Add a dash of liquid dish soap, then spray plants thoroughly. Be sure to get under the leaves. Repeat weekly until the lace bugs are gone.

Caterpillars

Creepy caterpillars are the larvae of a number of different moths and butterflies. These chewers can do quite a bit of damage, but before you decide to wipe 'em all out, remember that some are mighty pretty when they grow up. So if you see a caterpillar with bright green and yellow bands on its back, either leave it alone, or move it to a less conspicuous plant, so it can keep on eating. In a few weeks, it'll hatch into a beautiful black swallowtail butterfly!

 FLOWER GARDEN DETECTIVE

Caterpillars are worm-like pests with legs all along the length of their body. You'll often see 'em at work, but if you're not sure they're around, check for these signs:

- ☑ Chewed leaf edges, or whole leaves or stems eaten.

- ☑ Bits of dark green, brown, or black "frass" (that's a fancy word for caterpillar droppings) on chewed leaves.

Cabbageworm

Go Natural

One of the safest ways to kill caterpillars is to spray them with stuff called Bt. What's that? It's a bacterium (known to scientists as *Bacillus thuringiensis*) that causes a caterpillar disease. It's safe to use even where pets and children play, and you can get it at your local garden center. For best results, apply Bt when caterpillars are still small. If the spray doesn't seem to be sticking to the leaves, add a squirt of liquid dish soap to the mix. Rather try a homemade remedy? My Caterpillar Killer Tonic is just the ticket!

FLOWER POWER TONICS

Caterpillar Killer Tonic

To keep caterpillars in check and away from your flowers, brew up a batch of this tonic.

½ lb. of wormwood (*Artemisia*) leaves
2 tbsp. of Murphy's Oil Soap
4 cups of warm water

Simmer the wormwood leaves in 2 cups of warm water for 30 minutes or so. Strain out the leaves, then add the liquid and the Murphy's Oil Soap to 2 more cups of warm water. Apply with a 6 gallon hose-end sprayer to the point of run-off. Repeat as necessary until all of the caterpillars are history! ❋

Cutworms

Ever head out for a stroll through your flowers, only to find your carefully sown seedlings lying everywhere in pieces? It's almost enough to make you give up gardening—but don't you dare! While you can't save seedlings that have already been attacked, there's *plenty* you can do to prevent pests from striking again!

FLOWER GARDEN DETECTIVE

Cutworm

Cutworms are smooth, 1- to 2-inch-long, grayish or brownish caterpillars. They lie curled in the soil during the day, then creep out to attack seedlings and small plants at night. You'll know they've been at work when you see the following signs:

✔ Seedlings or plants that are healthy one day, then chopped down to the ground the next morning.

✔ Stems are chewed at the base, at or just below soil level.

✔ The tops of the plants are usually intact.

Here's a super-sneaky way to get rid of cutworms! Two weeks before you plan to plant, moisten some bran or cornmeal—the kind used for cooking—with a solution of Bt (*Bacillus thuringiensis*), then spread it over the planting beds. The cutworms will come crawlin' to chow down, and they'll be dead as doornails by the time you're ready to plant! You can find Bt for sale at most any garden center.

Please Fence 'Em In

The very best way to head these pests off at the pass is to put a collar around each seedling. I sink my mini-corrals 2 inches into the ground, with about 3 inches showing above. Collars made from any of these materials will give first-rate protection:

❀ Aluminum foil

❀ Cardboard tubes from wrapping paper, toilet paper, or paper towels

❀ Mailing tubes

❀ Paper or plastic cups with the bottoms cut out

❀ Tin cans minus the ends

Leafhoppers

With their powerful rear legs, these little insects can jump just like fleas. In fact, that's what Grandma Putt used to call 'em: flower fleas! Their favorite targets include asters and dahlias, but they'll also attack other flowers. As they feed, they can spread viruses, too—all the more reason to make sure you keep leafhoppers from gettin' ahead of you in the garden!

 FLOWER GARDEN DETECTIVE

Leafhoppers move like lightning, hopping away or scuttling sideways quick-as-a-wink. They're wedge-shaped insects, $1/8$- to $1/4$-inch long, with sharp mouthparts that let them feed by sucking plant juices. Look for these common symptoms:

☑ Tiny yellow or white spots on leaves.

☑ Leaves, buds, and/or flowers that are curled or misshapen.

☑ Leaves that are shiny and sticky, or that have a sooty black mold on the surface.

Leafhopper

Quick 'n' Deadly

To kill leafhoppers in a hurry, give your flowers a dose of my Flower Flea Fluid. If hoppers are still around a few days later, spray 'em with a simple mixture of 2 tablespoons of vegetable oil and 1 tablespoon of baby shampoo mixed into a quart of water.

FLOWER POWER TONICS

Flower Flea Fluid

This spicy brew'll do a real number on leafhoppers.

3 tbsp. of garlic-and-onion juice*
3 tbsp. of skim milk
2 tbsp. of baby shampoo
1 tsp. of Tabasco® sauce
1 gal. of water

Mix all the ingredients together in a bucket, and pour into a 20 gallon hose-end sprayer. Spray on your plants every 10 days. Make sure you get the undersides of the leaves, too!

*To make the garlic-and-onion juice, chop 2 cloves of garlic and 2 medium onions. Combine in a blender with 3 cups of water. Strain, and use remaining liquid. Freeze any leftover liquid for future use. ❁

Leaf Miners and Leaf Rollers

For pretty flowers that really sparkle, a backdrop of lush, healthy leaves is a must. When those leaves aren't lookin' their best, it might be that leaf miners or leaf rollers are at work. Read on to find out what to look for—*and* how to get rid of 'em, quick!

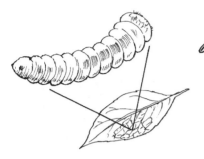

Leaf miner

🔍 FLOWER GARDEN DETECTIVE

Their names are similar, but leaf miners and leaf rollers cause different kinds of leaf damage. They're easy to tell apart—*if* you know what to look for!

☑ If you see squiggly lines or blotches on leaves, especially on columbines (*Aquilegia*) and chrysanthemums, leaf miners are to blame.

☑ Curled-up leaves, with brown-headed caterpillars visible when you pull the leaves open, are a clear sign of leaf rollers.

FL❀WER POWER TONICS

Rhubarb Pest Repellent Tonic

Here's a potent plant tonic that'll say "Scram!" to just about any kind of pest you can think of.

3 medium-size rhubarb leaves
¼ cup of liquid dish soap
1 gal. of water

Chop up the rhubarb leaves, put the pieces in the water, and bring it to a boil. Let the mixture cool, then strain it through cheesecloth to filter out the leaf bits. Mix in the liquid dish soap. Apply this terrific tonic to your plants with a small hand-held mist sprayer, and kiss your pest problems good-bye! ❁

A Pinch in Time Saves Nine—Leaves!

These culprits don't kill plants, but they sure do make a mess of the leaves! Leaf miners feed inside the leaves, so sprays can't reach them. The best control is to pick off the damaged foliage and toss it in the trash. Leaf rollers are also pretty well protected from sprays, so if you catch 'em early, just pinch off the damaged foliage. Otherwise, treat affected flowers with my Rhubarb Pest Repellent Tonic—and make sure you spray it on thoroughly!

Mealybugs and Spittlebugs

These two pests are easy to spot, and you sure won't mistake 'em for anything else! Once you've got 'em, send 'em on their way fast with these terrific tips.

FLOWER GARDEN DETECTIVE

It's a simple matter to tell these two pests apart—just look at the damage they do. Here's what you'll see:

Mealybug

- ✔ Bits of white fluff on leaves and stems, right where leaves are attached, are the mealybugs themselves.

- ✔ As mealybugs feed, they cause new shoots to turn yellow and wither; older leaves may be covered with black sooty mold.

- ✔ Spittlebugs make bubbly masses of "spit" along stems, usually where a leaf is attached.

- ✔ When lots of spittlebugs feed on a plant, growth may be stunted, and you'll see few flowers.

Plant Patrol

Mealybugs are the biggest headache by far, especially on greenhouse-raised flowers you bring home from the garden center. Here are some great ways to keep them from bugging you:

Read your plants. Before you buy, take a close look at any flowers you plan to purchase. Reject any that show signs of white fluff.

> **GARDEN SMARTS**
>
> Spittlebugs, also called froghoppers, aren't usually a big problem in flower gardens. Simply scrape off the gooey mess with a small stick, or blast it off the plant with a strong spray of water from the hose. Pull up severely infested plants, or chop 'em to the ground, to cut down on the problem in following years.

Blast 'em off. Spray away your mealybug problems with a stiff stream of water from the hose. Or, spot-treat 'em with a cotton swab dipped in rubbing alcohol.

Soap 'em up. If all else fails, mist-spray mealybugged flowers with a mixture of 1 teaspoon of baby shampoo and liquid Sevin at the rate recommended on the label per quart of water.

Scale

These tricksters are easy to miss, 'cause they just look like little bumps on what-ever plant they're attacking. Don't be fooled, though, or your flowers will suffer!

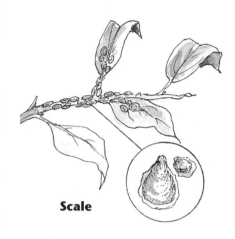

Scale

🔍 FLOWER GARDEN DETECTIVE

Adult scale insects can't move, but under their waxy shells, they have sharp mouthparts that pierce plants and suck plant juices. The babies, called crawlers, are super-small and can creep to new spots on the plant. Here's what you're likely to see:

☑ Round or oval bumps that are clustered on stems and leaves; bumps are gray, brown, yellow, or white.

☑ Shiny, sticky honeydew on leaves, often covered with black sooty mold.

☑ Yellow spots or patches on leaves; leaves may drop off.

☑ Stunted, sickly plants.

PROBLEM SOLVED!

The tight shell that covers adult scale insects sheds sprays like water off a duck's back—and that makes it mighty tough to kill 'em with regular insecticides. For sure-fire control, buy superior or horticultural oil at your local garden center. Following the directions on the label, mix up a batch *at the growing season dilution rate*. Add a squirt of liquid dish soap as well, to help the oil stick to the plant. Test the spray on a few leaves and wait a few days. If no damage occurs, spray the whole plant. Oil spray smothers scale, so it kills both adults and crawlers in one easy step!

Give 'Em an Alcohol Rub

If you see just a few scaly bumps, you're in luck! It's a cinch to wipe 'em out with a cotton swab dipped in rubbing alcohol. Just remember: This method doesn't get the crawlers, which can move around the plant for a few weeks until they form their hard adult shell. So, watch your plants closely for a few weeks after that, and re-treat if needed.

Slugs and Snails

Slugs and snails aren't insects, but they sure can bug your flower garden, big time! Their favorite hangout is in damp shade, where they chomp on the leaves of hostas and many other shade-loving plants. But during rainy or humid weather, just about any flower is fair game, so it's smart to be prepared for these slimy slitherers!

 ## FLOWER GARDEN DETECTIVE

Slugs and snails are easy to tell apart: Snails have shells, and slugs don't. Both cause similar kinds of damage, including:

Snail

☑ Large, ragged holes in leaves or flowers.

☑ Leaves eaten completely.

☑ Seedlings that disappear overnight.

☑ Shiny, slimy trails on leaves and on the ground around plants.

Slug

Belly Up to the Bar

Slugs and snails can be a real nuisance in the flower garden, but don't you let these slimeballs get you down! Get even by setting out some slug traps. Buy ready-made traps at your local garden center, or do what I do, and make your own—it's easy!

Start with a coffee can or plastic container, and cut a 2- or 3-inch hole in the lid. Bury the container so that the top is flush with the soil surface, then add a cup of my Slug-weiser tonic. Slugs and snails check in, but they won't check out! Empty the can, and add a fresh batch of brew every few days, or after a rain to keep 'em coming!

FLOWER POWER TONICS

Slugweiser

To drown your slug sorrows, try this sure cure.

1 lb. of brown sugar
½ pkg. (1½ tsp.) of dry yeast
Warm water

Pour the sugar and yeast into a 1-gallon plastic jug, fill it with warm water, and let it sit for two days, uncovered. Then pour it into your slug traps, and let the good times roll! ✤

Spider Mites

These little devils are so tiny you can't easily see 'em, but you *can* see the thousands of pinprick-sized yellow marks they make as they feed on leaves. These summer-loving pests'll do a real number on hydrangeas, roses, and just about any annual flower you can name!

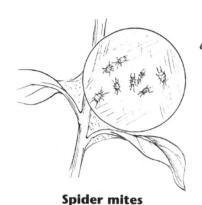

Spider mites

FLOWER GARDEN DETECTIVE

Spider mites are super-small, spider-like pests that suck the juice right out of leaves, stems, and flower buds. When lots of them are working, they cause big-time damage. Here's what to watch for:

☑ Leaves marked with tiny yellow or white spots.

☑ Leaves that turn all yellow or have a bronze cast.

☑ Leaves that drop off, and flower buds that don't open.

☑ Spider-like webbing on the undersides of leaves.

Splash Treatment

As far as spider mites are concerned, hot, dry summer weather is perfect for partying—and your flowers are the main course. To crash their party plans, give 'em a blast of water from the hose. Spray both sides of the leaves every other day for a week. If that fails, blast 'em with insecticidal soap or my Super Spider Mite Mix to send these pests packin'!

Bring in the Bugs

Lady beetles and green lacewings are both happy to chomp away on spider mites. Wait for them to appear, or buy them by mail, and release 'em in your garden to take care of the pests.

FLOWER POWER TONICS

Super Spider Mite Mix

Spider mites are tiny, all right, but they can get up to mite-y BIG mischief in your garden! When they show up, send 'em scurryin' with this floury remedy.

4 cups of wheat flour
½ cup of buttermilk
5 gal. of water

Mix all of the ingredients together, and mist-spray your plants to the point of run-off. This mix will suffocate the little buggers without harming your flowers. ❋

Thrips

Talk about pygmy pests that can do big-time damage! Thrips are super-small insects that you need a magnifying glass to see, but there's no missing the damage they can do to leaves and flowers. Peonies, gladiolus, and roses are a few of their favorite foods, but they'll feed on just about any flowering plant.

 FLOWER GARDEN DETECTIVE

Think you have thrips? Shake an infested flower over a piece of black paper, and watch closely to see these pests quickly hop or fly away. Other clues to watch for include:

Thrip

✔ Flowers and flower buds marked with white-flecked areas of dried-out tissue.

✔ Buds that turn brown and die; whole flower stalks may die or fail to appear.

✔ Leaves flecked with white; tips that may wither and die; undersides covered with tiny black specks.

✔ New leaves and stems that are distorted or misshapen; growth may be stunted.

Target Practice

Thrips can be tough to target, because they burrow down deep into flower petals and leaves. Try to catch them as early as possible, then treat 'em once a week with my Double Punch Garlic Tea (see page 255), or every three days with insecticidal soap. Make sure you cover both sides of the leaves, and soak the petals thoroughly, too!

GARDEN SMARTS

Thrips are happy campers in dry weather, so keeping plants well-watered and misting your flowers regularly with a hose can help hold these pesky pests at bay. Here are three other easy ways to trip up thrips:

• Pick off infested flowers and toss 'em in the trash.

• Mulch with a 2-inch-thick layer of shredded bark in spring to keep thrips from coming out of the soil, where they spend the winter.

• Cultivate the soil around your flowers in late fall and again in early spring to expose thrips to predators.

Whiteflies

"Flying dandruff" is another name for these teensy terrors—and it's a good one! When you brush against an infested plant, whiteflies float up like a cloud of dandruff with wings. These tiny, but troublesome pests can do big-time damage to your flowers in summer—*unless* you use my sure-fire controls, that is!

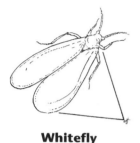

Whitefly

 FLOWER GARDEN DETECTIVE

Whiteflies suck juices from leaves, flowers, flower buds, and stems, so they're definitely bad news! You'll know there's a problem if you notice the adults flying around when you touch your flowers. Here are some more signs to search for:

☑ Yellowed leaves.

☑ Weak, stunted plants.

☑ Shiny, sticky coating on leaves and other plant parts; black sooty mold may grow on the sticky parts.

☑ Yellow eggs, the size of pinpoints, and tiny, white, wingless babies (nymphs) on the underside of leaves.

FL✲WER POWER TONICS

Whitefly Wipeout Tonic

Are whiteflies bugging your flowers? You're sure to find the fixin's for this super-simple spray right in your kitchen cabinet!

1 cup of sour milk (let fresh milk sit out for two days)
2 tbsp. of flour
1 qt. of warm water

Mix all of the ingredients in a bowl, and spray the mixture over any plants that are troubled by whiteflies. ✻

Spray Early, Spray Often

Early action is the key to keeping whiteflies in check. So, as soon as you spot a problem, treat infested plants every two days for two weeks with my Whitefly Wipeout Tonic. What if whiteflies have gotten ahead of you? It's best to pull up seriously infested annuals and toss 'em in the trash.

Hungry deer will munch on almost anything, and what they don't eat, they trample to the ground. So, if you're gardening in deer country, it's just plain smart to keep these pests away *before* they develop an appetite for your flowers!

FLOWER GARDEN DETECTIVE

If you have deer in your garden, you probably already know it. Annuals or perennials that disappear overnight are one sign; here are some others:

Deer

☑ Plants with stem tips, flowers, or flower buds missing.

☑ Hoofprints in soft soil.

☑ Broken stems or leaves.

Simple Soap Scarers

Any soap can scare away deer, but smelly deodorant soap is especially effective. Drill a hole through the bar, wrapper and all. Stick a wire through the hole, and bend it into a loop. Hang your soap scarers on tree branches or posts around the edge of your yard.

Fence 'Em Out

To keep deer out of your garden for good, install a fence. A 6-foot-tall solid board fence keeps 'em out; they won't jump it because they can't see where they'll land. An open wire or mesh fence needs to be 8 to 10 feet tall. Or, install two 4-foot-tall fences 5 feet apart. Deer can't jump both at once, and there's not enough space for them to land between the two fences.

FLOWER POWER TONICS

Deer Buster Egg Brew

If you notice that deer are starting to nibble on your flowers, protect your plants with this potent brew.

2 eggs
2 cloves of garlic
2 tbsp. of Tabasco® sauce
2 tbsp. of cayenne pepper
2 cups of water

Put all of the ingredients in a blender and purée. Allow the mixture to sit for two days, then pour or spray it all over and around the plants you need to protect. Reapply every other week or so, or after a rain, to keep the odor fresh. ❀

Vole

Like deer, rabbits and rodents'll snack on just about anything in your flower garden. The only difference is that these little critters eat a whole lot less than deer!

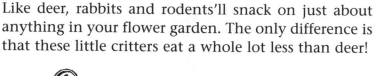

FLOWER GARDEN DETECTIVE

There's no doubt that rabbits love to sink their teeth into your flowers, but so do other critters. If you're not sure who's coming to dinner, do a little detective work and examine the damage:

- ☑ If seedlings and young plants disappear overnight, suspect rabbits.

- ☑ Hungry bunnies also chew holes in foliage, or eat entire leaves.

- ☑ Perennials and bulbs that are missing in spring were probably vole victims.

- ☑ Oval depressions scraped out under spreading perennials or shrubs are rabbit resting places, while shallow tunnels are probably vole highways.

Vole Control

Voles, which are close kin to mice, are a real pain in flower gardens. They travel from place to place along shallow paths at the soil surface, or along old mole tunnels underground, munching on any roots and bulbs they come across. They especially love to live under a cozy layer of mulch. So use that against 'em, and hold off on mulching your flowerbeds until the soil is frozen in early winter. By then, these vile villains will have found a cozier place to live for the winter, and your flowers should be safe!

Jerry's TIMELY TIPS

"Sure, bunnies look cute and cuddly—but believe you me, there's nothin' cute about the damage they do! Chewed up plants, especially young ones, are a good sign that rabbits are at work.

To send rabbits running, spray your flower garden with my Deer Buster Egg Brew (see page 325), or sprinkle bloodmeal (available at garden centers) all around your garden. Here's another option: Cut corncobs in half, soak them in vinegar overnight, and spread them around in your flowerbeds. Resoak the cobs every other week to keep rabbits away."

Lucky for us, most of the bacteria in our gardens are good guys. They help break down scraps to make compost, and they take nitrogen out of the air and make it available to our plants. But the bad bacteria can sure enough kill or disfigure our flowers, so use my tips for keeping 'em from gettin' started—you'll be glad you did!

 FLOWER GARDEN DETECTIVE

Bacterial diseases cause many different symptoms, including leaf spots of various sizes, shapes, and colors. Here are some more signs that bad bacteria are at work:

☑ Sticky, gummy, often smelly slime oozing out of affected areas, or from cut stems.

☑ Wilted stems and leaves; plants seem to wilt and die overnight.

☑ Leaf spots that start out looking like dark, water-soaked areas.

☑ Tumor-like galls on stems or plant crowns; plants are stunted with yellow leaves.

Crown gall

The Kindest Cut

Here's a super-simple way to do in any bacterial disease (and fungi, too): Give your plant a haircut! Pinch off spotted leaves as soon as you see 'em, and cut off sickly stems with pruning shears. Toss the diseased plant parts in the trash, *not* on your compost pile.

Galling Galls

Stunted growth and yellowed leaves are two signs your plants may have crown gall, a bacterial disease that causes tumor-like swellings on stems. If you see crown gall in your garden, cut off affected stems below the galls, and sterilize your pruners between cuts in a 10 percent bleach solution (one part bleach to nine parts water). Dig up and discard severely infested plants.

Bad bacteria—and funky fungi, too—often find their way into plants through wounds in leaves or stems. So it pays to be gentle when you work among your flowers; torn leaves and damaged stems make it easy for diseases to get a foothold!

Fungal Diseases

Powdery mildew

There's lots of fungus among us! In fact, funky fungi cause the most common diseases you'll find in the garden. Fortunately, they're easy to fight, if you know what to do!

FLOWER GARDEN DETECTIVE

The kinds of fungus that cause plant diseases usually appear as molds, mildews, rusts, or rots. Here's what to watch for:

☑ White, brown, gray, or rust-colored patches on leaves or flowers.

☑ Black, rotted roots, stems, or crowns.

☑ Sunken, rotted areas on stems.

☑ Wilted leaves and stems.

FLOWER POWER TONICS

Disease Defense

Wet, rainy weather can foster fungus in your flower garden, especially in late winter and early spring. But don't let the dreary days get you down—keep your perennials and bulbs happy and healthy with this elixir.

1 cup of chamomile tea
1 tsp. of liquid dish soap
½ tsp. of vegetable oil
½ tsp. of peppermint oil
1 gal. of warm water

Mix all of the ingredients together in a bucket. Mist-spray your plants every week or so *before* the really hot weather (75°F or higher) sets in. This elixir is strong stuff, so test it on a few leaves; wait two or three days to make sure there's no damage before completely spraying any plant.

Fungus Fighters

The best cure for fungal diseases is to keep 'em from gettin' started in the first place! Here are some of my best disease-stopping tips:

Choose fungus-fighting flowers. Look for flowers that are naturally resistant to common fungal diseases, like powdery mildew, rust, and black spot.

Don't wet your plants. Fungal spores need water to get going, so keep leaves and flowers dry. Use soaker hoses, or water in the morning so plants are dry by nighttime.

Plant and prune right. A breezy site cuts down on mildews and other fungal diseases. Thinning out stems or dividing crowded clumps to improve air circulation helps, too!

Viruses

Once viruses strike your flower garden, there's not much you can do. But there's *plenty* you can do to stop 'em from spreading in the first place. Insects are one of the main ways that viruses get around your garden, so if you keep aphids, leafhoppers, and whiteflies in check, you'll have fewer virus problems, too!

 FLOWER GARDEN DETECTIVE

Teensy, tiny viruses cause big problems in the garden, but they can be hard to identify. Look for these signs:

✔ Mottled patterns of green and yellow or white on leaves.

✔ Flowers that are streaked with white or another color.

✔ Stunted, misshapen flowers and curled or deformed leaves.

✔ Pale yellow spots on leaves.

✔ Stunted plants, or stems so short that the leaves form a rosette.

Mosaic virus

Got Milk?

The key to stopping viruses from spreading is as close as your fridge! Milk seems to neutralize certain viruses. So, try this tactic: Whenever you're working near likely targets, such as petunias, keep a bowl handy that's filled with a 50-50 mix of milk and water. Then every few minutes, dip your hands and tools into the liquid. It'll stop vicious viruses right in their tracks!

Smokers Beware!

If you enjoy a smoke now and then, be sure to wash your hands thoroughly before you work in your garden. Tobacco mosaic virus is carried in tobacco products, and it attacks many tobacco relatives, including petunias, flowering tobacco (*Nicotiana*), and peppers.

Jerry's TIMELY TIPS

"Once viruses have infected a plant, you can't cure it. It's best to just pull it up and toss it in the trash. Think that's too harsh? Pests feeding on a virus-infected plant can carry the disease to healthy plants nearby, and that means more and more flowers'll be infected. So steel yourself, and pull out that poor plant, pronto!"

Cultural Problems

Compacted soil, salt spray, and even too much or too little fertilizer can all turn beautiful blooms into sick-looking has-beens. Luckily, these environmental problems are easy to fix—and even easier to prevent!

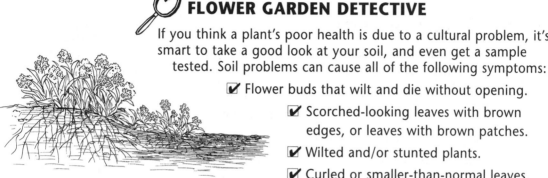

FLOWER GARDEN DETECTIVE

If you think a plant's poor health is due to a cultural problem, it's smart to take a good look at your soil, and even get a sample tested. Soil problems can cause all of the following symptoms:

☑ Flower buds that wilt and die without opening.

☑ Scorched-looking leaves with brown edges, or leaves with brown patches.

☑ Wilted and/or stunted plants.

☑ Curled or smaller-than-normal leaves.

☑ Rotted roots.

Soil compaction

Salt may be fine in the kitchen, but not in your garden! It can come from various sources: deicing salts, salt spray from the ocean, too much fertilizer, and pet urine. Signs of salt damage include stunted, wilting plants with dried-out leaves, and a crusty white buildup on foliage.

So what's a gardener to do? Sprinkle gypsum on the soil, then water heavily to wash out excess salt. Loosening the soil and working in organic matter to improve drainage also help.

Give 'Em Some Wiggle Room

Plants grow best in loose soil, where they can wiggle their roots and spread them out as far as they like. If their soil gets packed down by kids or pets cutting through the bed, your flowers are going to suffer.

To fix the problem, dig up the plants and loosen the soil with a rotary tiller or a garden fork. Spread a 2- to 3-inch layer of compost or other organic matter over the area, then work that in. Then figure out a way to keep kids and pets out of the area!

Flower Power Tonics Roundup

✿ By now, you've heard me say over and over again that my handy-dandy tonics can solve all your pesky flower garden problems. To make your life even easier, I've gathered all of my marvelous mixers, fabulous fixers, and excellent elixirs right here in one place, so you can find 'em in a snap if trouble strikes.

The Inside Scoop

Here's a quick rundown of the major ingredients in my Flower Power Tonics— and the role each plays in helping to keep your buds and blooms looking their very best!

Ammonia. This common household product is actually a readily available source of nitrogen that'll help encourage leafy plant growth. This is powerful stuff, so always dilute it as specified in my tonic recipes to avoid burning your plants. Ammonia can burn you, too, so always wear gloves when you're

Jerry's TIMELY TIPS

"Even though my tonic ingredients are natural substances and, for the most part, are safe when used as directed, some can irritate your eyes or skin, especially if you have allergies. So always take the proper precautions when you use these products. Be sure to label each tonic clearly—so that no one mistakes it for a product for human consumption—and keep all products safely stored away in a locked cabinet, well out of reach of children and pets."

mixing it into tonics, and don't get it anywhere near your eyes.

Antiseptic mouthwash. This stuff does the same thing in your garden that it does in your mouth. Yep, it actually destroys those disease germs that can cause trouble, big-time, if you don't get after 'em!

Baby shampoo and liquid dish soap. These products help soften soil, and they wash dust, dirt, and pollution from leaves, so your plants can grow better. They send pests packin', too.

Beer. Don't waste your money on fancy brands here; the cheap stuff will work just as well! Beer is an enzyme activator that helps release nutrients that are locked in the soil, and puts 'em to work making your plants grow stronger and healthier.

Cola. The sugar in this carbonated drink helps feed the good bacteria that keep your soil—and in turn, your plants—in top-notch condition. Skip the diet kinds, though, because artificial sweeteners don't work like the real thing.

Epsom salts. Besides being a great soak for your tired gardening muscles, this super stuff improves the root structure of your plants—and healthy roots mean abundant, healthy blooms!

Sugar, molasses, and corn syrup. These sugar sources stimulate the formation of chlorophyll in plants, and they help feed the good soil bacteria, too.

Tea. The tannic acid in tea helps your plants digest their food faster and more easily, so they can get busy making more flowers.

Tobacco. This potent stuff poisons bugs when they ingest it, or even when they simply come in contact with it. It does the same thing to some of the germs that cause plant diseases.

Whiskey. Whether it's Scotch, bourbon, or the plain old rot-gut variety, whiskey provides nutrients and is a mild disinfectant that'll keep bugs and thugs a good distance away.

All-Purpose Bug/Thug Spray

To kill flower garden insects and diseases in one fell swoop, whip up a batch of my all-purpose spray.

3 tbsp. of baking soda
2 tbsp. of Murphy's Oil Soap
2 tbsp. of canola oil
2 tbsp. of vinegar
2 gal. of warm water

Mix all of the ingredients together, and mist-spray your perennials to the point of run-off. Apply in early spring, just as the bugs and thugs are waking up. (For related text, see page 116.)

All-Purpose Fertilizer

Give your groundcovers a taste of this in spring, then stand back, and watch 'em thrive!

3 parts bonemeal
3 parts greensand or wood ashes
1 part bloodmeal

Mix the ingredients together. Scatter 2 tablespoons around each clump of plants, and scratch it into the soil surface. (For related text, see page 216.)

All-Season Clean-Up Tonic

Apply this tonic in early evening every two weeks during the growing season to keep insects and diseases at bay.

1 cup of liquid dish soap
1 cup of tobacco tea*
1 cup of antiseptic mouthwash
Warm water

Mix the soap, tobacco tea, and mouthwash in a 20 gallon hose-end sprayer, filling the balance of the jar with warm water. Liberally apply this mixture to your beds and borders to discourage insects and prevent disease during the growing season. (For related text, see page 115.)

*Place three fingers of chewing tobacco in an old nylon stocking and soak it in a gallon of hot water until the mixture is dark brown.

All-Season Green-Up Tonic

If your flowering plants are looking a bit peaked, give them a taste of this sweet snack. They'll green up in a jiffy!

1 can of beer
1 cup of ammonia
½ cup of liquid dish soap
½ cup of liquid lawn food
½ cup of molasses or corn syrup

Mix all of the ingredients together in a large bucket, then pour into a 20 gallon hose-end sprayer, and apply to your plants every three weeks during the growing season. (For related text, see page 147.)

Aphid Antidote

To keep aphids and other pests off your favorite flowers, mix up a batch of this amazing antidote.

1 small onion, chopped finely
2 medium cloves of garlic, chopped finely
1 tbsp. of liquid dish soap
2 cups of water

Put all of the ingredients in a blender, blend on high, and then strain out the pulp through cheesecloth or panty hose. Pour the liquid into a hand-held mist sprayer, and douse your flowers at the first sign of aphid trouble. (For related text, see page 312.)

Baking Soda Spray

If you're seeing gray spots on your zinnia leaves, whip up a batch of this simple solution.

2 tbsp. of baby shampoo
1 tbsp. of baking soda
1 gal. of warm water

Mix these ingredients together, and mist-spray your plants lightly once a week to keep diseases from zapping your zinnias! (For related text, see page 307.)

Bed Builder Mix

If you have a site that you'd like to fill with flowers someday, it's never too soon to start the soil-building process. Scrape off the weeds and grass with a sharp spade, then add a dose of my super-duper mix.

40 lbs. of bagged topsoil
10 lbs. of compost
5 lbs. of bonemeal
1 lb. of Epsom salts

Mix all of these ingredients in a wheelbarrow or garden cart, spread a 2- to 3-inch layer over the entire site, and then top the bed with mulch. Add the plants whenever you're ready! (For related text, see page 5.)

Beetle Juice Tonic

This stuff will stop any kind of pesky beetle right in its tracks!

½ cup of beetles (alive or dead)
2 cups of water

Collect the beetles and whirl 'em up in an old blender (one you'll *never* again use for food preparation) with 2 cups of water. Strain the liquid through cheesecloth. Pour about ¼ cup into a 1 gallon hand-held sprayer, and fill the rest of the jar with water. Spray your plants from top to bottom, and make sure you coat both sides of the leaves. (For related text, see page 313.)

Bug-Be-Gone Spray

Tired of pests having a picnic in your beds and borders? Then use this potent spray to keep bugs at bay.

1 cup of Murphy's Oil Soap
1 cup of antiseptic mouthwash
1 cup of tobacco tea*

Mix all of the ingredients together in a 20 gallon hose-end sprayer, and soak your plants to the point of run-off. (For related text, see page 116.)

*Place three fingers of chewing tobacco in an old nylon stocking and soak it in a gallon of hot water until the mixture is dark brown.

Bulb Bath

To keep all your bulbs bug-free, treat 'em to a nice, warm bath right before planting. Here's what you'll need.

2 tsp. of baby shampoo
1 tsp. of antiseptic mouthwash
¼ tsp. of instant tea granules
2 gal. of warm water

Mix all of the ingredients in a bucket, then carefully place your bulbs into the mixture. Stir gently, then remove the bulbs one at a time and plant them. When you're done, don't throw the bath water out with the babies; give your trees and shrubs a little taste, too! (For related text, see page 170.)

Dead Bug Brew

This mix of puréed dead bugs is a sure-fire way to keep *live* bugs away!

½ cup of dead insects (the more, the merrier!)
1 tbsp. of liquid dish soap
1 tbsp. of cayenne pepper
2 cups of water

Put all of the ingredients in an old blender (one you'll *never* again use for food preparation) and purée the heck out of 'em. Use cheesecloth or panty hose to strain out the pulp. Dilute the remaining brew at a rate of ¼ cup of brew per 1 cup of water. Apply to your flowers with a hand-held mist sprayer, to the point of run-off.

Bulb Booster

Give your bulb beds a boost each year with a taste of this terrific tonic!

2 lbs. of bonemeal
2 lbs. of wood ashes
1 lb. of Epsom salts

Sprinkle this mixture on top of flowerbeds where bulbs are growing in early spring, just as the foliage starts to peek out of the ground. (For related text, see page 172.)

Bulb Breakfast

Don't spend a fortune buying special bagged fertilizer for your bulbs. Just whip up a batch of this marvelous mix.

10 lbs. of compost
5 lbs. of bonemeal
2 lbs. of bloodmeal
1 lb. of Epsom salts

Blend all of the ingredients together in a wheelbarrow. Before setting out your bulbs, work this hearty breakfast into every 100 square feet of soil in your bulb beds and borders. (For related text, see page 168.)

Bulb Soak

Get your hyacinths—and other bulbs, too—off to a great start by soaking them in this super solution before planting.

1 can of beer
2 tbsp. of liquid dish soap
¼ tsp. of instant tea granules
2 gal. of water

Mix all of the ingredients together in a large bucket, and carefully dip the bulbs in the mix before planting. (For related text, see page 231.)

Caterpillar Killer Tonic

To keep caterpillars in check and away from your flowers, brew up a batch of this tonic.

½ lb. of wormwood (*Artemisia*) leaves
2 tbsp. of Murphy's Oil Soap
4 cups of warm water

Simmer the wormwood leaves in 2 cups of warm water for 30 minutes or so. Strain out the leaves, then add the liquid and the Murphy's Oil Soap to 2 more cups of warm water. Apply with a 6 gallon hose-end sprayer to the point of run-off. Repeat as necessary until all of the caterpillars are history! (For related text, see page 315.)

Chamomile Mildew Chaser

If your verbenas are looking gray and dusty, there's a good chance they've got powdery mildew. Apply this elixir at the first sign of trouble.

4 chamomile tea bags
2 tbsp. of Murphy's Oil Soap
1 qt. of boiling water

Make a strong batch of tea by letting the tea bags steep in the boiling water for an hour or so. Once the tea cools, mix with the Murphy's Oil Soap. Apply once a week with a 6 gallon hose-end sprayer. (For related text, see page 301.)

Clematis Chow

These regal beauties can take a lot of neglect, but if you want a really fine clematis vine, I've got just the ticket— this secret family recipe.

5 gal. of well-cured horse or cow manure
½ cup of lime
½ cup of bonemeal

Mix the ingredients together in a wheelbarrow and spread over the root zone of your clematis, first thing in the spring. Top that with a rich mulch of half-rotted compost to make sure the soil stays cool and moist, and your clematis will be as happy as a clam! (For related text, see page 305.)

Compost Booster

Whether you use it as a mulch or dig it into the soil to help hold water, you can never have too much compost! To keep your pile cookin', and the compost comin', try the following formula.

1 can of beer
1 can of regular cola (not diet)
1 cup of ammonia
½ cup of weak tea water*
2 tbsp. of baby shampoo

Pour this mixture into a 20 gallon hose-end sprayer, and saturate your compost pile every time you add a new, foot-deep layer of ingredients to it. (For related text, see page 108.)

*Soak a used tea bag and 1 teaspoon of liquid dish soap in a gallon of warm water until the mix is light brown.

Compost Tea

This simple solution is super for feeding tuberous begonias—plus all kinds of other flowers, too! Put several shovels-ful of compost or manure into a large trash can, and fill the can to the top with water. Allow the mixture to sit for a day or two, stirring it several times each day. To use, dilute with water until it is light brown. Give each plant about a cup of this tea every two or three weeks, and your feeding worries will be over! (For related text, see page 162.)

Deer Buster Egg Brew

If you notice that deer are starting to nibble on your flowers, protect your plants with this potent brew.

2 eggs
2 cloves of garlic
2 tbsp. of Tabasco® sauce
2 tbsp. of cayenne pepper
2 cups of water

Put all of the ingredients in a blender and purée. Allow the mixture to sit for two days, then pour or spray it all over and around the plants you need to protect. Reapply every other week or so, or after a rain, to keep the odor fresh. (For related text, see page 325.)

Disease Defense

Wet, rainy weather can foster fungus in your flower garden, especially in late winter and early spring. But don't let the dreary days get you down—keep your perennials and bulbs happy and healthy with this elixir.

1 cup of chamomile tea
1 tsp. of liquid dish soap
½ tsp. of vegetable oil
½ tsp. of peppermint oil
1 gal. of warm water

Mix all of the ingredients together in a bucket. Mist-spray your plants every week or so *before* the really hot weather (75°F or higher) sets in. This elixir is strong stuff, so test it on a few leaves; wait two or three days to make sure there's no damage before completely spraying any plant. (For related text, see page 328.)

Dog-Be-Gone!

Man's best friend can be your worst traffic nightmare. To keep dogs away from their favorite digging spots, liberally apply this mix to the soil.

2 cloves of garlic
2 small onions
1 jalapeño pepper
1 tbsp. of cayenne pepper
1 tbsp. of Tabasco® sauce
1 tbsp. of chili powder
1 qt. of warm water

Chop the garlic, onions, and jalapeño pepper finely, then combine with all of the remaining ingredients. Let the mix sit for 24 hours, then sprinkle it on any areas where dogs are a problem. (For related text, see page 45.)

Double Punch Garlic Tea

Are thrips and other pesky insects bugging your perennials? Send 'em packing with a dose of this excellent elixir.

5 unpeeled cloves of garlic, coarsely chopped
2 cups of boiling water
½ cup of tobacco tea*
1 tsp. of instant tea granules
1 tsp. of baby shampoo

Place the chopped garlic in a heat-proof bowl, and pour the boiling water over it. Let it steep overnight. Strain through a coffee filter, and then mix it with the other ingredients in a hand-held mist sprayer, and thoroughly drench your plants. (For related text, see page 255.)

*Place three fingers of chewing tobacco in an old nylon stocking and soak it in a gallon of hot water until the mixture is dark brown.

Fabulous Foliar Formula

For big, bright, shiny leaves in even the sandiest soil, feed your flowering plants this fantastic formula every three weeks.

1 can of beer
½ cup of fish emulsion
½ cup of ammonia
¼ cup of blackstrap molasses
¼ cup of instant tea granules

Mix all of the ingredients together in a 20 gallon hose-end sprayer and apply thoroughly until it starts running off the leaves. This formula works best on perennials that aren't blooming. If your plants are in flower, aim the spray at the foliage, and try to avoid wetting the blooms. (For related text, see page 40.)

Flowerbed Bonanza

After the fall clean-up, spray all of your flowerbeds and borders with this terrific tonic. It'll get rid of any pests and diseases, and get your soil in great shape for spring, too!

1 can of beer
1 can of regular cola (not diet)
½ cup of liquid dish soap
½ cup of tobacco tea*

Mix all of the ingredients together in a bucket, then apply with a 20 gallon hose-end sprayer. (For related text, see page 118.)

*Place three fingers of chewing tobacco in an old nylon stocking and soak it in a gallon of hot water until the mixture is dark brown.

Flower Defender

Once your annuals are up and growing, protect them from pests with this potent brew.

1 cup of liquid dish soap
1 cup of tobacco tea*
1 cup of antiseptic mouthwash
¼ cup of Tabasco® sauce
Warm water

Mix the dish soap, tobacco tea, mouthwash, and Tabasco sauce in a 20 gallon hose-end sprayer, filling the balance of the sprayer jar with warm water. Then bathe all of your early bloomers with this super bug-busting elixir to keep 'em growing. (For related text, see page 146.)

*Place three fingers of chewing tobacco in an old nylon stocking and soak it in a gallon of hot water until the mixture is dark brown.

Flower Feeder

Use this all-purpose food to keep all your flowers flourishing!

1 can of beer
2 tbsp. of fish emulsion
2 tbsp. of liquid dish soap
2 tbsp. of ammonia
2 tbsp. of hydrogen peroxide
2 tbsp. of whiskey
1 tbsp. of clear corn syrup
1 tbsp. of unflavored gelatin
4 tsp. of instant tea granules
2 gal. of warm water

Mix all of the ingredients together. Water all your flowering plants with this mix every two weeks in the morning. (For related text, see page 110.)

Flower Flea Fluid

This spicy brew'll do a real number on leafhoppers.

3 tbsp. of garlic-and-onion juice*
3 tbsp. of skim milk
2 tbsp. of baby shampoo
1 tsp. of Tabasco® sauce
1 gal. of water

Mix all the ingredients together in a bucket, and pour into a 20 gallon hose-end sprayer. Spray on your plants every 10 days. Make sure you get the undersides of the leaves, too! (For related text, see page 317.)

*To make the garlic-and-onion juice,

chop 2 cloves of garlic and 2 medium onions. Combine in a blender with 3 cups of water. Strain, and use remaining liquid. Freeze any leftover liquid for future use.

Flower Power Prep Mix

Here's a flower power mixture that'll really energize your beds and produce a bounty of bright, beautiful blooms.

4 cups of bonemeal
2 cups of gypsum
2 cups of Epsom salts
1 cup of wood ashes
1 cup of lime
4 tbsp. of medicated baby powder
1 tbsp. of baking powder

Combine all of these ingredients in a bucket, and work the mixture into the soil before you plant to get all your flowers off to a rip-roarin' start! (For related text, see page 133.)

Foundation Food

Soil along a foundation is often downright awful, at least as far as your plants are concerned. Use the following tonic to build it up and make your plants happy—with a minimum amount of work!

10 parts compost
3 parts bonemeal
2 parts bloodmeal
1 part kelp meal

Mix the ingredients in a garden cart or wheelbarrow. Spread a thin layer (about a half-inch or so) over the entire planting, and lightly scratch it into the soil around shrubs. Add a new layer each year. Top it with shredded bark or other mulch. (For related text, see page 48.)

Fragrant Pest Fighter

People love perfumed perennials, but pests sure don't! So the next time you're out in your flower garden, gather the ingredients for this aromatic pest-control spray.

½ cup of fresh tansy (*Tanacetum vulgare*) or mugwort (*Artemisia vulgaris*) leaves
½ cup of fresh lavender flowers and/or leaves
½ cup of fresh sage (*Salvia officinalis*) leaves

Boiling water
2 cups of room-temperature water
1 tsp. of Murphy's Oil Soap

Place the leaves and flowers in a 1-quart glass jar; fill with boiling water, cover, and let sit until cool. Add ⅛ cup of that liquid to the 2 cups of room-temperature water and the Murphy's Oil Soap. Pour into a hand-held mist sprayer, and apply to all your flowers to keep pests at bay! (For related text, see page 252.)

Frozen Feed

To give your perennials a welcome winter snack and a rip-roarin' start in spring, wait until the ground freezes, then apply the following mix.

25 pounds of garden gypsum
10 pounds of garden fertilizer (4-2-4 or 5-10-5)
5 pounds of bonemeal

Mix all of the ingredients together, then spread the mixture evenly over your beds and borders. This amount will cover 100 square feet. (For related text, see page 117.)

Fungus Fighter

Get sweet on your peonies, and give 'em a dose of molasses to keep dastardly diseases away! At the first sign of trouble, try this tonic.

½ cup of molasses
½ cup of powdered milk
1 tsp. of baking soda
1 gal. of warm water

Mix the molasses, powdered milk, and baking soda into a paste. Place the mixture into the toe of an old nylon stocking, and let it steep in the warm water for several hours. Then strain, and use the remaining liquid as a fungus-fighting spray for peonies and other perennials every two weeks throughout the growing season. I guarantee you'll have no more fungus troubles! (For related text, see page 250.)

Garden Cure-All Tonic

At the first sign of insects or disease, mix up a batch of this tonic to set things right.

4 cloves of garlic
1 small onion
1 small jalapeño pepper
Warm water
1 tsp. of Murphy's Oil Soap
1 tsp. of vegetable oil

Pulverize the garlic, onion, and pepper in a blender, and let them steep in a quart of warm water for two hours. Strain the mixture through cheesecloth or panty hose, and dilute the liquid with three parts of warm water. Add the Murphy's Oil Soap and vegetable oil. Mist-spray your flowers with this elixir several times a week. (For related text, see page 114.)

Get-Up-and-Grow Iris Tonic

For the most beautiful bearded irises on the block, feed your plants a dose of this magical mix.

4 parts bonemeal
6 parts hydrated lime

Mix the ingredients together and sprinkle around established plants in early spring. Your irises will get off to a flying start! (For related text, see page 235.)

Herb Garden Potpourri

For a potpourri that smells good enough to eat, give this magical mix a try.

2 cups of thyme shoots, dried
1 cup of rosemary leaves, dried
1 cup of mint leaves, dried
½ cup of lavender flowers, dried
¼ cup of cloves, whole
2 tbsp. of orrisroot, powdered

Combine all the ingredients in a large bowl. Mix with your hands (they'll smell great afterward). Put the mixed potpourri in closed glass jars for storage, or sew into fabric sachets and use to freshen up closets and drawers. (For related text, see page 223.)

Homegrown Daisy Spray

If you grow painted daisy (*Tanacetum coccineum*)—also called pyrethrum daisy—you have the makings for a great homemade pest spray. Here's how to make it.

⅛ cup of 70% isopropyl alcohol
1 cup of packed, fresh painted
  daisy flower heads

Pour the alcohol over the flower heads and let sit overnight. Strain out the flowers, then store the extract in a labeled and sealed container. When you need it, mix the extract with three quarts of water to make a spray that controls a wide range of garden pests. (For related text, see page 194.)

Hot Bite Spray

Want to keep pesky squirrels from nipping off the buds of your prized tulips? This spicy mixture'll make 'em think twice about taking a bite!

3 tbsp. of cayenne pepper
1 tbsp. of Tabasco® sauce
1 tbsp. of ammonia
1 tbsp. of baby shampoo
2 cups of hot water

Mix the cayenne pepper with the hot water in a bottle, and shake well. Let the mixture sit overnight, then pour off the liquid without disturbing the sediment. Mix the liquid with the other ingredients in a hand-held mist sprayer. Keep a batch on hand as long as new tulip buds are forming, and spritz the flower stems as often as you can to keep 'em hot, hot, hot! It's strong medicine, so make sure you wear rubber gloves while you're handling this brew. (For related text, see page 300.)

Hummingbird Nectar

Hummers will visit a feeder all summer long, once they get the idea it's filled with nectar. You can buy packets of nectar mix, but making your own is easy and inexpensive.

1 part white sugar (not honey, which hosts bacteria harmful to hummers)
4 parts water
A few drops of red food coloring (optional)

Boil the mix and let it cool before filling the feeder. Once hummers start coming, decrease the solution to about 1 part sugar and 8 parts water. No, this isn't the old bait-and-switch tactic—there's a good reason for diluting the solution. Hummingbirds can sometimes suffer a fatal liver disorder if they get too much sugar.

Replace the nectar every three days or so—every other day, if temperatures are above 60°F. Wash the feeder with soap and scalding water. Rinse thoroughly. Otherwise, the nectar and/or feeder can host hummingbird-harming bacteria. (For related text, see page 61.)

Magic Mum Booster

Whenever Grandma Putt set out new mums in spring, she'd give 'em a little extra TLC. She'd fill the hole with plenty of compost, and then follow that up with a handful of this mix to get those mums growin' up right!

2 lbs. of dry oatmeal
2 lbs. of crushed dry dog food
½ cup of sugar
1 handful of human hair

Mix all of these ingredients in a 5-gallon bucket. Work a handful of this mix into the base of each hole before planting. Mums love this mix, as do many other perennials—so why not give all your new plantings a taste? (For related text, see page 179.)

Mildew Relief Elixir

If you've had problems with powdery mildew on your roses, try this tonic to keep it from spoiling your fun again this year.

1 tbsp. of baby shampoo
1 tbsp. of hydrogen peroxide
1 tsp. of instant tea granules
2 cups of water

Mix all of these ingredients in a hand-held mist sprayer and apply to rose leaves, stems, and buds. Midafternoon on a cloudy day is the best time to apply it. (For related text, see page 279.)

Mulch
Moisturizer Tonic

When you give your perennial beds a fresh layer of organic mulch in spring, overspray it with this super tonic to give it a little extra kick.

1 can of regular cola (not diet)
½ cup of ammonia
½ cup of antiseptic mouthwash
½ cup of baby shampoo

Mix all of these ingredients in your 20 gallon hose-end sprayer, and give your mulch a long, cool drink. (For related text, see page 257.)

Nutrient Boost
for Neglected Soil

If you have a garden with less-than-great soil, or seem to have lots of yellowed, sick-looking plants, try this sure-fire pick-me-up!

6 parts greensand or wood ashes
3 parts cottonseed meal
3 parts bonemeal

Mix the ingredients together. Add 2 cups of gypsum and 1 cup of limestone per gallon of blend. Apply 5 pounds per 100 square feet a few weeks before planting, or work the mix around established plants. (For related text, see page 109.)

Perennial
Planting Potion

To make sure your flowers get growing on the right root, feed them this powerful potion.

½ can of beer
¼ cup of ammonia
2 tbsp. of hydrogen peroxide
1 tbsp. of liquid dish soap
2 gal. of warm water

Mix all of the ingredients together, and soak the soil around each transplant. You can also sprinkle it around your blooming beauties throughout the summer. (For related text, see page 92.)

Perfect Potting Mix

If you've got a lot of divisions to pot up, you'll need plenty of potting soil. So mix up a big batch of this simple blend, and keep it handy!

1 part topsoil
1 part peat moss
1 part vermiculite
1 part compost

Mix all of the ingredients together and use for potting up all kinds of perennials and bulbs. (For related text, see page 128.)

Potted Plant Picnic

Container plants need lots of energy to stay chock-full of flowers, so whatever you do, don't skimp on the fertilizer! Here's a meal your potted plants are sure to appreciate.

2 tbsp. of brewed black coffee
2 tbsp. of whiskey
1 tsp. of fish emulsion
½ tsp. of unflavored gelatin
½ tsp. of baby shampoo
½ tsp. of ammonia
1 gal. of water

Mix all of the ingredients together and feed to each of your potted perennials and bulbs once a week. (For related text, see page 68.)

Powdery Mildew Control

Don't let mildew mess up your phlox! Try this terrific tonic instead.

4 tbsp. of baking soda
2 tbsp. of Murphy's Oil Soap
1 gal. of warm water

Mix all of the ingredients together. Pour into a hand-held mist sprayer, and apply liberally as soon as you see the telltale white spots on your phlox. (For related text, see page 261.)

Quassia Slug Spray

There's no getting around it: Slugs love hostas! But don't despair—here's a magical mixer that'll really knock those slimy slitherers for a loop.

4 ounces of quassia chips (available at health food stores)
1 gal. of water

Crush, grind, or chop the chips, add them to the water in a bucket, and let steep for 12 to 24 hours. Strain through cheesecloth, then spray the liquid on hostas and other slug-prone plants, such as bellflowers (*Campanula*). This spray also helps control aphids, but will not hurt good guys like lady beetles and honeybees. (For related text, see page 229.)

Really Rosy Potpourri

Don't let fall call an end to your rosy pleasures—mix dried pink, red, and white petals together to make this pretty potpourri you can enjoy all winter long. For extra color, add 1 cup of dried flowers from delphiniums, bee balms (*Monarda*), or bachelor's buttons (*Centaurea cyanus*).

¼ **cup of orrisroot nuggets**
2 ½ **tsp. of rose essential oil**
3 **cups of dried rose petals**
1 **cup of dried rosebuds**
1 **cup of dried rose geranium**
   leaves and flowers
1 **cup of dried lavender flowers**
¼ **cup of dried, crushed lemon peel**

Combine the orrisroot nuggets and the essential oil (both available at craft stores) in a small, airtight glass jar for two days. Mix the remaining ingredients together, add the orrisroot/oil mix, and store in a large, airtight jar for two weeks. Shake the mix daily to blend the scents, then display as desired. (For related text, see page 50.)

Repotting Booster Tonic

When your rooted cuttings are ready for transplanting, a dose of this terrific tonic'll help 'em adjust to their new homes in a jiffy.

½ **tsp. of all-purpose plant food**
½ **tsp. of Vitamin B$_1$ Plant Starter**
½ **cup of weak tea water***
1 **gal. of warm water**

Mix all of the ingredients together, and gently pour the tonic through the soil of your repotted plants. Allow pots to drain for 15 minutes or so, then pour off any excess in the tray, and treat your trees and shrubs to the leftovers! (For related text, see page 126.)

*Soak a used tea bag in a gallon of warm water and 1 teaspoon of liquid dish soap until the water is light brown.

Rhubarb Pest Repellent Tonic

Here's a potent plant tonic that'll say "Scram!" to just about any kind of pest you can think of.

3 **medium-size rhubarb leaves**
¼ **cup of liquid dish soap**
1 **gal. of water**

Chop up the rhubarb leaves, put the pieces in the water, and bring it to a boil. Let the mixture cool, then strain it through cheesecloth to filter out the leaf bits. Mix in the liquid dish soap. Apply this terrific tonic to your plants with a small hand-held mist sprayer, and kiss your pest problems good-bye! (For related text, see page 318.)

Root Revival Tonic

Use this terrific tonic to give your bare-root perennials and roses some refreshment before they go into the garden.

¼ cup of brewed tea
1 tbsp. of liquid dish soap
1 tbsp. of Epsom salts
1 gal. of water

Let the plants sit in this tonic for up to 24 hours. It'll rev up those tired roots and get them ready to grow—*guaranteed!* (For related text, see page 93.)

Root-Rousing Tonic

Want to get your new flowers off to a fabulous start? Well then, you can't do better than giving each one a generous dose of this excellent elixir!

1 can of beer
1 can of regular cola (not diet)
1 cup of liquid dish soap
1 cup of antiseptic mouthwash
¼ tsp. of instant tea granules

Mix all of the ingredients in a large bucket, then pour into a 20 gallon hose-end sprayer and spray liberally over all of your flowerbeds. (For related text, see page 95.)

JERRY'S **BONUS** TONIC!

Scare-'Em-All Tonic

Not sure exactly what's buggin' your beautiful flowers? Send all your pests packin' with this potent brew!

20 cloves of garlic, peeled
1 medium onion, finely chopped
1 tbsp. of liquid dish soap
3 tsp. of glycerin
1 qt. plus 1 gal. of water

Place the garlic cloves, onion, and 1 quart of water in a blender. Blend at high speed for 1 minute. Strain the mixture through cheesecloth or panty hose. Mix the garlic-onion liquid with 1 gallon of water. Add the liquid dish soap and glycerin. Spray on plants as needed to keep the bugs at bay.

Rose Rousin' Elixir

To get bare-root roses off to a rip-roarin' start, give 'em a taste of this magical mixer before you plant.

**1 tbsp. of 5-8-5 or 5-10-5
   garden fertilizer
1 tbsp. of baby shampoo
1 tbsp. of corn syrup
1 gal. of warm water**

Mix these ingredients together in a bucket, and soak the roots in the solution overnight. When you're done, sprinkle this mixture around all your other rosebushes, too—they'll love you for it! (For related text, see page 271.)

Rosy Clean-Up Elixir

Fall is the best time to get a jump on the insects and diseases that plague your roses. So, after your bushes have shed their leaves, but before you mulch them for the winter, spray 'em thoroughly with this terrific tonic.

**1 cup of baby shampoo
1 cup of antiseptic mouthwash
1 cup of tobacco tea***

Place all of these ingredients in your 20 gallon hose-end sprayer and douse each rosebush from top to bottom.

*Place three fingers of chewing tobacco in an old nylon stocking and soak it in a gallon of hot water until the mixture is dark brown. (For related text, see page 280.)

Rosy Feeding Regime

Believe you me, roses are the hardest-working flowering plants in your garden. These beauties bloom only for the sake of showing off, as much as they can, for as long as they can. All this hard work takes lots of energy—and that's where you come in! Follow this simple feeding routine, and your roses will have all the food they need to keep those blooms comin' along! Start with a dose of this elixir in mid- to late spring.

**4 cups of bonemeal
1 cup of 5-10-5 garden fertilizer
1 cup of Epsom salts**

Mix these ingredients together in a bucket, then give each bush 1 heaping tablespoon, or work in 4 pounds per 100 square feet of rose bed. Then every three weeks after that, give 'em a drink of this terrific tonic.

**1 cup of beer
2 tsp. of instant tea granules
1 tsp. of 5-10-5 fertilizer
1 tsp. of fish emulsion
1 tsp. of hydrogen peroxide
1 tsp. of liquid dish soap
2 gal. of warm water**

Mix the ingredients together, then water each plant with 1 pint of the solution in the morning. Stop feeding by July 15 in the North, and August 15 in the South. (For related text, see page 274.)

Scat Cat Solution

Cats can be great pets, but they can also be real pests if they dig in your garden—and they seem to just love the loose, fluffy soil of annual beds. Try this spicy solution to keep them away from your prized plantings.

5 tbsp. of flour
4 tbsp. of powdered mustard
3 tbsp. of cayenne pepper
2 tbsp. of chili powder
2 qts. of warm water

Mix all of the ingredients together. Sprinkle the solution around the areas you want to protect to keep kitty at bay. (For related text, see page 149.)

Seedling Starter Tonic

Give your seedlings a break on moving day by serving 'em a sip of my starter tonic. This helps them recover quickly from the transplanting shock.

1 tbsp. of fish emulsion
1 tbsp. of ammonia
1 tbsp. of Murphy's Oil Soap
1 tsp. of instant tea granules
1 qt. of warm water

Mix all of the ingredients in the warm water. Pour into a hand-held mist sprayer, and mist the young plants several times a day until they're back on their feet and growing again. (For related text, see page 132.)

Seedling Strengthener

To get your seedlings off to a healthy, disease-free start, mist-spray them every few days with this terrific tonic.

2 cups of manure
½ cup of instant tea granules
Warm water

Put the manure and tea in an old nylon stocking, and let it steep in 5 gallons of water for several days. Dilute the mixture with 4 parts of warm water (for example, 4 cups of water for every cup of mix) before using. (For related text, see page 122.)

Slugweiser

To drown your slug sorrows, try this sure cure.

1 lb. of brown sugar
½ pkg. (1½ tsp.) of dry yeast
Warm water

Pour the sugar and yeast into a 1-gallon plastic jug, fill it with warm water, and let it sit for two days, uncovered. Then pour it into your slug traps, and let the good times roll! (For related text, see page 321.)

Soil Energizer Elixir

Whatever kind of garden you're planning, you'll get great results if you perk up the soil before planting with this energizing elixir!

**1 can of beer
1 cup of regular cola (not diet)
1 cup of liquid dish soap
1 cup of antiseptic mouthwash
¼ tsp. of instant tea granules**

Mix these ingredients in a bucket or container, and fill a 20 gallon hose-end sprayer. Overspray the soil in your garden to the point of run-off (or just until small puddles start to form), then let it sit at least two weeks. This recipe makes enough to cover 100 square feet of garden area. (For related text, see page 12.)

Start-Up Snack

Give your just-divided perennials the following fertilizer tonic to get 'em growin' like gangbusters!

**1 can of beer
1 cup of all-purpose plant food
¼ cup of ammonia**

Mix the ingredients together, and pour them into a 20 gallon hose-end sprayer. Fill the balance of the sprayer jar with water. Thoroughly spray on newly divided plants. Repeat one week later. (For related text, see page 129.)

Summer Rejuvenating Tonic

Whenever Grandma Putt's carefully planned annual gardens started to look a little tired in late summer, she'd pinch 'em back hard and give 'em a good drink of this potent pick-me-up.

**¼ cup of beer
1 tbsp. of corn syrup
1 tbsp. of baby shampoo
1 tbsp. of 15-30-15 fertilizer
1 gal. of water**

Mix all of these ingredients, then slowly dribble the solution onto the soil around your annuals. Within two weeks, they'll be real comeback kids! (For related text, see page 14.)

Super Seed-Starting Mix

Typical potting soil is way too rich for small seedlings, and it can foster a bunch of funky fungi that'll quickly wipe out whole pots of baby plants. To get your seeds up and growing safely, I suggest blendin' up a batch of this mix.

**2 parts peat moss
1 part perlite or vermiculite
Warm water**

Mix the peat moss and perlite or vermiculite in a bag or bucket. The day

Hot Bug Brew

Want to get all of those bad bugs out of your flowerbeds—
pronto? Give 'em a shot of this spicy solution!

3 hot green peppers (canned or fresh)
3 medium cloves of garlic
1 small onion
1 tbsp. of liquid dish soap
3 cups of water

Purée the peppers, garlic, and onion in a blender. Pour the purée into a jar, and add the liquid dish soap and water. Let stand for 24 hours, then strain out the pulp with cheesecloth or panty hose. Use a hand-held mist sprayer to apply the remaining liquid to bug-infested bulbs and perennials. Make sure you thoroughly coat the tops and undersides of all the leaves.

before sowing seeds, moisten the mix by adding warm water—a few cups at a time—and working it in with your hands until the mix feels evenly moist to the touch. (For related text, see page 120.)

Super Shrub Elixir

Don't waste your hard-earned dough on fancy, pre-packaged shrub fertilizers from your local garden center! Instead, just whip up a batch of this terrific tonic, and you'll have the best-looking flowering shrubs on the block.

½ can of beer
½ cup of fish emulsion
½ cup of ammonia
¼ cup of baby shampoo
2 tbsp. of hydrogen peroxide

Mix all of the ingredients together, and pour into your 20 gallon hose-end sprayer. Every three weeks during the spring and summer, spray your shrubs until the tonic starts dripping off their leaves. That'll really get 'em growin' like gangbusters! (For related text, see page 291.)

Super Shrub Stimulator

Want to get your shrubs off to a rip-roarin' start in spring? Give 'em a taste of this excellent elixir!

4 tbsp. of instant tea granules
4 tbsp. of bourbon, or ½ can
**   of beer**
2 tbsp. of liquid dish soap
2 gal. of warm water

Mix all of these ingredients together, and sprinkle the mixture over all your shrubs as soon as their leaves are out. (For related text, see page 290.)

Super Spider Mite Mix

Spider mites are tiny, all right, but they can get up to mite-y BIG mischief in your garden! When they show up, send 'em scurryin' with this floury remedy.

4 cups of wheat flour
½ cup of buttermilk
5 gal. of water

Mix all of the ingredients together, and mist-spray your plants to the point of run-off. This mix will suffocate the little buggers without harming your flowers. (For related text, see page 322.)

Transplant Tonic

Use the following tonic to give your new divisions a boost that'll really get 'em growing.

½ can of beer
1 tbsp. of ammonia
1 tbsp. of instant tea granules
1 tbsp. of baby shampoo
1 gal. of water

Mix all of the ingredients together. Use 1 cup of the tonic for each division after replanting. (For related text, see page 104.)

Ultra-Light Potting Soil

To keep your really big pots and planters from being back-breakers, use this planting mix.

4 parts perlite (moistened)
4 parts compost
1 part potting soil
½ part cow manure

Mix all of these ingredients together, then fill your containers. This mix dries out very quickly, particularly in the hot summer sun, so be sure to keep an eye on your flowers, and water them as needed. (For related text, see page 67.)

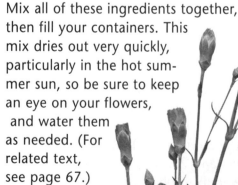

Weed Wipeout

Zap those hard-to-kill weeds with this lethal weapon.

1 tbsp. of gin
1 tbsp. of apple cider vinegar
1 tsp. of liquid dish soap
1 qt. of very warm water

Mix all of the ingredients together in a bucket, then pour into a hand-held sprayer to apply. Drench weeds to the point of run-off, taking care not to spray any surrounding plants. (For related text, see page 112.)

Whitefly Wipeout Tonic

Are whiteflies bugging your flowers? You're sure to find the fixin's for this super-simple spray right in your kitchen cabinet!

1 cup of sour milk (let fresh milk sit out for two days)
2 tbsp. of flour
1 qt. of warm water

Mix all of the ingredients in a bowl, and spray the mixture over any plants that are troubled by whiteflies. (For related text, see page 324.)

Wonderful Weed Killer

Nothing spoils the look of a formal garden quicker than weed-filled paths. Use this tonic to kill weeds in gravel walks, or in cracks between bricks or stones in walkways.

1 gal. of white vinegar
1 cup of table salt
1 tbsp. of liquid dish soap

Mix all of the ingredients together until the salt has dissolved. Spray the solution on weeds, or pour it along cracks to kill weeds. Don't spray it on plants that you want to keep, and don't pour it on soil that you plan to garden in someday! (For related text, see page 64.)

Year-Round Refresher

Use this elixir every three weeks from spring through fall to keep your mixed plantings healthy and happy. (In warm climates, you can use it year-round.)

1 cup of beer
1 cup of baby shampoo
1 cup of liquid lawn food
½ cup of molasses
2 tbsp. of fish emulsion
Ammonia

Mix the beer, shampoo, lawn food, molasses, and fish emulsion in a 20 gallon hose-end sprayer. Fill the balance of the sprayer jar with ammonia, then spray away! (For related text, see page 20.)

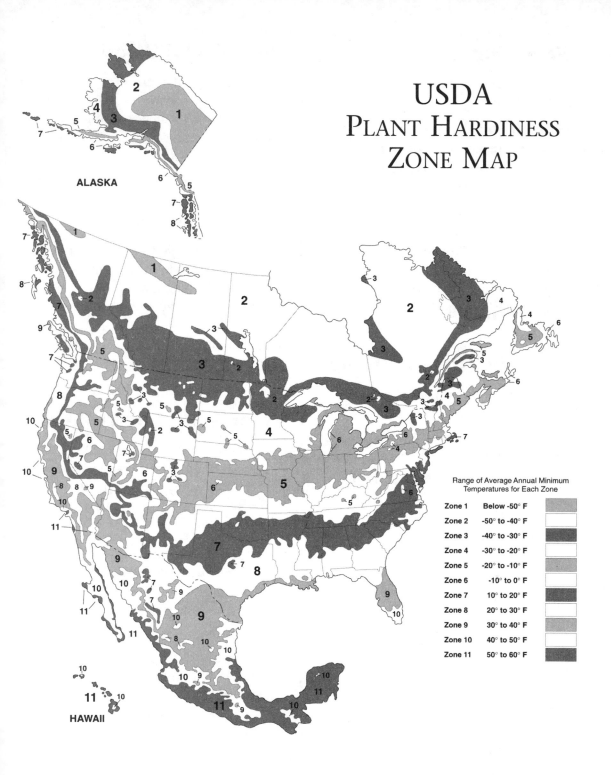

USDA
PLANT HARDINESS
ZONE MAP

ALASKA

HAWAII

Range of Average Annual Minimum
Temperatures for Each Zone

Zone 1	Below -50° F
Zone 2	-50° to -40° F
Zone 3	-40° to -30° F
Zone 4	-30° to -20° F
Zone 5	-20° to -10° F
Zone 6	-10° to 0° F
Zone 7	10° to 20° F
Zone 8	20° to 30° F
Zone 9	30° to 40° F
Zone 10	40° to 50° F
Zone 11	50° to 60° F

Index

Page numbers in **boldface** indicate illustrations.

Cover crops, for clay soil, 38
Crabapples, 72
Cranesbills, 63, 208
Cress, rock, 23
Crocosmias, 61, **172**
Crocuses, 17, 26, 48, 168, 172, 189, **189**, 218, 294
  autumn, **170**
  snow, 23, 189
Crown gall, 327, **327**
Crown imperial, **170**
Crown rot, 155, 167
Cultural problems, 330
Cup-and-saucer vine, 149
Cup plant, 257
Cut flower arrangements, 154, 165, 173, 184, 191, 207, 232, 264, 270, 306
Cuttings, 123–26
Cutworms, 114, 146, 147, 316, **316**
Cypress vine, 149, **305**

D

Daffodils
  anemones with, 140
  dividing, 103–4, 130
  drifts of, 26
  for early color, 17, 23
  facing sun, 27
  with groundcovers, 48, 172–73, 218
  as inedible, 54
  layering, 172
  planting schedule for, 169
  profile of, 190–91, **190**
  with shrubs, 294
  as true bulbs, 168

Dahlias, 18, 50, 96, 100, 124, 143, 169, 192–93, **192**, 317
Daisies, **26**
  attracting butterflies, 55–56
  gloriosa, 70, 88, 282, 283
  oxeye, 56, 99, 195, **195**, 311
  painted, **194**
  paper, **141**
  profile of, 194–95
  pyrethrum, 114, 194
  Shasta, 50–51, 56, 97, 101, 106, 195, 207
  sneezeweed, 56, 98, 101, 106, 195, 257
  Swan River, **143**
  in tonics, 194, 344
Daisy Spray, Homegrown, 194, 344
Dame's rocket, 70, 74
Damping-off, 122, 146, 147
Dandelions, 112
Daylilies
  attracting humming-birds, 61
  for bare patches, 29
  bloom time of, 27
  for color, 10
  dividing, 85, 128, 129
  as drought-tolerant, 34
  edible flowers on, 53
  as groundcovers, 215
  pinching and, 97
  plants paired with, 165, 187, 261, 266, 282, 284, 294
  profile of, 196–97, **196**

for sandy soil, 40
  terms describing, 197
  as tuberous roots, 169
Dead Bug Brew, 336
Deadnettles, 28, 74, 128, 198, **198**, 216, 294
Deer, 325, **325**
Deer Buster Egg Brew, 325, 338
Delphiniums, 9–10, 27, 54, 101, 199–200, **199**
Design, flower garden, 2–8, 12–15, 19, 95
Dianthus, 201–2, **201**. *See also* Pinks
Digging, 39, 83
Dill, 224
Disease Defense, 328, 339
Disease-resistant plants, 116, 150
Diseases, 135, 150, 278, 311
  bacterial, 327
  fungal, 122, 129, 328
  signs of, 112, 113
  viruses, 329
Division
  methods of, 102–6, 127–30
  of perennials, 31, 102–6, 127, 129, 152, 258
  of pot-bound plants, 85
Docks, 56
Dog-Be Gone!, 45, 339
Dog food, in tonics, 179, 345
Dogwoods
  Cornelian cherry, 292
  flowering, 20

Dogwoods (*continued*)
pagoda, 21
red-twig, 27, 36, 292
yellow-twig, 36
Dolls, hollyhock, 228
Double Punch Garlic Tea,
255, 339
Drainage, 8, 79
Drawing garden plan
on base map, 6, 7, 30
on bubble diagram,
13–14
Dried flower arrange-
ments, 137, 165, 184
Drought-tolerant plants,
34, 44
Drying methods
for fragrant plants, 58
for herbs, 223, 224
for rose petals, 280
Dry-soil sites, 32–34, 38
Dry well, for wet sites, 35
Dusty miller, 10, 34, 68,
74

E

Echinacea tincture, 186
Edges, 4, 5, 20
Edging plants, 17, 144
Edging strips, 30, 81, 167
Edible flowers, 52–54,
137, 158, 196, 224, 247
Eggplant, 258
Eggs, in tonics, 325, 338
Elephant's ears, **173**
Epsom salts
in bulb fertilizer, 110
for roses, 275
in tonics, 5, 93, 133,
168, 172, 274,

332–33, 335, 336,
349, 350
Erosion, on slopes, 43
Evening primrose,
Missouri, **253**
Evergreens, 27, 65

F

Fabulous Foliar Formula,
40, 340
Fall, colorful flowers for,
27, 140
Farewell-to-spring, 88
Fencing, 64, 325
Ferns, 14, 28, 29, 166,
232, 261, 265
Fertilizer, All-Purpose,
216, 333
Fertilizers
for annuals, 109–10,
147, 148
cultural problems and,
330
for perennials, 110,
254, 255
in tonics, 14, 117, 271,
274, 342, 350, 352
Feverfew, 224
Fish emulsion
as fertilizer, 110, 255
in tonics, 20, 40, 68,
110, 132, 274, 291,
340, 341, 347, 350,
351, 355
Flax, blue, 9
Flea beetles, 113, 313
Floating row covers, 89
Flora's paintbrush, 89
Flour, in tonics, 149, 322,
324, 351, 354, 355

Flowerbed Bonanza, 118,
340
Flowerbeds
edges for, 4
locating, 3–4
plant height and,
18–19
plant selection for,
84–86
post-planting care of,
94–95
preparing, 78–82
protecting, from foot
traffic, 45
seed-sowing for, 86–90
size of, 145
soil for, 82–84
transplants for, 90–93
visualizing, before
planting, 4
Flower Defender, 146, 340
Flower Feeder, 110, 341
Flower Flea Fluid, 317,
341
Flower Power Prep Mix,
133, 341
Flower Power Tonics
All-Purpose Bug/Thug
Spray, 116, 333
All-Purpose Fertilizer,
216, 333
All-Season Clean-Up
Tonic, 115, 334
All-Season Green-Up
Tonic, 147, 334
Aphid Antidote, 312,
334
Baking Soda Spray,
307, 334
Bed Builder Mix, 5,
335

Lily-of-the-valley, 28, 216, **216**
Lilyturfs, 65, 216
Lime, in tonics, 133, 235, 305, 337
Liquid dish soap
  for pest spray adherence, 311, 320
  in tonics, 12, 64, 92, 93, 95, 110, 112, 115, 118, 146, 147, 231, 274, 290, 312, 314, 318, 328, 332, 334, 336, 337, 339, 340, 341, 346, 348, 349, 350, 352, 353, 354, 355
Lobelias, 36, **60,** 144, **149, 256**
Lovage, 224
Love-in-a-mist, 70, 256
Love-lies-bleeding, 18, 99, 143
Lungworts, 24, 41, 128, 153, 198, 225, 229, 253, 299
Lupines, 56, 244, **244**

M

Magic Mum Booster, 179, 345
Magnolia, star, 24
Mallow, 10, 111–12
Manure
  as soil amendment, 82
  in tonics, 67, 122, 162, 305, 337, 338, 351, 354
Map
  base, 6, 7, 30

USDA Plant Hardiness Zone, 251, **356**
Maples, 27, 42, 72
Marigolds, 56, 68, 87, 99, 145, 256
  pot, 54, 56, 70, 89
  profile of, 245, **245**
Mattocks, 83
Meadow rues, 153, 253, **256**
Mealybugs, 319, **319**
Mice, 113
Mignonette, 88
Mildew, 50. *See also* Powdery mildew
Mildew Chaser, Chamomile, 301, 337
Mildew Relief Elixir, 279, 345
Milk
  for disease control, 277, 329
  in tonics, 250, 317, 324, 341, 343, 355
Milkweeds, 36, 56
Milky Spore disease, for beetle control, 313
Mint, 53, 58, 221, 224
  in tonics, 223, 344
Miscanthus, 45
Mixed borders, 13, 17, 27
Mixed plantings, 13, 16–21
Moisture-loving plants, 35, 36
Molasses, in tonics, 20, 40, 147, 250, 333, 334, 340, 343, 355
Money-saving ideas
  buying transplants, 86
  daffodil bulbs, 190

four-o'clocks, 204
free compost, 84
freezing herbs, 222
geraniums, 209
groundcovers, 213
layering shrubs, 131
mulch, 239
perennials, 257–58
plant sources, 15, 28
plant ties, 102
rose care, 275
seed-sowing, 70
seed-starting, 119–22
tender bulbs, 171
watering ideas, 31, 33
wildflower garden, 62
Monkshoods, 54, 140
Moonflowers, 74, 75, 149, 246
Morning glories, 47, 61, 87, 246, **246,** 293
Mosaic virus, 329, **329**
Mountain bluet, 97, 106, 128, 156
Mouthwash, antiseptic, in tonics, 12, 95, 115, 116, 146, 170, 257, 280, 332, 334, 335, 340, 346, 350, 352
Mugworts, in tonics, 252, 342
Mulch(ing)
  bark, 45–46
  from Christmas trees, 118, 239
  for dry soil, 33
  for new beds, 94
  perennials, 254
  for pest control, 323
  pests attracted to, 113, 114, 326

Rudbeckias, 282–83, 284, 287. *See also* Coneflowers, orange
Rusts, 328

S

Saffron, 189
Sage, 56, **223,** 224
 mealycup, 50
 profile of, 284–85
 Russian, 74, 101, 140
 scarlet, **284,** 285
 in tonics, 252, 342
Salt, in tonics, 64, 355
Salt damage, 117, 330
Salt-tolerant shrubs, 40
Salvias, 18, 56, **60,** 61, 68
Sand, for clay soil, 38
Sandy-soil sites, 39–40
Sawdust, as soil amendment, 82
Scabiosas, 286. *See also* Pincushion flowers
Scale, 320, **320**
Scaly bulbs, defined, 242
Scare-'Em-All Tonic, 349
Scarlet runner beans, 47, 122, 293
Scat Cat Solution, 149, 351
Seasons. *See also specific seasons*
 color throughout, 22–27
Sedums, 34, 40, 124, 128, 215, 287–88, **287**
Seedbeds, preparing, 87
Seedheads, for birds, 99
Seedlings, 69, 89, 90–93

Seedling Starter Tonic, 132, 351
Seedling Strengthener, 122, 351
Seeds
 vs. purchased plants, 86
 sowing, 69, 70, 86–90, 145
 starting, 119–22
Seed-Starting Mix, Super, 120, 352–53
Seed tapes, 90
Self-sowing flowers, 70–71, 98–99
Serviceberry, downy, 20
Sevin, liquid, 319
Shade
 bench in, 42
 for hummingbirds, 60
 plants suited for, 3, 20, 21, 23–24, 26, 28, 41, 79, 144, 216, 224, 253
 for potted plants, 67
 from trees, 41–42
Shampoo, baby. *See* Baby shampoo
Shopping tips, 84–86
Shrub Elixir, Super, 291, 353
Shrubs. *See also specific shrubs*
 for balancing garden design, 19
 bulbs with, 173
 flowering, 19, 24
 in formal gardens, 65, **65**
 as groundcovers, 218
 growth of, 293

 layering, 131
 loosening roots of, 289
 in mixed planting, 20
 moisture-loving, 36
 overview of, 289–94
 planting, 29, 289–91
 plants paired with, 293, 294
 privacy from, 16
 for protecting flowerbeds, 45
 pruning, 292–93, 294
 salt-tolerant, 40
 for shade, 21
 showy, 291–92
 winter-hardy, 291
Shrub Stimulator, Super, 290, 354
Silver-lace vine, 303
Site selection
 checking drainage for, 8, 79
 for flower garden, 3–6, 13
 plants suited for, 24, 80, 135
Size of flower garden, 6
Sleep sachet, 238
Slopes, gardening on, 43–44
Slugs, 113, 114, 146, 164, 229, 230, 321, **321**
Slug Spray, Quassia, 229, 347
Slugweiser, 321, 351
Snails, 114, 146, 164, 321, **321**
Snakeroots, 63
Snapdragons, 54, 61, 96, 295, **295,** 311

Sneezeweeds, 56, 98, 101, 106, 195, 257
Snow, as mulch, 117
Snowdrops, 23, **170,** 218, 294
Snowflakes, 25
Snow-in-summer, 29, **213,** 215
Snow-on-the-mountain, **146**
Soap. *See also* Liquid dish soap
  as deer deterrent, 325
  insecticidal, 314, 322, 323
Soil
  amending, 29, 79, 82, 117, 279–80
  annuals improving, 142
  berms, 81
  checking drainage of, 8, 79
  clay, 37–38
  digging test hole in, 4
  dry, 25–26, 32–34
  heavy, defined, 38
  potting, in tonics, 67, 354
  preparing, 82–84
  preventing erosion of, 43
  rocky, 83
  sandy, 39–40
  soggy, 34–36, 165
  for transplants, 92
Soil compaction, 330, **330**
Soil cultivation, for pest control, 323
Soil Energizer Elixir, 12, 352

Soil problems, symptoms of, 330
Soil testing, 48, 84, 330
Solomon's seal, 153
Southernwood, 59
South-facing sites, planting in, 23
Spanish flag, 246
Speakers, outdoor, 46
Speedwells, 97, 106, 296, **296**
Sphagnum moss, for preventing damping-off, 122
Spider flowers, 18, 70, 143
Spider Mite Mix, Super, 322, 354
Spider mites, 113, 148, 180, **281,** 322, **322**
Spiderwebs, for hummingbirds, 60
Spiderworts, 63, 97, 253
Spinach, 17
Spireas
  false (*see* Astilbes)
  Thunberg, 24
Spittlebugs, 319
Spring, early-bloomers for, 22–25
Sprinklers, watering depth from, 107
Spruces, for winter color, 27
Spurges, 297, **297**
Squash, 52
Squash bug, **314**
Squirrels, 171, 248
Staking methods, 30, 100–102
Star-of-Bethlehems, 25
Start-Up Snack, 129, 352

Statices, 50
Stepping stones, 38, 59, 73
Stink bug, **314**
Stocks, 74, 88
Straw, as soil amendment, 82
Strawflowers, **147**
Stumps, tree, 80–81
Sugar, in tonics, 61, 179, 321, 333, 345, 351
Sulfur, uses for, 129, 167
Summer flower care, 25–27
Summer Rejuvenating Tonic, 14, 352
Summersweet, 21
Sundrops, 128, 178
Sunflowers, 18, 26–27, 56, 122, 143, 147–48
  annual, 298, **298**
  common, 99
  Maximilian, 257
  Mexican, 18, 56, 99, 143
  perennial, 98, 99, 298
  profile of, 298
  swamp, 36, 257, 298
  willow-leaved, 298
Sunken beds, 33–34
Sunlight
  assessing, in planting site, 78–79
  flowers facing, 26–27
  groundcovers for, 215
  perennials for, 23, 28–29
  on shade-loving plants, 26
Super Seed-Starting Mix, 120, 352–53

Vines *(continued)*
   paired with shrubs, 293
   profile of, 302–5
   types of, 303
Violets, 24, 25, 53, 144, 253
Virburnums, 292
Viruses, 180, 329
Vitamin B$_1$ Plant Starter, in tonics, 126, 348
Voles, 113, 326, **326**

W

Walls, 43, 44, 64
Walnut trees, black, 268
Watering
   with all-purpose elixir, 109
   for deep rooting, 107
   frequency of, 33
   groundcovers, 43
   indications for, 108
   mulch minimizing, 108
   new beds, 94
   perennials, 33, 254, 255
   potted plants, 66
   preventing fungus from, 328
   seedbeds, 89
   soaker hoses for, 31
   with soda bottle, 33
   summer-blooming plants, 25–26
   transplants, 33, 91, 92
Weed Killer, Wonderful, 64, 355

Weeds
   among annuals, 146
   attracting beneficial insects, 311
   attracting butterflies, 56
   destroying, 62, 79–80, 81, 110–12
   among foundation shrubs, 48
   preventing, 16, 18, 93, 94
   types of, 111–12
Weed Wipeout, 112, 355
Weigelas, 131, **289**
Wet-soil sites, 34–36, 37, 165
Whiskey, in tonics, 68, 110, 333, 341, 347
Whiteflies, 113, 148, 324, **324**
White flowers, for night-time gardens, 74
Whitefly Wipeout Tonic, 324, 355
Wildflowers, 27, 62–63
Willows, rooting hormone in, 125
Windflowers. *See* Anemones
Wind protection, in fragrance garden, 57
Winter
   colorful plants for, 27
   mixed borders and, 17
Wintercreeper, 218
Winter hazel, fragrant, 24
Wishbone flower, 144
Wisteria, 131, **302**

Witch hazels, 21, 24
Wonderful Weed Killer, 64, 355
Wood ashes
   in bulb fertilizer, 110
   in tonics, 109, 133, 172, 216, 333, 336, 346
Woodruff, sweet, 216, 223
Wormwoods, 10, 74, 219
   in tonic, 315, 337

Y

Yarrows, **11**
   common, 311
   dividing, 106
   as fillers, 29
   leaves on, 8
   plants paired with, 165, 178, 187, 194, 238, 266, 282, 284
   profile of, 306, **306**
   pruning, 11, 97
   for sandy soil, 40
Year-Round Refresher, 20, 355
Yeast, in tonics, 321, 351
Yellowroot, 218
Yuccas, 8, 14, 34, 53, 61, 178, 206

Z

Zinnias, 23, 50, 56, 88, 99, 121, 256, 307, **307**
Zucchini, 52